FRENCH
VEGETARIAN
COOKING

FRENCH
VEGETARIAN
COOKING

Paola Gavin

M. EVANS AND COMPANY, INC.
NEW YORK

M. Evans and Company, Inc.
216 East 49th Street
New York, New York 10017

Library of Congress Cataloging-in-Publication Data

Gavin, Paola.
    French vegetarian cooking / by Paola Gavin.
       p.   cm.
    Includes index.
    ISBN 0-87131-837-7
    1. Vegetarian cookery.   2. Cookery, French.   I. Title.
TX837.G33   1995
641.5′636′0944 — dc20   94-49427
                                                    CIP

Manufactured in the United States of America

9 8 7 6 5 4 3 2 1

To Francesca,
Seana, and
Bianca

CONTENTS

FRANCE

INTRODUCTION

French cooking is considered to be the finest in the world. There are two cuisines—*haute cuisine*, which evolved from France's great chefs—La Varenne, Antonin Carême, and Auguste Escoffier, and *cuisine régionale*—regional country cooking made with local produce from recipes passed on from mother to daughter for generations. This book is a personal collection of regional vegetarian dishes from all of the provinces of France.

French provincial cookery varies enormously. In the northeast it is influenced by Flemish and German cuisine. Savoie, Provence, the Comté de Nice, and Corsica have much in common with the cooking of Italy. Roussillon and the Pays Basque have strong links with Spanish cooking.

Vegetarian food is nothing new to France. In the Middle Ages, France suffered many famines. Meat and fish were replaced by cereals, which, together with dried beans, vegetables, and herbs, formed the basis of the peasant diet.

However, French food as we know it today did not evolve until the middle of the sixteenth century, after Catherine de Medici married the Dauphin and brought her Italian chefs to France. At that time Florence was the most sophisticated city in Europe with the finest cuisine. New vegetables were introduced—tiny peas, artichokes, broccoli, Savoy cabbage, and various salad greens, along with new methods of cooking. *Haricots* (French green beans), Jerusalem artichokes, sweet corn, tomatoes, and potatoes were introduced from the New World, although it took two hundred years before the tomato and potato were widely accepted as edible in France.

At the beginning of the nineteenth century a great chef and cook-book writer emerged—Antonin Carême—"King of Cooks and Cook of Kings." At this time the division between *haute cuisine* and *cuisine régionale* began. Restaurants sprang up all over Paris, run by chefs who formerly had cooked for the aristocracy, and by well-known chefs from all of the provinces of France, each outdoing one another with their culinary inventions. At about the same time French regional cooking was evolving. New stoves were invented with adjustable heat, which helped to advance cooking techniques. Before then most cooking was done in cauldrons over hot coals. In many villages food had to be taken to the local baker to be cooked as he had the only oven.

After World War I cooking and eating in France changed greatly. More meat and fish were eaten and more butter and cream were used. Many traditional recipes were lost during the war. Fortunately a new interest in regional cooking emerged, led by Curnonsky, the prince of gastronomes, who motored around the French provinces seeking out local specialties. Unfortunately a visitor to France today would find few local specialties in restaurants, which now cater to "international" tastes. Nevertheless, traditional dishes are still prepared with much loving care at home.

The recipes in this book are very simple and easy to prepare. Unlike for haute cuisine, no great skill is needed. There is plenty of room for improvisation and flexibility. As Roger Lallemand writes in *La Vrai Cuisine à Travers La France, La Lyonnais et La Bresse*, "cooking is above all a question of heart and personality, not weights and measures."

THE REGIONS AND THEIR SPECIALTIES

In this chapter I have divided France into regions that roughly coincide with her historic provinces, with the exception of Gasgony and Guyenne, which I have subdivided and re-grouped according to their gastronomic similarities.

After each section I have given a list of local specialties, which are by no means definitive—such a work would take a lifetime of research—which I hope will give the reader a fuller understanding of the great diversity of French vegetarian cooking. Many of these specialties have not been included in the recipe section of this book, where I have chosen dishes based entirely on my personal preference and taste, and on the simplicity of their preparation.

Picardy, Flanders, Artois

Picardy, Flanders, and Artois lie in the northeast corner of France, on the Belgian border, facing England across the Channel. These are the flatlands of the north—the most industrialized region of France, and the least inspiring. Picardy, perhaps more than its two neighbors, has retained its own customs, folklore, and cooking, with many vegetables dishes, cakes, and sweets that date back to the Middle Ages.

All kinds of vegetables—leeks, carrrots, peas, pumpkins, beans, and a wide variety of salad greens—are grown in *hortillonages*—market gardens divided up by canals that can only be reached by punt. Many vegetable soups are made as well as vegetable or cheese tarts, which are called *tartes*, *tourtes*, *flamiches*, *flamiques*, or *goyères*.

Desserts are simple and rustic. Various fruit tarts and pies are made, usually with apple, pears, or rhubarb. *Tarte à l'ancienne* is filled with a mixture of *fromage blanc* (fresh white cheese), egg yolks, and cream. Amiens is famous for its macaroons.

The cooking of Flanders is more Flemish than French. Flanders became French in 1668, when it was acquired by Louis XIV, (before then it was part of the Spanish Netherlands, which were ruled by the Hapsburgs).

Curnonsky called Flanders "the country of brick and beer." Beer is often used in the cooking of Flanders—*flamiche au maroilles* is a tart filled with *Maroilles* cheese, beer, eggs, and cream; *petits légumes à la bière de garde* is a dish of mixed vegetables simmered in beer, white wine, and herbs.

Cereals, sugar beets, and hops are widely grown. Cabbage and potatoes are favorite vegetables, and of course, the Belgian endive. Endive, or chicory, to use the original name, was first grown in Belgium in the middle of the nineteenth century, and was introduced to France some years later. However, by the end of the century the French were forced to use the same name "endive," as the Belgians objected to the French using the same name. In Flanders, coffee is always served with the ground roots of dried chicory, which gives it its characteristic bitter taste.

Many cakes, pies, waffles, pancakes, and brioches are made, often with Flemish names. *Koke-boteram*, or *Couque-bootram*, is a large raisin brioche; *crakinoskis à la rhubarbe* is a kind of pound cake topped with rhubarb. *Pain d'épice* (spice bread) is said to have originated in Flanders during the time of the spice trade.

Artois is sandwiched between Picardy and Flanders, and has no coastline. It is a little hillier than its neighbors, and is sometimes called "la petite Suisse" (little Switzerland) by the locals.

Artois has few culinary traditions, although fine vegetables are grown around Saint-Omer. Like Flanders, Artois has a beer soup.

The *coeurs d'Arras* are little spice cakes. *Gateau d'Artois* is a puff pastry filled with *crème pâtissière*. *Craquelin* is an oval-shaped brioche.

The cheeses of the north are strong: *Maroilles*, *Rollot* (a favorite of Louis XIV), and *Gris de Lille*, sometimes called "Le Vieux Puant" (the old stinker). *La Boulette d'Avesnes* is a low-fat cheese seasoned with salt, pepper, crushed cloves, and fines herbes, and left to ripen for four months on windowsills or on special shelves nailed to window frames. The sunlight helps dry the cheese.

No wine is produced in the region. Besides beer, gin (*genièvre*) is made, which is often added to a cup of coffee (*l'bistouille*). Cider and *poiré* (perry) are also made.

LOCAL SPECIALTIES

LE PAIN DAUSSÉ or DAUSSADE. Chopped scallions and lettuce mixed with vinegar, cream, and coarse salt, served on slices of country bread.

SOUP DE BETTERAVES. Beetroot soup with onion and celery.

SOUP DES HORTILLONS. Vegetable soup with cabbage, leeks, potatoes, peas, lettuce, sorrel, and chervil.

SOUP DE FLANDRES. Puréed vegetable soup made with potatoes, leeks, celeriac, and tomato, thickened with tapioca.

FLAMICHE AUX POIREAUX or FLAMIQUE À PORIONS. Leek pie.

FLAMICHE AUX OIGNONS or FLAMIQUE À L'OIGNONS. Onion pie.

FLAMIQUE À L'CHITROUILLE or TOURTE AU POTIRON. Pumpkin pie.

GOYÈRE DE VALENCIENNES. A Maroilles and fresh white cheese tart.

TARTE À LA DJOTTE DE NIVELLES. Tart filled with beet greens, onions, and fresh white cheese.

TARTE AU MAROILLES. Maroilles cheese tart.

SOUFFLÉ PICARD. Leek soufflé.

HARICOTS BLANCS, SAUCE PICARDE. Dried white haricot beans simmered with onion and carrots, topped with a thick onion sauce.

ENDIVES AU GRATIN. Belgian endives topped with *béchamel* sauce and grated cheese and gratinéed.

GRATIN DE CHOUFLEUR PICARDE. Cauliflower topped with a thick onion sauce, breadcrumbs and melted butter and gratinéed in a hot oven.

POMMES DE TERRE DE DUNKERQUE. Parboiled potatoes, cut in half and deep-fried.

SALADE AMIÉNOISE. Salad of Belgian endives, apples, lettuce, and walnuts.

GAUFRES AU POTIRON. Pumpkin waffles.

GALOPIAUX. Thick pancakes sprinkled with brown sugar.

GALOPINS. Thick pancakes made with bread or brioche.

GÂTEAU DE MERS. Apple cake topped with whipped cream.

RABOTTE PICARDE. An apple baked in puff pastry—similar to the *douillon* of Normandy.

TARTE À L' PRONÉE or TARTE AUX PRUNEAUX. Prune tart.

ESKOUKEBAEKE. Large pancakes made with beer, served with honey or jam.

NIEULLES. Little flat cakes.

Normandy

The Normans are descendents of the Vikings, or Norsemen, who, in the latter part of the ninth century, plundered the valleys of Normandy almost as far as Paris. Eventually Charles the Simple (who was no fool) decided the only way to secure peace was to give the Vikings the land. So, in 911, their leader, Rollo, became the first Duke of Normandy.

The land is suprisingly varied, with long, sandy beaches near the fashionable resorts of Deauville and Le Touquet, the chalky cliffs of Etretat—mirroring the white cliffs of Dover—the rocky headland of the Cotentin Peninsula, and the extraordinary Mont–St–Michel— often called the eighth wonder of the world. To the south and west lie the hilly peaks of the Norman Switzerland, and the beech forest of the *bocage* that stretches toward Brittany.

Normandy has been called "the farm of France." It is one of the most prosperous of the French provinces; its wealth comes directly from the fertility of the land and its superior cattle. Norman cooking is based on dairy products; cream is lavished on everything and the butter of Isigny is only rivalled by the sweet butter of the Charente. Normandy cheese is world famous—Camembert, *Livarot, Pont-Lévêque* (known as the three graces), *Neufchâtel, Demi-sel,* and *Petit-suisse.*

Vegetables, especially asparagus, Brussels sprouts, green beans, carrots, cabbage, salsify, and peas, are widely grown. Rouen is famous for its watercress, and more parsley is cultivated in Soutrainville than anywhere else in France. Many creamy vegetable soups and fluffy omelettes are made. Wild mushrooms are gathered in the Avranchin and Orne forests.

Although pears and cherries are grown, the apple is queen. Apples appear in pies, cakes, tarts, flans, crêpes, and omelettes. Normandy has no vineyards: this is cider country. There are several *crus—brut, bouché* (slightly effervescent), and *sec. Sec* is best. Perry is also made, as well as cider and pear vinegars. Normandy is also famous for its apple brandy, Calvados, which also has its *crus;* the best Calvados comes from the Pays d'Auge. Norman appetites are renowned, and their meals are lengthy, only to be broken by *le Trou Normand* (literally, the "Norman hole"), which was traditionally filled with a digestive glass of Calvados. Bénédictine, a liqueur originally made by Benedictine monks in the fourteenth century from twenty-seven local herbs, is produced at Fécamp.

LOCAL SPECIALTIES

ASPERGES À LA NORMANDE. Asparagus topped with cream and baked.

POTAGE AVRANCHINAIS. Creamy tomato soup.

SOUPE AU CRESSON CAUCHOISE. Cream of watercress soup.

SOUPE DE L'ORNE. Cabbage, leek, and sorrel soup.

NOQUES. Small dumplings. Also made in Alsace.

DIABLOTINS DE CAMEMBERT. Camembert croquettes.

OMELETTE DE LA MÈRE POULARD. The famous fluffy omelette made originally by Madame Poulard at her restaurant in Mont-St-Michel.

POMMES BRAYTOISE. Baked potatoes stuffed with *Bondart de Neufchâtel* cheese, eggs, and cream.

POMMES DE TERRE À LA NORMANDE. Potato gratin with cream. There are many versions; some include onions or leeks.

MORILLES À LA ROUENAISE. Morel mushrooms cookes in cream.

CAROTTES À LA SAUCE NORMANDE. Carrots in a sauce made with butter, cream, cider, lemon juice, and nutmeg.

CRÊPES FÉCAMPOISES. Apple pancakes flambéed with Bénédictine.

OMELETTE NORMANDE. A sweet omelette, filled with apple purée and flambéed with Calvados.

BOURDELOTS. Whole apples baked in pastry.

DOUILLONS. Whole pears baked in pastry. Sometimes called *rabottes*.

MIRLITONS DE ROUEN. A custard tart flavored with vanilla or orange flower water.

GÂTEAU D'EVREUX. Almond cake made with rice flour and flavored with orange flower water.

LA TARTE BON ACCUEIL. Apple tart topped with an almond crumble.

LA TARTAPAPA. Apple custard tart.

LA GÂCHE. Yeasted bread enriched with eggs and dried fruit. Sometimes it is made with buckwheat flour. A specialty of the Cotentin Peninsula.

SABLÉS. Shortbread. A specialty of Caen.

Brittany

Brittany, in the northwest corner of France, is a remote granite peninsula, dominated by the sea. Almost an island, Brittany has 750 miles of rugged coastline, with picturesque villages, sandy beaches, rocky inlets, and windswept headlands. The land was originally inhabited by the Druids, then by the Gauls, who called it Armorica, or Ars Mor—land of the sea. The interior was called Ar Goat—land of the woods. The Celts first invaded Brittany in the fifth century BC, but then they moved on to the British Isles. It was not untill the fifth century AD that the Celts finally returned, fleeing the Anglo-Saxons, and renamed the land Petite Bretagne. Eventually the "Petite" was dropped.

Brittany was not annexed to France until 1532. Even today it retains a strong sense of identity. In many ways the Bretons have stronger links with their Celtic brothers in Cornwall and Wales than with their fellow Frenchmen. They share the legend of King Arthur (except that it is set in Brittany). Bretons have a love of folklore and legend, and believe in ghosts. The Breton language, which is still spoken, especially in parts of Finistère, is very similar to Welsh.

The cooking of Brittany is simple and rustic, molded by centuries of poverty. In the past the diet was based on thick soups, gruels, and porridges, crêpes and galettes, eggs and dairy products, and vegetables, especially potatoes and haricot (small white) beans. Meat was rarely eaten and no cheese is produced. There is no word for cheese in the Breton language. Instead various dairy products are made— *caillé* (curds), *lait baratté*, or *lait ribot* (buttermilk), and *mangaux rennais* (a kind of cream that is mixed with day-old milk; the exact recipe is a well-kept secret).

A wide variety of vegetables are grown, especially on the fertile plains in the north, near the sea. Since the Second World War the population has dwindled, as many people moved into the cities. Modern farming techniques were introduced and now Brittany produces more vegetables than anywhere else in France. The large round artichokes grown in the Laon, *gros camus*, are known all over France. Asparagus is grown at Cherveix and potatoes, shallots, turnips, cauliflower, carrots, onions, peas, beets, cabbages, and green beans flourish. Various types of mushrooms are gathered, including *coulemelles* (parasol mushrooms) which are called *champignons de blé noir* because they grow in fields of buckwheat.

Plougastel is famous for its strawberries (*fraises*). The first plant is said to have been brought back from America by a sailor called Frezier. Melons called *petit gris*, which have deep pink flesh, are grown around Rennes.

Breton crêpes and galettes are world famous; they are more substantial than the usual French crêpe. Galettes are usually made with buckwheat flour and water, without eggs, and have savory fillings. Crêpes are generally sweetened and made with wheat flour, eggs, milk, and melted butter.

Fars or *farz* are various kinds of dumplings, puddings, and porridges that were once a substantial part of the Breton diet. However, few are made today, except for the sweeter versions called *fars fourn* or *far Breton*, which may include prunes or raisins, and are baked like a flan.

Perhaps the best known cake or pastry is *gâteau Breton,* which comes in many versions, from a rich, crumbly butter cake, almost a biscuit, to an apple tart. *Kouign amann* is another rich, yeasted butter cake.

Brittany, like Normandy, is cider country, but Muscadet wine is produced around Nantes. Pear cider, mead (*hydromel*), and various fruit liqueurs are also made.

LOCAL SPECIALTIES

POTAGE À LA BRETONNE. Haricot bean soup.

POTAGE AUX MARRONS DE REDON. Cream of chestnut soup.

POTAGE ROSCOVITE AU CHOUFLEUR. Cauliflower and potato soup.

OEUFS BROUILLÉS CHERRUEIX. Scrambled eggs with asparagus tips.

SOUFFLÉ DE SAINT-POL. Artichoke soufflé.

OMELETTE CORNOUAILLAISE. A plain omelette garnished with fried potatoes.

SOUPE MORDELLAISE. Mixed vegetable soup with fresh white haricot beans, green beans, carrots, onions, sorrel, herbs, and cream.

PANNEQUETS GLAS-GWER. Crêpes stuffed with spinach.

BIGNEZENNOU, or BEIGNETS D'ARTICHAUT. Artichoke fritters.

FONDS D'ARTICHAUTS BROCELIANDE. Artichoke bottoms and wild mushrooms simmered in Muscadet wine.

PURÉE BRETONNE. Puréed dried white haricot beans with butter and cream.

CHOU À LA NANTAISE. Cabbage salad with sliced banana and walnuts.

PETIT POIS À LA NANTAISE. Tiny garden peas simmered in butter with tomatoes, thyme, and summer savory.

SOUFFLÉ PLOUGASTEL. Strawberry soufflé.

GÂTEAU BRESTOIS. Almond cake flavoured with lemon and curaçao.

BEIGNETS DE MAM GOZ. Sweet fritters made with pureéd potatoes, flour, sugar, and orange or lemon rind.

CRÊPES DENTELLES. Wafer-thin, rolled crêpes, flavored with vanilla.

BIGOUDENS. Sweet almond biscuits.

BARA SEGAL. Rye bread.

Anjou, Touraine

The French statesman and writer, George Clemenceau claimed, "To fully understand and appreciate the temporary sweetness of life, one must know Anjou." Anjou and Touraine were once the heart of French culture, especially during the Renaissance. Rabelais was born here; Francis I brought Leonardo da Vinci to the Touraine, where he stayed until he died. Balzac was a native of Tours, and Curnonsky was born in Angers.

The land is dotted with elegant châteaux along the Loire and its tributaries—at Amboise, Chinon, Azay-le-Rideau, Chenonceaux, Chaumont—to name a few. The French claim that the finest French is spoken in Tours. This is "the Garden of France" with its market-gardens, orchards and vineyards. It is often said that there are few regional dishes in the cooking of Anjou and Touraine. Perhaps that is because their cuisine was so pure and simple that it became the foundation of French cooking today.

Vegetables grow in abundance, especially the choicest early vegetables known as *primeurs* (literally "first"), which have been cultivated since the sixteenth century. It was Charles VIII who first brought artichokes and cardoons to France at the end of the fifteenth century (after a trip to Italy, where he became enamored with Italian food and gardens). Shortly after, other "exotic" vegetables such as petits pois were introduced by Catherine de Medici when she left Florence to marry the Dauphin (who later became Henry II). Excellent thick-stemmed white aparagus is cultivated, as well as small white onions, mushrooms, and shallots (the kind called *échalotes gris*), which are so typical of Angevin cooking. Anjou is the second largest producer of shallots in France (Brittany is first). All kinds of cabbages are grown; Angevins are often affectionately called *piochoux* (little cabbages). Vegetables are prepared simply *à la crème* or *au gratin*, and are often served as a separate course.

Fruit is plentiful, especially cherries, peaches, apricots, strawberries, and black currants, but apples and Williams pears are the most widely grown fruit. Plums were brought back from Damascus at the time of the Crusades. Tours is famous for its *gros damas* prunes, and melons have been cultivated since Roman times.

The traditional pastries of Anjou and Touraine are simple and rustic. *Fouace* (a small, flat hearthcake or bun), *russeroles* (fritters), and *cassemusses* (literally, jaw-breakers) date back to the Middle Ages. Various fruit tarts are made, as are desserts and ices flavored with Cointreau.

Few cheeses are produced, except from goat's milk, and the well-known *Crêmet d'Angers*—a very light molded cheese that is made with a mixture of cream cheese, whipped cream, and stiffly beaten egg whites, and served sprinkled with sugar.

Vouvray wine is the best known wine of the Touraine. Red wines of note are Bourgueil and Chinon. Anjou is world famous for its wine, especially the sweet Rosé d'Anjou, Saumur and Saumur Mousseuse (which is naturally sparkling), and the fine white wines of the Côteaux du Layon. Various fruit and nut liqueurs are made, and Cointreau is produced at Angers.

LOCAL SPECIALTIES

CERNAUX AU VERJUS. Green walnuts marinated in the juice of unripe grapes.

MILLIÈRE. A kind of porridge, or gruel, made with millet, milk, butter, and cream.

CRÈME TOURANGELLE. Cream of dried white bean soup, with onion, leek, and potatoes, garnished with green beans.

NOUZILLARDS AU LAIT. Chestnuts in hot or cold milk.

OMELETTE TOURANGELLE. An omelette filled with sautéed mushrooms, cream and herbs, topped with cream and grated cheese, and baked briefly.

OEUFS POCHÉS SAUMUROIS. Eggs poached in white wine with mushrooms.

HARICOTS À LA TOURANGELLE. Fresh white haricot beans and green beans in a *béchamel* sauce.

PIOCHONS SAUTÉS. Small green cabbages sautéed in walnut oil.

CÔTES DE BLETTES AU GRATIN. Gratin of the white stalks of Swiss chard, eggs, cream, and fresh goat cheese.

CARDONS DE TOURS AU GRATIN. Cardoons topped with *béchamel* sauce and breadcrumbs and gratinéed in a hot oven.

SALADE ANGEVINE. Potato salad with flageolet and green beans, dressed with walnut oil, wine vinegar, and mustard. (Sometimes this is a mixed-green salad).

SALADE TOURANGELLE. Similar to *salade angevine* but dressed with mayonnaise.

CRÊPES BELLES ANGEVINE. Crêpes flavored with Cointreau, and filled with a thick, sweetened apple purée.

PRUNEAUX AU VOUVRAY. Prunes simmered in Vouvray wine, topped with whipped cream.

LA BIJANE AUX FRAISES. Strawberries marinated in sweetened wine, poured over slices of oven-dried brioche.

PÂTÉ DE PRUNE ANGEVIN. Plum pie made with puff pastry.

FOUACE, or FOUGASSE. Small flat loaves flavored with saffron, usually eaten with soft cheese or jam.

Orléanais, Berry

Curnonsky wrote of the Orléanais, "The cooking of the Orléanais is pure, noble, and simple, like the line of its landscapes, like the language that is spoken, like the light that bathes it . . . a picture of harmony and gentleness."

In the north lie the huge wheat plains of the Beauce, the granary of France, and the Gâtinais, famous for its honey and saffron. Vegetables grow in abundance, including Chinese artichokes (*crosnes*) grown from tubers imported from China. Fruit is plentiful, especially apples, pears, cherries, quinces, and greengage plums (*reines–claude*), named after the wife of Francis I. The town of Orléans is famous for its pure wine vinegar, which has been produced here since the Middle Ages. Butter, olive oil, and walnut oil are all used in cooking.

South of the Loire is the Sologne, a low-lying area of marshy heathland with four thousand lakes and ponds. Although it is sometimes called *"triste Sologne"* (sad Sologne), it has a quiet, unspoiled charm. This is the hunting ground of France, once favored by the French aristocracy. On the edge of the Sologne is Chambord, one of France's most impressive Châteaux, with 365 chimneys, one for every day of the year!

Fine asparagus and strawberries are grown in the Sologne. *Cèpe*, *chanterelle*, and parasol mushrooms are gathered. Small farms produce eggs, milk, cream, and goat cheese.

Delicious pastries and pies are made: *Pithiviers*—an elegant almond pastry, and the famous *Tarte des desmoiselles Tatin*—a carmelized, upside-down apple tart, which was created by the Tatin sisters in their hotel in Lamotte-Beuvron.

Several goat cheeses are produced, including *Troô* and *Vendôme* cheese, and *Olivet bleu*, a blue rinded cow's milk cheese.

Wines of note are the Gris Meunièr (red, white and rosé), Cheverny, and Sauvignon (both white). Several ciders are produced, a liqueur made from quince, and *hydromel* (mead).

Berry lies between the Sologne and the Central Massif, in the literal heart of France. It is the smallest and one of the most ancient of the French provinces. Here the cooking is simple, healthy, and robust. The Berrichons are traditionally soup-eaters—at one time soup was eaten three times a day. Vegetables are abundant, especially cabbage, cauliflower, Brussels sprouts, pumpkin, and the potato called *truche* or *tartuffe* in the local patois. Many substantial galettes, tarts, and pies are made, often including goat cheese.

North of the ancient town of Bourges, the capital of Berry, pears, apples, and hazelnuts are grown. Hazelnut oil is much appreciated for its flavor.

Morels, *chanterelles*, *cèpes*, and parasol mushrooms are all gathered, and chestnut trees grow on the border of the Limousin. Desserts are simple and rustic, including various waffles, fritters, and crêpes.

Berry is famous for its cheeses. The most well known are the *Crottin de Chavignol* and *Sancerre*. Other cheeses of note are *Levroux*, *Pouligny–Saint–Pierre* and *Valençay*.

White Sancerre is the best-known wine of the region, followed by Chavignol, which was a favorite of Balzac.

LOCAL SPECIALTIES

VELOUTÉE or CRÈMEUSE BERRICHONNE. Creamy white haricot bean and potato soup.

POTAGE BERRICHON. Mixed-vegetable soup with onion, lettuce, cabbage, broad beans, and peas.

SOUPE À L'ORTRUGE. Nettle and potato soup.

ROUTIE or SOUPE AU VIN. Hot sweetened wine poured over slices of toast; traditionally served to couples on their wedding night.

OEUFS À LA TRIPE. Sliced boiled eggs in a *béchamel* and onion sauce.

POMMES À LA FORESTIÈRE. Baked potatoes stuffed with mushrooms, herbs, and cream.

POMMES DE TERRE SOLOGNOTES. Potato gratin with milk, cream, butter, garlic, and herbs, topped with Gruyère cheese and browned in the oven.

ÉCHALOTES D'ORLÉANS. Shallots cooked in a vinegar and honey sauce.

SALADE DE MOISSONEURS. Potato salad with hard-boiled eggs, sliced onion, and herbs, dressed with a vinaigrette sauce made with walnut oil.

GALETTE AU FROMAGE BLANC. A round, flat cake or pastry made with puréed potatoes, fresh white cheese, flour, and eggs.

TRUFFIAT or BOURRE–CHRÉTIEN. Potato pie.

LE CITROUILLAT. Pumpkin pie (sweet or savory).

SANCIAUX. Thick pancakes served with fresh white cheese, honey, or jam.

GALOPINS D'ORCHAISE. Whole apples baked in a pastry—similar to the *bourdelots* of Normandy.

GOUERRE, or GOUÉRON AUX POMMES. Sliced apples marinated in brandy and baked in a pancake batter.

BEUGNONS. Sweet fritters fried in walnut oil.

LE POIRAT. Pear and cream pie.

LA TART DES DESMOISELLES TATIN. Carmelized upside-down apple tart.

GÂTEAU DE PITHIVIERS or FEUILLÉTÉ AUX AMANDES. Light puff pastry with an almond cream filling flavored with rum.

PAIN D'ÉPICE DU GÂTINAIS. A spice bread made with wheat and rye flour, honey, candied orange rind, and anise seed.

PETITS BERRICHONS. Little walnut macaroons.

LA BADRÉE. An apple and pear jam.

COTIGNAC or PÂTÉ DE COING. Quince paste or jelly.

Paris, Ile-de-France

Paris has been called the gastronomic capital of France, even of the world. It has also been said that Paris has no cuisine of its own, but this is not true. Paris has a vast repertoire of creamy vegetable soups, sauces, and excellent pastry created by its innovative cooks during the past four centuries. The first restaurants opened in Paris in 1765 were called *bouillons restauratifs*—hence the derivation of "restaurant." Although Paris has a long history of haute cuisine dating back to the Renaissance, when Catherine de Medici brought her Italian chefs and bakers to France, it was not until after the French Revolution that modern French cuisine evolved. Many new restaurants were opened, especially in the Palais Royal, run by chefs who once cooked for the aristocracy, and by famous chefs from all the regions of France. The cooking was modified to suit the less frivolous taste of the wealthy bourgeoisie; it became a combination of haute cuisine, good country cooking of the Ile–de–France, and the ingenuity of the individual chef.

The Ile–de–France was so-named because in the Middle Ages any land surrounded by rivers was called an island. Originally the Ile–de–France was bounded by the Marne, the Seine, and the Oise, but gradually it expanded to surround Paris by a radius of fifty kilometres. The Ile–de–France was once the dairy and the garden of Paris: Argenteuil was famous for its asparagus, Arpajon for flageolet beans, Crécy for carrots, Clamart and Saint Germain for peas, and Laon for artichokes. Mushrooms (*Champignons de Paris*) were grown in caves around Paris (now moved to the Loire). Each village lent its name to specialties that have become synonymous with French restaurant fare the world over: *potage Argenteuil, potage Saint-German, potage Crécy,* and *petit pois Clamart.* Paris is also famous for its sauces—*béarnaise, béchamel, mornay gribiche,* and *soubise,* which were all invented here. *Duxelles,* a mixture of finely chopped mushrooms and shallots sautéed in butter, was probably created in the seventeenth century by La Varenne, chef to the Marquis d'Uxelles, though it is sometimes said that *duxelles* comes from the village of Uxel in Brittany.

Desserts are equally world famous: crêpes Suzettes, Paris–Brest, and gâteau Saint–Honoré. The Ile–de–France is also famous for fine fruit: the cherries of Montmorency, the peaches of Montreuil, Chasselas grapes, and wild strawberries, which are often served with crême chantilly—sweetened whipped cream flavored with vanilla.

The most famous cheese is Brie, which has been made in the Ile–de–France since the eighth century. There are various kinds of Brie: *Brie de Melun, Brie de Meaux* (which is also made in Champagne), *Brie façon Coulommiers,* and *Brie de Montereau. Fontainebleau* is a very light cream cheese that is usually eaten with sugar and cream.

Paris has no wine, but Grand Marnier, an orange-flavored cognac, is produced at Neauphle–le–Château. There is also a cherry-flavored cognac.

LOCAL SPECIALTIES

ASPERGES À LA FONTANELLE. Boiled asparagus served dipped in melted butter and soft-boiled egg.

POTAGE CRESSONIÈRE, or POTAGE AU CRESSON. Cream of watercress soup.

SOUP À L'OIGNON MONTMARTOISE. Creamy onion soup, flavored with white wine, poured over fried croutons, and served with grated cheese on the side.

POTAGE CRÉCY. Creamy carrot soup with potato and leek.

GNOCCHIS À LA PARISIENNE. Dumplings made with cream puff pastry topped with *béchamel* sauce and grated cheese, and gratinéed.

OEUFS FARCIS CHIMAY. Eggs stuffed with a mixture of sautéed mushrooms and shallots, topped with cheese sauce and grated cheese, gratinéed.

POMMES ANNA. Thinly sliced potatoes baked in a covered dish with plenty of clarified butter until golden. Created by Adolphe Dugléré for the nineteenth-century courtesan, Anna Deslions.

POMMES MACAIRE. A potato galette, or flat cake made with puréed potatoes, butter, flour, cream and nutmeg.

POMMES ALLUMETTES or POMMES FRITES. French fries the size of matchsticks.

PETIT POIS CLAMART or PETIT POIS À LA FRANCAISE. Tiny peas simmered with small white onions, lettuce hearts, butter, sugar, and herbs.

SAUCE PARISIENNE. A sauce made with *Petit-suisse,* a fresh unsalted cheese made with pasteurized milk, cream, oil, and lemon juice.

TALMOUSES. Cheese-filled pastries dating from the Middle Ages. The name comes from *talmelier,* meaning baker.

PARIS–BREST. A large cream-puff pastry filled with almond butter cream.

SAINT-HONORÉ. An elaborate pastry filled with *crème pâtissèrie,* named after the patron saint of pastry cooks.

TARTE DE MONTFORT–LAMAURY. A large puff pastry filled with whipped cream, strawberries, or raspberries.

POIRES À LA BOURDALOUE. Poached pears with vanilla custard, topped with crushed macaroons and red currant jelly.

MOUSSE FONTAINEBLEAU. Fresh cream cheese topped with strawberry purée and chopped almonds.

Champagne

Champagne is one of the larger French provinces, stretching from the Belgian border to Burgundy, and from Lorraine in the west to the Ile–de–France. The name Champagne derives from the Latin *campania* meaning "land of the plains." Much of Champagne is fertile agricultural land where cereals and sugar beets are grown. It is, however, on the chalky plains south of Rheims that the world's most famous wine is produced.

It was the Romans who first planted vines here, but they disappeared in the fifth century when the land was overrun by Barbarians. Viticulture was started again by monks in the seventh century, and although excellent wine was produced—both Henry VIII of England and Henry IV of France had vineyards here—it was not until the seventeenth century that Dom Perignon, a monk and celler-master at the Benedictine Abbey of Hautvilliers near Epernay, created champagne as we know it today. He did not "invent" champagne, but he discovered if the bottles were closed with cork bark instead of a plug of wadded cloth, the wine would retain its sparkle.

Champagne is not well known for its gastronomy, as Prosper Mantagné wrote in *Larousse Gastronomique*, "its repertoire is rather limited." Many dishes are prepared with champagne, but it is often "still" Champagne, or *champagne nature*, that is used, as champagne loses its bubbles when heated. The cooking is often influenced by the surrounding regions—*gougère de l'Aube* (a cheese puff pastry) resembles the *gougère* of Burgundy. As in Alsace, there is *choucroute* (sauerkraut), and cheese fondue is made with champagne.

Potatoes and cabbage are the favorite vegetables.

Bread is a staple, and often sold in huge loaves called *miches*. Plenty of fruit and nuts are grown. Excellent honey is produced at Rheims, which is used to make *pain d'épice* (spice bread) and *non-nettes* (little iced honey cakes). The pink *biscuits de Rheims* are traditionally eaten with champagne. Châlons is famous for its sugared almonds.

Champagne produces many fine cow's milk cheeses: *Brie de Meaux, Chaource, Langres, Barberey*—sometimes called *'Fromage de Troyes'*—and *Carré de l'Est*.

Besides Champagne, "the wine of kings," there is a full-bodied rosé wine Rosé de Riceye, and the red and white wines of the Côteaux Champenois. There is also Marc de Champagne and a ratafia made with grape juice blended with *eau–de–vie*.

LOCAL SPECIALTIES

SOUPE À LA BIÈRE. Beer soup poured over slices of toast and served with grated cheese on the side. A specialty of Mezières.

POTAGE DOM PERIGNON. Creamy lentil soup made with champagne.

SOUPE AU LAIT ARDENNAISE. Milk-based soup with onion, leeks, potatoes, and escarole.

GRATINÉE AU CHAMPAGNE. Onion soup made with champagne, topped with slices of bread and Gruyère cheese, and gratinéed.

TOURTELETS, or TETULOTS. Rectangular egg noodles served in cold milk.

BAILLINE or BAÏENNE. New potatoes cooked in water and white wine with onions.

CHAMPIGNONS À LA SAINT-MÉNÉHOULD. Mushrooms sautéed with shallots and herbs, spooned over slices of bread soaked in milk, and baked until golden.

PURÉE DE POIS–CASSES SAINT–MÉNÉHOULD. Split-pea and potato purée.

SALADE D'ENDIVES AUX BETTERAVES ROUGES. Belgian endive and beet salad with walnuts.

ANGLOIS. Plum tart.

FLAN CHAMPENOIS. Pudding made with *biscottes* soaked in Marc de Champagne, eggs, milk, sugar, and cherries.

DARIOLES. Little custard tarts flavored with orange flower water.

BEIGNETS DE FROMAGE BLANC. White cheese croquettes.

PAIN D'ÉPICE DE RHEIMS. Spice bread made with rye flour, honey, ground almonds, candied peel, and anise seed.

SABAYON DE CHAMPAGNE. Frothy cream similar to the Italian zabaglione made with eggs yolk, sugar, and champagne.

Alsace, Lorraine

Alsace is the most easterly of the French provinces, bordering on Switzerland and Germany. Blessed with a warm, dry climate and rich alluvial soil, it has been called "the wine cellar, the granary, and the larder" of the surrounding countryside. The medieval towns and villages, with their quaint half-timbered houses and steepled roofs, seem more Teutonic than French, for Alsace was under German rule for more than eight hundred years. Despite its long history of wars, invasions, and occupations, which continued up until the end of World War II, Alsace has retained its own customs and language, a dialect of German. Since the thirteenth century Alsace has had a strong Jewish community, and both German and Jewish influences are reflected in the cooking. Soups are substantial, such as potato, barley, and split pea. All kinds of dumplings and noodles are made.

The Alsatians are great lovers of savory pastries, especially onion tarts, which are called quiche, *tarte*, *tourte*, flan, or even *gâteau*. Herbs and spices are distinctive: cumin, caraway seed, juniper berries, cinnamon, anise seed, poppy seed, and horseradish.

Cabbage is the favorite vegetable. White cabbage is used for sauerkraut, which could be called the national dish. Unlike its German counterpart, Alsatian sauerkraut is flavored with white wine. Red cabbage is simmered with apples or chestnuts, or cooked *ziss-sauer* with sugar, cinnamon, and vinegar (Jewish-style). Turnips are cut into sticks as thin as spaghetti and salted and marinated to make a turnip sauerkraut called *sûri–ruena*. Hop shoots are added to omelettes. Potatoes appear in salads, dumplings, gratins, and pancakes. Asparagus has been grown since the Roman occupation; white asparagus is preferred.

The fruit of Alsace is superb, especially bilberries, cherries, apricots, pears, and plums, which all appear in delicious fruit tarts.

There are a vast number of breads, cakes, and pastries, many of which were originally baked on feast days and religious holidays: *milchweka* (milk bread), *kaffeekrantz* (coffee cake), *bretzels* (pretzels), *loeffelpastrlas* (sourcream fritters), *krapfen* (jam-filled doughnuts), and *jungfraukiechlas* (sweet, fried pastries), to name a few.

The most famous cheese is Munster, which was originally made in Alsace by Irish monks in the seventh century. It is a soft cow's milk cheese with an orange-yellow washed crust. Sometimes it is flavored with cumin or anise seed.

Alsace is famous for its white wines—Tokay, Gewürztraminer, Syvaner, Pinot, Muscat, and Riesling. Many excellent white fruit brandies are distilled from cherries, raspberries, *mirabelle* and *quetsche* plums. Beer has been brewed since Roman times.

Lorraine, like Alsace, spent part of its history under German rule. In 1736, it was ceded to Stanislas Leczynski (the former king of Poland and father-in-law to Louis XV), and finally became French after his Leczynski's death in 1766.

The cooking of Lorraine is substantial, with many savory pastries and quiches, usually filled with cheese, onions, or potatoes. One rustic tart (*tarte fermière*) is simply filled with a mixture of eggs and cream, and seasoned with salt and black pepper. Dumplings (*kneppes*), and sauerkraut are made. Potatoes are often used; they appear in galettes, pancakes, and gratins. Cabbage, tiny peas, carrots, turnips, salsify, and Chinese artichokes are all grown. Metz is famous for its asparagus.

Like Alsace, Lorraine produces excellent fruit: bilberries, cherries, pears, raspberries, strawberries, and mirabelle plums, which are also made into fine fruit tarts and preserves. Bar–le–Duc is famous for its red and white currant preserves, which Victor Hugo was so fond of that he would order four hundred pots at a time.

Lorraine is well known for its cake and pastries. *Baba au rhum* was created in Nancy by Stanislas Leczynski. *Pâte feuilleté* (puff pastry) was invented by Claude Gelée, who started his career as a pastrycook's boy, but later became known as the great landscape painter, Claude Lorraine. *Madeleines* of Commercy are the little shell-shaped cakes flavored with orange or lemon that were immortalized in Marcel Proust's *Remembrance of Things Past*.

Géromé or *Gérardmer*—a similar cheese to Munster—is made in the Vosges mountains. There is also a *fromage cuit* that is heated, wrapped in muslin, hung up to drain, and potted for a week. Butter, raw milk, egg yolks are added before the cheese is heated again, potted, and served cold. *Fromage blanc de la Messine* is a fresh white cheese flavored with onions and shallots.

The wines of Lorraine are no match for those of Alsace. The best known is *vin gris* which is, in fact, a pale rosé, Côtes de Toul, and the red, white, and rosé of the Moselle. Excellent fruit brandies are distilled, especially cherry (kirsch), raspberry, and mirabelle. Two of France's renowned mineral waters, Vittel and Contréxeville, come from Lorraine.

LOCAL SPECIALTIES

SOUP DE CHOUCROUTE. Sauerkraut and potato soup.

BIERSUPP, or SOUP À LA BIÈRE. Beer soup with cream and cinnamon.

SURAMPFERSUPP. Sorrel soup.

GRUMBEERESUPP. Potato soup.

KNEPFLE, or OEUFS À LA JUIVE. Potato dumplings served with melted butter and grated cheese.

NOUILLES À L'ALSACIENNE. Egg noodles topped with fried breadcrumbs and melted butter.

TOTELOTS. Square egg noodles served with a vinaigrette.

GRIESSCHNIETTE, or CROQUETTES DE SEMOULE. Semolina croquettes.

WASSERSCHTRIWLE, or SPÄEZLE. Egg noodles served with melted butter and fried croutons.

RAMEQUIN MESSIN. Cheese soufflé.

ZEWELWAÏ or GÂTEAU DES OIGNONS. Creamy onion tart.

QUICHE AUX CHAMOTTES. Onion and poppy-seed tart.

LA FIOUSSE. White cheese tart.

EIERKUCHAS. Pancakes flavored with herbs. There is also a sweet version.

REIZFLOÏMES. Rice with prunes and raisins. A Jewish specialty.

KACHELMUES. Onion fondue with sliced hard-boiled eggs—usually served with baked potatoes.

POMMES DE TERRE À LA LORRAINE. Sliced potatoes and onions baked with beer and cream.

CHOUCROUTE AU MAIGRE. Sauerkraut simmered with onions and apples.

CRÊPES À L'ALSACIENNE. Pancakes stuffed with white cheese and sprinkled with sugar.

BETTELMAN (literally, "beggarman"). Cherry bread pudding or cake.

CHINOIS (literally "Chinaman"). Almond and raisin pastry flavored with kirsch.

KUGELHOPF or GUGELHUPF. Light yeast cake with almonds and raisins.

GÂTEAU AU CHOCOLAT DE NANCY. Chocolate almond cake.

BIREWECKA. Rich fruit bread with dried pears, prunes, figs, raisins, walnuts, lemon rind, spices, and liqueur.

LA CHAUDÉE. Apple or plum tart.

HEIDELBEEREKUECHE, or TARTE AUX MYRTILLES. Bilberry tart.

LA TARTE AUX PAVOTS. Poppyseed tart.

SCHWOWEBREDLE. Almond *petits fours* with candied orange peel. A Chistmas specialty.

QUATRE–QUATRE AUX MIRABELLES. Pound cake topped with mirabelle plums.

SCHENKELES. Fried almond pastries flavored with cinnamon and cognac.

FRAISES DES BOIS LORRAINE. Wild strawberries marinated in kirsch and topped with whipped cream.

SIASKAS. Homemade cream cheese served with cream, sugar and kirsch.

Franche–Comté

Franche–Comté, "the free country," has been known for its independent spirit and self-rule since pre-Roman times. It was acquired by the Dukes of Burgundy by marriage, and later by the Hapsburgs, who also ruled Spain. Louis XIV finally secured Franche–Comté by treaty in 1678. To the south the land is mountainous, with plateaux, pine forests, ridges, and waterfalls that give way to the terraced hillsides and gentle plains in the north, on the borders of Alsace, Lorraine and Champagne.

The cuisine is based on fine cheese, numerous wild mushrooms, and distinctive wine. A hundred years ago, white bread was virtually unknown in the Jura mountains. An oatmeal bread called *grésillon* was eaten, usually dunked in a vegetable broth made with cabbage, carrots, turnips, onions, and leeks.

Gaudes, a cornmeal porridge similar to Italian polenta, is the national dish. As in Savoie and Dauphiné, potatoes are a staple and appear in various gratins. Cabbage, turnips, spinach, cardoons, kidney beans, peas, and lentils are cultivated. Wild mushrooms include cèpes, morels, chanterelles, and mousserons. Salads are often dressed with walnut oil.

Fruit is bountiful, especially plums, cherries, apples, blackberries, and bilberries. Fritters, waffles, various fruit pastries and tarts, and a delicious cream caramel, called *pain d'oeuf au caramel*, are made. Spice bread is a specialty of Vercel and Dôle.

Comté, or *Gruyère de Comté,* made from raw cow's milk, is one of the finest hard cheeses in France. *Emmental Français Beaufort, Bleu de Gex, Septmoncel,* and *Morbier* are also made. The latter, one of the oldest cheeses produced in France, is made of two disks of cheese that are rubbed with charcoal before being joined, giving the appearance of a black line running along the center of the cheese.

La Cancoillotte is a *fromage fort* (strong-flavored potted cheese) and is also the name given to a kind of Welsh rarebit made with melted cheese, egg, and garlic.

Franche–Comté is the only wine-producing province of France that makes five types of wine: white, yellow, rosé, red, and *vin de paille* (straw wine), which is made from grapes picked in November and dried on beds of straw until February. It is said to be one of France's best dessert wines. Château–Chalon is the most famous of the *vin jaunes* (yellow wines), and is also made from late-flowering grapes.

LOCAL SPECIALTIES

FONDUE DE GEX. Cheese fondue made with Comté cheese, dry white wine, and brandy or kirsch.

FONDU FRANC–COMTOISE. As above, but with the addition of beaten eggs and butter.

POTAGE CHARLES QUINT. Tomato soup with fresh sweet corn cooked in milk with celeriac, butter, and cream.

LA SOUPE AUX CERISES. Sweetened black cherry soup, thickened with flour, flavored with kirsch, and served with fried croutons.

OMELETTE DE LA CHANOINESSE. An omelette with various wild mushrooms.

OMELETTE MONTAGNARDE. An omelette made with bread soaked in milk, grated Comté cheese, and nutmeg.

ATTEREAUX JURASSIENNES. Comté cheese and semolina croquettes.

CROQUETTES DE FROMAGE BLANC. White cheese croquettes.

FLAN COMTOIS. Cheese tart or flan.

MATEFAIMS or MATAFANS. Thick pancakes. The name comes from the Spanish *mata famé* (hunger-killer).

RAMEQUIN. Little cheese cream-puff pastries.

PAIN DE POIREAUX. A savoury loaf made with chopped leeks and bread soaked in milk, eggs, and Gruyère cheese.

GRATIN DE POMME DE TERRE AU COMTÉ. Potato gratin with milk, Comté cheese, and garlic.

CRÔUTES AUX MORILLES À LA MODE DU JURA. Slices of toast topped with morels in a creamy béchamel sauce, and baked.

ÉPINARDS MÔDE DE MOREZ. Spinach sautéed in butter with onion, garlic, cream, and nutmeg.

SALADE AU COMTÉ. Lettuce and Comté cheese salad dressed with oil, vinegar, mustard, and cream.

PETS–DE–NONNE. Little doughnuts or fritters.

TARTE JURASSIENNE. Apple, prune, and hazelnut tart.

FRANC–COMTOIS. Rich cheese cake flavored with kirsch and layered with bilberry jam.

GÂTEAU DE CERISES AU KIRSCH. Cherry cake flavored with kirsch.

BEIGNETS DE GAUDES. Cornmeal fritters.

BRICLETS. Almond biscuits.

Savoie, Dauphiné

Savoie is mountain country. It boasts the highest peak in Europe, Mont Blanc, where France, Italy, and Switzerland meet. Savoie was annexed to France in 1860; before then it was part of the kingdom of Sardinia, which included Piedmont and Comté de Nice. The Italian influence is reflected in the local cuisine, where a liking for pasta, rice, and polenta is prevalent. The cooking of Savoie is based on milk, cream, butter, and cheese. Potatoes are a staple and appear in pancakes, croquettes, gratins, and *farçons*, sweet or salted potato pudding. The most famous dish is *Gratin savoyard*, a potato gratin layered with sliced Gruyère or Beaufort cheese and cooked with broth. Spinach, Swiss chard, cardoons, turnips, and pumpkin are also prepared au gratin. Wild mushrooms, especially morels, are found in the woods and clearings. In the past, chestnuts were a staple, but today they appear only in soups and *farçons,* or in gratins with cabbage or turnips. Wheat, rye, and buckwheat are grown in the valleys. Walnut oil is used in cooking and salad dressings.

Fruit is abundant, especially apples, pears, yellow and white peaches, bilberries, blackberries, and wild strawberries, which are made into various tarts, pastries, and turnovers.

Savoie produces excellent cheese: Reblochon, Beaufort, Emmental, Gruyère, and various *tomme* cheeses, including one studded with grape seeds.

The best known wine is Seyssel. Other wines of note are Roussette de Savoie (white) and Montmélian (red). Vermouth, made from a blend of white wines, is bottled at Chambéry. Evian is famous for its mineral water.

Dauphiné has belonged to France since 1340, when Humbert II sold it to Philip VI for 200,000 florins. At that time it was decreed that the eldest son of the French king should become its viceroy, and all future crown princes of France would hold the title "Dauphin."

Dauphiné is a land of rugged mountains and dramatic gorges that stretches from the Alps to the fertile Rhône Valley, where spring vegetables and fruit are grown, especially apricots and peaches. The cooking is similar to that in Savoie, but with the addition of olive oil, which is produced at Nyons. There is the same love of gratins, especially those made with millet, pumpkin, and potatoes. The best-known dish is the *Gratin dauphinois*, made with sliced potatoes and cream, or a mixture of cream and milk, and baked until the potatoes are golden.

Some of the best walnuts in France are grown around Grenoble, and used in various cakes and pastries. Montélimar is famous for its nougat, which is made with fine honey from the high Alps.

Dauphiné also produces fine cheese: *Saint Marcellin*, *Picodon*, *Bleu de Sassenage*, and *Pétafine*, a strong cheese made with a mixture of fresh goat cheese, cream, and brandy.

Dauphiné is famous for its wine: Crozes–Hermitage, Côte Rôtie, and Hermitage, which was a favorite of Julius Caesar. Chartreuse, a liqueur originally made by Carthusian monks at La Grande Chartreuse monastery, outside of Grenoble, is made with various medicinal herbs, saffron, cinnamon bark, and the seed coat of nutmeg, although the precise ingredients and proportions are a secret. There are two kinds of Chartreuse: green *Chartreuse de santé*, and yellow, said to be digestive.

LOCAL SPECIALTIES

FONDU SAVOYARDE. Cheese fondue made with Beaufort cheese, dry white wine, and kirsch.

SOUPE DAUPHINOISE, or SOUPE DE TULLINS. Creamy vegetable soup with French green beans.

LE FRIQUÉRON JAUNE. Cornmeal gruel or porridge.

SOUPE SAVOYARDE. Milky soup with celeriac, turnips, leeks, and potatoes, topped with croûtons and Gruyère cheese, gratinéed.

SOUFFLÉ MONTAGNARDE. Light cheese soufflé made with semolina.

OEUFS BROUILLÉS AUX MOUSSERONS. Scrambled eggs with mushrooms.

LA RAVIOLE. Ravioli stuffed with fresh goat cheese.

FIDÉS. Fresh vermicelli sautéed with onions, and cooked in stock like rice.

LES CROZETS. Fresh egg noodles usually made with a mixture of buckwheat and wheat flour, cut into small cubes.

ÉPOGNE À LA COURGE. Pumpkin tart made with bread dough.

LES RAMBOLLETS. Potato quenelles stuffed with prunes.

COURGETTES FARCIS À LA SAVOYARDE. Zucchini stuffed with rice, tomatoes, shallots, and cheese, served with tomato sauce.

GRATIN À LA DOUVAINOISE. Potato gratin with mushrooms, grated cheese, and cream.

FARÇON or FARCEMENT. Sweetened or salted potato pudding that may include onions, cheese, raisins, dried figs, prunes, or dried pears.

PAILLASSONS. Potato and onion pancakes.

POIREAUX À LA SAVOYARDE. Layers of leek, breadcrumbs, and Gruyère cheese, gratinéed.

LA POGNE DE ROMANS. Sweet brioche flavored with lemon rind and orange flower water.

GÂTEAU À LA FARINE DE MILLET. Cake made with millet flour, and flavored with orange flower water.

GÂTEAU GRENOBLOIS. Rich coffee walnut cake, flavored with rum.

BISCUIT DE SAVOIE. Light sponge cake made with a mixture of potato and wheat flours.

RÉZULES DE POIRES. Pear turnovers made with puff pastry. They may be baked or deep-fried.

LES JEMBELLES. Little cornmeal cakes flavored with lemon rind.

Burgundy

Burgundy is one of the oldest of the French provinces. Invaded by the Gauls, and then by the Romans in 52 BC, it was overrun by the Burgondes, a tall, blond people from the Baltic, who gave it their name. By the fifteenth century Burgundy stretched from the North Sea to Mâcon. It became one of the most powerful duchies in Europe, rivalling the kingdom of France. The capital, Dijon, named Divio (the Divine) by the Romans, was already a renowned gastronomic center. The Dukes of Burgundy held gargantuan feasts at the ducal palace, which went on for days and nights. Courses consisted of ten plates, and there were five or six courses!

Curnonsky wrote of them: "Whereas other sovereigns built fireplaces in their kitchens, the Dukes of Burgundy built a kitchen in their fireplaces, i.e., the four walls of the kitchen are merely an enormous cooking, roasting, boiling, stewing and frying machine. So the kitchen staff and scullions bustled and worked in the middle of the large room, prisoners of the turning spits, the hissing cauldrons, the spattering greasepans, the humming saucepans and the bubbling soups."

The cooking of Burgundy is sumptuous, based on wine and cream. Eggs are poached in wine; asparagus, mushrooms, Chinese artichokes, and even turnips are cooked in cream. Delicious savory tarts and pastries are made. The most famous pastry is the *gougère*, a large ring-shaped cream-puff pastry flavored with Gruyère cheese.

Fruit and vegetables grow in abundance. Mushrooms and white truffles are gathered in the woods and clearings. Hazelnuts and walnuts are grown, and walnut oil is often used in salad dressings.

Pain d'épice (spice bread) is a specialty of Dijon. There is even a pudding (*pouding de pain d'épice de Dijon*) made with spice bread with raisins and lemon rind soaked in a mixture of eggs and milk, that is baked, then flambéed with rum. Black currants are another specialty of Dijon, and they appear in many desserts.

Dijon is also famous for its mustard, which has been made here since the fourteenth century. Mustard seed was first brought to Burgundy by the Romans, who chewed it with their food, a habit they learned from the Egyptians. The mustard is made from ground mustard seed mixed with *verjus*—the juice of unripe grapes. In France mustard is said to be an aid to digestion. A dish *à la Dijonaise* always includes mustard.

Burgundy produces many fine cheeses: *Aisy cendré*, made from raw cow's milk and ripened on wood ash (preferably from vine-strippings), *Soumaintrain*, *Époisses* (called the "king of the cheeses" by Brillat–Saverin), *Saint Florentin*, *Citeaux*, *Chevrottoin de Mâcon* (sometimes called *les Boutons de culottes*), *Charolais*, and *Claquebitou*, a fresh cheese flavored with garlic and herbs.

The wines of Burgundy are legendary, rivalled only by the wines of Bordeaux: Gevrey–Chambertin, Chambolle–Musigny, Nuits-St.-Georges, Beaune, Pommard, Meursault, and Montrachet, to name but a few.

Cassis, a black currant liqueur is made in Dijon. It is said to be a miracle cure, perhaps because it is so rich in vitamin C and minerals. Cassis is sometimes added to white wine, in which case it is drunk as an aperitif, called kir.

LOCAL SPECIALTIES

OIGNON À LA BOURGUIGNON. Braised onions in sweet and sour sauce.

POTAGE CRÈME DE LAITUE. Cream of lettuce soup.

CONCOMBRES À LA DIJONAISE. Cucumbers in mustard vinaigrette sauce.

OEUFS FARCIS À LA DIJONAISE. Hard-boiled eggs stuffed with butter, mustard, and herbs, in a creamy mustard sauce.

SOUFFLÉ BOURGUIGNON. Cheese soufflé made with separated eggs, Gruyère cheese and cream.

NOUILLES À LA BOURGUIGNONNE. Egg noodles baked with eggs, cream, and Gruyère cheese.

HARICOTS ROUGES À LA BOURGUIGNONNE. Kidney beans in red wine sauce.

HARICOTS BLANCS, SAUCE MOUTARDE. Dried white haricot beans in white wine sauce with tomato and mustard.

MOUSSERONS À LA CRÈME. Mushrooms in wine and cream sauce.

MOUSSE AU CHOUFLEUR. Cauliflower mousse, served with a tomato or cream sauce.

TARTE AUX ÉPINARDS. Spinach tart.

FEUILLETÉ AUX MORILLES. Large puff pastry filled with morel mushrooms and cream.

FLAMICHE AUX POIREAUX. Leek pie, similar to the flamiche of Picardy.

LES CORNIOTTES BOURGUIGNONNES. Little puff pastries made in the shape of a cocked hat, with a cheese filling.

RIGODON BOURGUIGNON. Pudding or flan made with brioche soaked in milk, vanilla sugar, chopped walnuts, and raisins.

POIRES À LA BELLE DIJONNAISE. Poached pears, topped with black currant parfait and whipped cream.

BAVAROIS AU CASSIS. Black currant bavarian cream.

TOURTE CHAROLLAISE. Pear custard tart.

TARTOUILLAT. Cherry tart flavored with rum.

FLAMOUS. Pumpkin pudding or flan.

PAIN D'ÉPICES DE DIJON. Spice bread made with
   rye and wheat flour, honey, candied orange rind,
   cinnamon, and anise seed.

GAUFRES MÂCONNAISE. Buckwheat waffles.

Lyonnais

Lyons has been called the gastronomic center of France. Its culinary
tradition dates back to 43 BC when Lyon, then called Lugdunum,
was the Roman capital of Gaul. During the Renaissance, Lyon was
a great center for the arts and sciences. Huge fairs were held,
attracting merchants from all over Europe and Asia. The inns and
hotels of Lyon became famous for their fine food. Rabelais, who
wrote *Pantagruel and Gargantua* here, was an ardent fan of Lyonnais
cuisine.

A silk industry was set up that soon rivalled that of China. After
the French Revolution the silk workers, or *canuts* as they were
called, formed a large part of the working population. They lived
on a frugal diet of soup, such as *soupe de farine jaune*, a kind of gruel
made with cornmeal, water, and milk; *matefaims*, thick pancakes;
salade de groins d'ane, dandelion salad; and *bugnes*, fritters. They also
enjoyed fresh white cheese flavored with shallots and herbs called
la cervelle de canut (literally, silk-weaver's brain), which was served
in eating houses called *mâchons*. These mâchons were also fre-
quented by the middle classes. In Lyon, throughout the nineteenth
century, the bourgeoisie dined at both humble and luxury restaurants—as long as the food was good. Many of these establishments
were run by women chefs or *mères*, a tradition that continues today.

Curnonsky claimed that the cooking of Lyons was created "by
great chefs who never seek to create an effect." It is a cuisine based
on simplicity. What better foundation for the nouvelle cuisine of

Paul Bocuse, whose family members have been restauranteurs here for two hundred and fifty years.

Onions play an important part in the cooking of the Lyonnais; *à la lyonnaise* generally means "with onions." Potatoes, nicknamed "truffles of the poor," are prepared in over twenty ways. Dandelion, arugula, and lamb's lettuce appear in salads, usually with beets and hard-boiled eggs.

Lyons is well known for its excellent pastry. Various cakes are made with pumpkin, chestnuts, or chocolate. *Tarte lyonnaise* is an open tart filled with a mixture of brioche soaked in milk, sugar, ground almonds, eggs, and kirsch. Frangipane—a custard cream with ground almonds used to garnish pastries—originated in Lyons.

The most famous cheese of the Lyonnais are *Mont-d'or*, usually made with goat's milk, and *Rigotte de Condrieu*, a small round cow's milk cheese. Its name derives from the Italian "ricotta." Various small goat cheeses are produced such as *fromage fort*—made from a mixture of grated dried goat cheese, dry white wine, and stock—which is potted, covered with olive oil, and left to ripen for two weeks.

The best-known wine is Beaujolais. They drink so much Beaujolais in Lyon that there is a standing joke—attributed to Léon Daudet—three rivers flow through Lyon: the Rhône, the Saône, and the Beaujolais.

LOCAL SPECIALTIES

SOUPE AU POTIRON. Pumpkin soup with onion, leek, and tomatoes, thickened with tapioca, and served with grated cheese on the side.

SOUPE LYONNAISE. Onion soup, thickened with egg yolks.

POIREAUX VINAIGRETTE À LA CRÈME. Boiled leeks in a creamy vinaigrette sauce.

OMELETTE LYONNAISE. An onion omelette with parsley, served sprinkled with vinegar.

MACARONI À LA CRÈME AU GRATIN. Macaroni baked with Gruyère cheese and cream.

VERMICELLE AU GRATIN. Vermicelli mixed with fried onions and stock, topped with Gruyère cheese and gratinéed.

TOURTE DE CHAMPIGNONS. Large puff pastry filled with mushrooms and cream.

TARTE AU POTIRON. Pumpkin and Gruyère cheese tart.

CROQUETTES DE POMMES DE TERRE. Potato croquettes.

GRATIN DE POMMES DE TERRE. Layers of sliced pototates, cream, melted butter, and Gruyère cheese, baked.

CRÊPES VONASSIENNES. Pancakes made with puréed potatoes, flour, eggs, and cream.

ARTICHAUTS À LA LYONNAISE. Quartered artichokes topped with onion sauce and Gruyère cheese, and gratinéed.

POMMES DE TERRE SAUTÉES À LA LYONNAISE. Sautéed potatoes with onions, garnished with parsley.

ÉPINARDS À LA VIEILLE MÔDE. Equal quantities of spinach, cress, dandelion, and curly endive topped with béchamel sauce and baked.

HARICOTS VERTS À LA LYONNAISE. Green beans sautéed with onions.

CHAMPIGNONS À LA CRÈME. Mushrooms in a creamy béchamel sauce.

BEIGNETS DE FLEURS D'ACACIA. Acacia flower fritters.

BUGNES LYONNAISES. Sweet pastry fritters, flavored with cognac.

GÂTEAU AUX MARRONS LYONNAIS. Chestnut cake, flavored with vanilla and sugared almonds, served with whipped cream.

MOUSSE AU CHOCOLAT. Chocolate mousse.

CORNIOTTES DE LOUHANS. Little white cheese pastries.

Bourbonnais, Nivernais

Bourbonnais and Nivernais lie in the heart of rural France, on either side of the Loire. Nivernais, famous for its earthenware and nougatine, was an independent duchy until the French Revolution. The sandy soil of the Loire produces excellent vegetables, especially onions, turnips, and carrots. The classic garnish *à la nivernaise* is made with glazed carrots cut into the shape of olives. Several vegetable soups are made; vegetable pies are usually filled with potatoes, spinach, or leeks.

Desserts are rustic. *Sauciaux* are thick pancakes, also made in Berry and Bourbonnais. *Flamusse aux pommes* is a kind of apple flan. *La pâté aux poires* is a simple pie filled with pears, cream, sugar, and a dash of black pepper.

The best-known cheese is *fromage sec*, which is dried on beds of straw and dusted with pepper.

Nivernais produces one of France's great white wines, Pouilly–Fumé, named after the smokey-blue color of the Sauvignon grape from which it is made. Another fine white wine is Pouilly–sur–Loire.

The ancient province of Bourbonnais was the homeland of the Bourbon dynasty that ruled France for more than three hundred years. It lies between Nivernais and Auvergne. The landscape is varied with fertile plains, thick forests—the forest of Tronçais has oak trees that are several hundred years old—granite moors, and the deep valleys of the Central Massif.

The cooking of Bourbonnais is hearty country fare. The Bourbonnichons, as the inhabitants are called, are great soup-eaters. Once soup was eaten three times a day. Excellent vegetables are grown in the fertile plain of Limagne, especially potatoes and cabbage. Rye was once the main cereal—it has been gradually replaced by wheat—but, *pain noir* (black bread) can still be found. Plenty of eggs, milk, butter, and cheese are used in cooking. *Fondu bourbonnais* is a cheese fondue made with cheese, water, a little flour mixed with milk, and egg yolks. Various potato pies are made. Gannat is famous for its walnut oil.

Fine fruit is also grown, especially apples, pears, plums, and peaches. *Millas* or *Milliat* is a cherry-batter cake similar to the *clafoutis* of the Limousin. Walnuts appear in many desserts.

Several goat cheeses are produced: *Chevrotin, Mont Chalmoux*, and *Roujadoux*, which, as its name implies, reddens with age. *Chamberat, Coulandon*, and *Coupi* are all made with cow's milk.

The region's most famous wine is Saint–Pourçain, which has been produced here since the Middle Ages. Vichy is known for its mineral water.

LOCAL SPECIALTIES

SOUPE AUX MARRONS. Cream of chestnut soup.

SOUPE DE NEVERS. Brussels sprout and carrot soup with vermicelli.

POTAGE GERMINY, or FERMIÈRE NIVERNAISE. Sorrel soup thickened with egg yolks and cream.

SOUPE À L'AIL. Garlic soup made with walnut oil, served with poached eggs.

SOUPE AUX CHOUX À L'HUILE DE NOIX. Cabbage and potato soup made with walnut oil, poured over slices of bread.

FLAN DE CAROTTES À LA BOURBONNAISE. Carrot tart.

GÂTEAU DE CHOU–RAVÉ. Kohlrabi soufflé or flan.

LA TARTE AUX POIREAUX. Leek pie.

GOUERRE AU FROMAGE. Potato and white cheese pie.

PÂTÉ AUX TRUFFES, or TRUFFAT. Potato pie.

LE GRATIN À LA CITROUILLE. Pumpkin gratin.

CHOUFLEUR À LA BOURBONNAISE. Cauliflower in vinegar and cream sauce.

CÈPES À LA CRÈME. Cèpe mushrooms in cream.

CARROTS À LA VICHY. Carrots cooked in Vichy water with butter and sugar.

PETIT POIS À LA NIVERNAISE. Tiny peas simmered in butter with lettuce hearts, small white onions, and carrots.

SALADE DE PISSENLITS À L'HUILE DE NOIX. Dandelion salad dressed with a mustard-walnut oil vinaigrette, garnished with croutons fried in walnut oil.

BRIOCHE DE GANNAT. Cheese brioche.

SANCIAUX. Thick pancakes, usually served with fresh white cheese, jam, or honey.

BEIGNETS AU CAILLÉ. Sweet curd fritters.

PIQUENCHÂGNE. Pear and cream pie.

TARTE AUX PRUNEAUX, or GOUERRE AU CIRAGE. Prune tart.

PATRICIEN. Almond meringue filled with chestnuts and rum.

GÂTEAU ROULÉ AUX NOIX. A kind of swiss roll rilled with walnut cream.

GARGOUILLEAU, or GÂTEAU CREUSOIS. Pearbatter cake.

Auvergne, Limousin

The Auvergne lies in the heart of the Central Massif. It is a rugged land of extinct volcanos, high mountain pastures, and thick forests, with picturesque Norman towns built of dark volvic stone. The climate is extreme, with long cold winters and short, hot summers. Even in summer the temperature can drop 70° at night. The Auvergnats have a reputation for being austere, obstinate, practical, and thrifty.

The cooking of the Auvergne is solid and substantial. Various cheese tarts and pastries are made. *Farinette*, or *pachade*, is a cross between an omelette and a pancake, which may be sweet or savory. Potatoes are a staple. Rye bread is preferred to wheat. In the past, bread was made with barley or chestnut flour; the chestnut tree was called "the bread tree." Fine garlic is grown in the fertile plain of Limagne, as well as potatoes and cabbage. Various wild mushrooms are gathered in the woods. Le Puy is famous for its tiny greenish-black lentils.

Fine fruit is grown, especially cherries, peaches, apples, and pears. Desserts are rustic; *milliard* is a cherry-batter cake, similar to the *clafoutis* of Limousin. Chestnuts and walnuts appear in cakes, puddings, and tarts.

Auvergne produces many fine cheeses: *Cantal*, which has been made here for more than two thousand years; *Tomme, Fourme d'Ambert, Bleu d'Auvergne, Saint–Nectaire; Murol*, which has a hole in the center—the part that is removed is sold separately as *Trou de Murol*—and *Gaperon*, which is made from buttermilk curds. *Gape* means "buttermilk" in Auvergne.

Wine has been produced in the Auvergne since Roman times. Unfortunately the best wine, Chanturgue, has virtually disappeared. Other wines of the region are Corent, Fel, and Côtes d'Auvergne.

The Limousin is one of the poorest and least-populated regions of France. Much of the land consists of densely forested plateaux, steep valleys, and vast meadows of gorse and heather where sheep graze.

The cuisine is simple country fare, based on the ingredients at hand. Potatoes, cabbage, turnips, and chestnuts appear in many dishes. Truffles and wild mushrooms, especially cèpes, are gathered in the woods and fields. *À la limousine* generally means "with red cabbage," but sometimes cèpes or chestnuts are included. Bread is an important staple, and is usually made with whole wheat or rye flour. There is an old French saying: *"On mange du pain, comme un Limousin"*—"One eats bread like someone from Limousin."

Fine strawberries, plums, and cherries are grown. The most famous dessert is *clafoutis*, made from unpitted black cherries, baked in a batter. The cherry pits are said to improve the flavor. Bilberries are also grown and are used to make the purple mustard of Brive.

Limousin produces a few cheeses: *Chabricon*, *Chasteaux*, and a blue cheese from Bassignac.

Only a modest amount of wine is produced in the Limousin: *vin gris* in Haute–Vienne; Clos de Vertoujit, and the *vin paille* (straw wine) in Queyssac and Beaulieu.

LOCAL SPECIALTIES

COUSINAT, *or* SOUPE AUX MARRONS. Creamy chestnut soup usually served with slices of toast and grated cheese on the side.

SOUPE AUVERGNATE. Lentil and potato soup.

FONDUE AUVERGNATE. Cheese fondue made with Cantal and Gruyère cheese, and white wine.

RIZ AU CANTAL. Rice with Cantal cheese, béchamel sauce, and capers.

PÂTES AU CANTAL. Macaroni topped with Cantal cheese, breadcrumbs, and melted butter, gratinéed.

PASCADE AU PISSENLITS. A thick pancake made with dandelion leaves, garlic, and herbs.

OEUFS À LA CANTALIENNE. Egg yolks baked in a nest of stiffly beaten egg whites, topped with Cantal cheese and cream, and baked.

RISSOLES DE SAINT–FLOUR. Cheese turnovers.

ALIGOT or ALICOT. Fresh tomme cheese, or *tomme d'aligot*, cooked with puréed potatoes until the cheese melts and forms long ribbons. Also made in Rouergue.

PATRANQUE. A kind of pancake or galette made with bread soaked in milk and Cantal cheese.

CHOU FARCI LIMOUSINE. Cabbage stuffed with chestnuts.

GRATIN AUVERGNAT. Potato and chestnut gratin.

BOURRIOLS. Buckwheat pancakes.

CÈPES MÔDES DE BRIVE. Cèpe mushrooms simmered with onions, celery, tomatoes, white wine, and herbs. Served hot or cold.

LA PASTOURELLE. Green salad dressed with a mixture of Bleu d'Auvergne cheese, walnut oil, wine vinegar, and cream.

SALADE LIMOUSINE. Green salad garnished with sliced truffle.

TRUFFES SOUS LA CENDRE. Truffles cooked in ashes.

BOULAIGOU. A thick pancake served with sugar, honey, or jam—similar to the sanciaux of Bourbonnais.

FLOGNARDE, or FLAUGNARDE. Sweet flan or battercake.

POMPO DE POUN, or POMPE AUX POMMES. Apple pie.

PACHADE AUX PRUNEAUX. Prune flan, sometimes cooked on top of the stove like a pancake.

SOUFFLÉ AUX MARRONS. Chestnut soufflé.

TARTE À LA CRÈME D'AURILLAC. A cheesecake or tart flavored with orange flower water.

Périgord, Quercy, and Rouergue

Périgord, Quercy, and Rouergue were once part of the old province of Guyenne, which came under English rule when Eleanor of Aquitaine brought it as part of her dowry on her marriage to Henry Plantagenet in 1152. This is a land of great variety, which includes the beautiful Dordogne valley scattered with medieval and Renaissance castles, the limestone Causses of Quercy and the rugged mountains, cliffs, and gorges of the Rouergue.

The cuisine of Périgord is synonymous with luxury cooking, for this is the land of the black truffle, which Brillat–Savarin called the "black diamond." As no one yet knows how to cultivate truffles, dogs and pigs are trained to sniff out these precious fungi, which only grow under certain conditions under oak trees. Périgord is also famous for its walnuts; walnut oil is preferred to butter in cooking. As Curnonsky wrote, it is a cuisine *"sans beurre et sans reproche"* (without butter and without reproach).

Soup has always been a mainstay of the diet, especially of the poor. At one time, soup was eaten four times a day. *Tourin* (a garlic soup poured over slices of bread) was served for breakfast. A little red wine was added to the dregs, and drunk straight down in a custom called *faire chabrol*, common to much of southwest France.

The rich alluvial soil of the river valleys produces excellent vegetables; asparagus, artichokes, salsify, onions, garlic, pumpkins, various beans, and all kinds of salad greens are cultivated. Many different wild mushrooms, including *cèpes* and morels, are gathered.

Fruit is abundant. Périgord is one of France's largest producers of strawberries. Table grapes, pears, and peaches are also widely grown.

Desserts are simple and rustic, and often include cornmeal. Various goat cheeses and a blue cheese, *Bleu de Basillac*—similar to Bleu d'Auvergne—are made.

The best known wines of Périgord are the sweet golden wine of Monbazillac—which is usually drunk as an aperitif or a dessert wine—and the full-bodied, red Pécharmont. Various fruit liqueurs and two walnut liqueurs, *eau–de–noix* and *crème de noix*, are produced.

The cooking of Quercy is similar to that of Périgord. Black truffles are also found, although the Périgourdins claim that all the truffles come from Périgord. Sheep graze on the limestone plateaux, where the soil is thin and water scarce. In the fertile valleys tobacco, cereals, vegetables, and fruit are grown.

The best known cheeses of Quercy are *Bleu des Causses* (sometimes called *Bleu de Quercy*), a strong-smelling blue cheese made from cow's milk, and *Cabécou*—made from sheep's or ewe's milk—which is usually eaten fresh. Sometimes it is wrapped in chestnut leaves and called *Picadou*.

Quercy has one famous wine, the "black" wine of Cahors, which is said to have tonic qualities.

The Rouergue has a hearty cuisine, suited to its cold, harsh winters. Chestnuts were once a staple, but the potato has gradually taken over since its introduction in the early nineteenth century. The potato is the basis of the Rouergue's most famous dish *aligout*, made with fresh tomme cheese stirred into a mixture of puréed potatoes, milk, butter, and garlic, until the cheese has melted and forms long ribbons.

Rouergue is, of course, most famous for Roquefort cheese, made from ewe's milk, which has been produced here for more than two thousand years. The cheese is matured in naturally humid caves that have a steady temperature of 6°–10°C., which creates ideal conditions for the mold *penicillum roquefortii* to grow and give the cheese its distinctive flavor.

Rouergue's best-known wines are Entraygues, Martillac, and Estaing.

LOCAL SPECIALTIES

TOURAIN PERIGÔURDIN. Onion and tomato soup.

LE TOURAIN À L'OSEILLE. Garlic soup with sorrel.

LA BAJANAT ROUERGATE. Chestnut soup.

RIMOTES. Cornmeal porridge.

LE FAR AU CHOU DU QUERCY. Cabbage baked in a pancake batter.

FEUILLÉTÉ AUX ROQUEFORT. Puff pastry with Roquefort cheese and herbs.

OMELETTE AUX BOUTONS DE SCORZONÈRES. An omelette with black salsify.

BROUILLADE AUX TRUFFES. Scrambled eggs with truffles.

CROQUETTES DE POMMES DE TERRE AUX NOIX. Potato and walnut croquettes.

BEIGNETS DE SALSIFIS. Salsify fritters.

AUBERGINES À LA CRÈME. Sautéed eggplant topped with cream and baked.

HARICOTS VERTS QUERCYNOISE. French beans in an egg and vinegar sauce.

MESCLOU AUX NOIX. Mixed-green salad with wild herbs and walnuts, dressed with walnut oil and vinegar.

SALADE DE TOMATE À L'EAU DE VIE. Sliced tomatoes, marinated in brandy and dressed with walnut oil and vinegar.

LE GOUGEAS DE QUERCY. Little pumpkin puddings.

LES JACQUES. Apple pancakes.

FLAUGNARDE. Prune batter cake.

GÂTEAU BRANTÔMOIS. Sultana raisin cake flavored with liqueur and orange flower water.

LOU CACOU. Rich walnut cake.

LA CAJASSE SARLADAISE. A cake made with flour, eggs, milk, and sugar, flavored with rum.

LES COQUES. Yeasted cakes flavored with lemon and rum.

LES PESCAJOUNES. Cornmeal pancakes flavored with orange flower water.

LES OGUILHETS. Sweet fritters.

PAIN DE MÉTEIL. A wheat and rye bread.

Poitou, Charente

The ancient province of Poitou is named after the Pictones, a Gallic tribe of Celtic origins. Poitou has a long history of wars and invasions that began with the Romans, followed by the Visigoths, the Franks, and the Moors—who were defeated by Charles Martel in 732. In the twelfth century Poitou was part of the Duchy of Aquitaine when it came under English rule. This began a power struggle between France and England that finally ended with French rule at the end of the Hundred Years War.

Today Poitou is a peaceful agricultural backwater. Along the coast is the Marais Poitevin, a marshy region originally drained by monks in the twelfth century, which has been turned into market gardens—criss-crossed by canals—that can only be reached by punt. Excellent fruit and vegetables are grown, especially broad beans, peas, carrots, garlic, and *mojhettes*—large, flat haricot beans of exceptional quality. The island of Noirmoutier is famous for its new potatoes. The people of Poitou eat so much cabbage that they are nicknamed *ventres à choux* (cabbage stomachs). Purslane, called *pipou* in the local patois, and lamb's lettuce appear in salads, often dressed with walnut oil.

In the past bread was generally made with whole wheat, barley, or cornmeal, or a mixture of each, but these heavy country breads ceased to be baked by the end of the 1930s.

The best known dessert is *tourteau fromagé*, a sweet goat-cheese tart flavored with cognac, rum, or vanilla. Angelica, a specialty of Niort, appears in various cakes and galettes.

Chabichou is the best known goat cheese. The name derives from *chabli*—"goat" in Arabic—a leftover from the Moorish invasion of the eighth century. Another goat cheese called *Melusine* is wrapped in chestnut leaves.

The wines of Poitou do not travel well. As Curnonsky said, "They have no names! It seems as though they have never been baptized."

Charente and Charente–Maritime are made up of the ancient provinces of Angoumois, Santonge, and Aunis. The capital, La Rochelle, with its medieval fortifications, is one of the most beautiful fishing ports in France.

The cooking is simple, but opulent, based on milk, cream, butter—considered to be the best in France—and wine. The inhabitants are often called *gagouillards* (snails), probably because of the long, slow simmering that is so typical of the cooking of the region.

This fertile, arable land, with its mild climate, produces superb fruit and vegetables. Charentais melons are world famous. Asparagus, grown on the island of Ré, is one of the first to appear in the Paris markets each year. *Mojhettes piates*, the finest of the large, flat haricot beans, are grown in Saintonge. Fine mild garlic is cultivated; *aillettes*, green garlic tops, are delicious in omelettes. All kinds of wild mushrooms are gathered, as well as truffles.

Various fritters and fried pastries are made, sometimes with cornmeal. *Cruchades* is a cornmeal porridge that is cooled and made into fritters. Chocolates filled with brandy are a specialty of Angoulême.

Cheese is mainly fresh curds called *caillebotte* (made with *chardonette*, a wild artichoke used to curdle the milk), and *jonchée*, which is similar to caillebotte, but is drained on rush or reed mats.

Charente is, of course, most famous for its brandy, Cognac—the finest in the world—which Victor Hugo called the "liqueur of the Gods." Like Normandy, Charente traditionally had a *trou au milieu*, a "hole in the middle" (of the meal), when a glass of Cognac would be served as an aid to digestion. There is also an aperitif, *pineau*, which is made with a mixture of Cognac and grape juice, and left in casks to age.

LOCAL SPECIALTIES

SOUPE À L'OUZILLE. Sorrel soup, thickened with egg yolks and cream, served with slices of bread.

SOUPE AU POTIRON ET CHÂTAIGNES. Pumpkin and chestnut soup, poured over slices of bread.

OEUFS À L'OSEILLE. Eggs covered with cream and baked on a bed of sautéed sorrel.

CROQUETTES DE MILLET. Millet croquettes.

MOJHETTES FRAÎCHES À LA CHARENTAISE. Fresh, large haricot (white) beans simmered with garlic, onion, tomato, butter, oil, and herbs.

MOJHETTES À LA CRÈME. Large flat dried white beans simmered with butter, oil, and cream.

PAIN DE PORÉE. Not a bread, but chopped leeks in a cream sauce, thickened with egg yolk.

LA SOUGRENÉE. Boiled potatoes, carrots, peas, and lettuce hearts, briefly sautéed in butter.

CÈPES À LA CHARENTAISE. Cèpe mushrooms sautéed in oil with garlic, shallots, parsley, and cognac.

LA CHOUÉE DES CHOUANS. Green cabbage purée simmered in butter and sprinkled with white wine vinegar.

BEIGNETS DE FEUILLE D'OSEILLE. Sorrel fritters.

SOUFFLÉ À L'ANGELIQUE. Sweet soufflé with candied angelica.

LE GÂTEAU SAINTONGEAIS. Almond sponge cake.

MILLAS. Cornmeal flan.

LE PRUNÉ. Prune tart

LES FOUTIMASSOUS. Cream fritters.

LES TOURTISSEAUX. Sweet fried pastries.

GÂTEAU AU MIEL DE POITOU. Honey cake.

GIMBELETTES. Ring-shaped biscuits, flavored with lemon or orange rind.

Bordelais, Les Landes, Agenais, and Armagnac

Bordelais and the Landes were once part of the Duchy of Aquitaine, which was ruled by the English for three hundred years. Stendhal called the capital, Bordeaux, with its wide squares and elegant boulevards, the most beautiful city of France. Bordeaux is one of France's great gourmand centers. Her wines are the most famous in the world: Château d'Yquem, Château Lafite, Château La Tour, Château Margaux, and Châteaux Haut–Brion. In Bordeaux it is customary to select the wine first, and then choose a dish to go with it, rather than the other way around. One simple rule is always observed: All dishes prepared with a wine should be served with the same wine.

The cooking of the Bordelais is simple and elegant, based on olive oil, shallots, garlic, herbs, and spices. Three kinds of shallots are cultivated: purple (*gris*), red, and greyish-white. Other fine vegetables are grown: the potatoes of Eysines, the tiny peas of Cérons, the artichokes of Macau, asparagus, and eggplants. Various wild mushrooms are gathered, but the cèpe is king and, of course, cooked *à la bordelaise*, sautéed in olive oil with garlic and parsley. Surprisingly, shallots are not used in this dish. It is only in Parisienne restaurants that *cèpes à la bordelaise* are made with shallots and a dash of lemon juice.

Bordelais has no cheese, but the locals like to eat Dutch cheese, which they claim goes well with their wine. This habit began in the eighteenth century, when the Dutch bartered cheese for Bordelais wine.

Inland from Bordelais lies Agenais—the market garden and orchard of the southwest. Tobacco, corn, and all kinds of vegetables are grown, especially artichokes, asparagus, and tomatoes in Marmande. Melons, peaches, apples, cherries, and strawberries flourish, but the Agenais is most famous for its prunes, which are often preserved in Armagnac and appear in all kinds of desserts.

The Landes was once one of the poorest regions of France. In the nineteenth century it was a vast marshy plain with high sand dunes along the coast, which were blown in by strong westerly winds. The dunes threatened the Bordeaux vineyards, so pine forests were planted and slowly the marshes disappeared. Today the timber from these pine forests is used for papermaking and the resin for synthetics and glue.

The cooking of the Landes is simple and rustic. Millet was once the most important grain, but it was gradually replaced by corn when it was introduced from the New World in the sixteenth century. Asparagus grows well in the sandy soil. Haricot beans, tomatoes, sweet peppers, and eggplants are popular. Cèpes, girolles, and *mousserons des pins* mushrooms are all gathered in the woods and forests.

Desserts are often made with cornmeal. A large, round pastry called *tourière* is made with strudel or filo pastry, which probably originated with the Saracens when they pushed their way up from Spain in the eighth century.

The only cheese produced in Les Landes is *Poustagnacq*, or *Postignac*, a fresh cheese made from ewe's or cow's milk which is flavored with garlic and sweet pepper.

Armagnac is in the heart of the ancient province of Gascony. It is a land of dense forests and gentle rolling hills, with scorching hot summers and bitterly cold winters. This extreme climate perhaps explains the volatile Gascon temperament: Gascons have a reputation for being hot-tempered, proud, quick-witted, and brave. This is the home of Count d'Artagnan, immortalized by Alexandre Dumas in *The Three Musketeers*.

Armagnac is most famous for producing one of the great brandies of France—Armagnac, which is rivalled only by Cognac.

LOCAL SPECIALTIES

TOURIN BORDELAIS. A milky onion soup, thickened with egg yolks and cream, poured over slices of bread.

TOURIN À LA TOMATE. Onion and tomato soup with vermicelli.

SOUPE GASCONNE. Soup made with stock, white wine, and spices, thickened with egg yolks.

SOUPE AU POTIRON GIRONDINE. Pumpkin soup with rice or string beans.

MILHADE LANDAIS. Millet porridge.

TOURTE AUX CÈPES. Puff pastry filled with sliced potatoes, cèpes and shallots.

LES CHÂPEAUX DE CURÉ, or LES CORNIOTTES. Little triangular pastries filled with a mixture of white cheese, eggs, cream, and Gruyère cheese.

OEUFS À L'AGENAISE. Sautéed eggplants topped with eggs, garlic, and herbs, and baked.

OMELETTE AUX CÈPES. Omelette with cèpes.

HARICOTS PANACHÉS À LA TOMATE. Green and flageolet beans simmered with tomatoes, onion, and herbs.

AUBERGINES À LA BORDELAISE. Sautéed eggplants, garnished with a mixture of fried breadcrumbs, parsley, and garlic.

RAGOUGNASSE. A stew of sweet peppers, eggplant, tomatoes, zucchini, shallots, garlic, and herbs—similar to the Provençal *ratatouille.*

SALADE DE PISSENLITS. Dandelion salad with pinenuts, dressed with a mustard vinaigrette.

SALADE MÉDOCAINE. Salad of lamb's lettuce, black grapes, walnuts, and Gruyère cheese.

COQUE AU LAIT. Baked custard flavored with Armagnac.

BEIGNETS DE POTIRON. Sweet pumpkin fritters.

MILLAS GIRONDIN. A kind of flan flavored with bitter almonds.

CRUCHADE MAIGRE. A cornmeal porridge, made into fritters and sprinkled with sugar.

COMPÔTE GASCONNE. Dried fruit compote with Armagnac.

CLAFOUTIS AUX PRUNEAUX. Prunes soaked in Armagnac and baked in a batter.

FANCHONNETTES. Puff pastries filled with custard and topped with meringue.

GÂTEAU À LA BROCHE. Cake made with flour, sugar, eggs, white wine, oil, and orange flavored water, cooked on a turning spit.

CROQUETS DE BORDEAUX. Almond biscuits flavored with orange flower water.

PRUNEAUX FOURRÉS D'AGEN. Prunes stuffed with almond paste.

Pays Basque, Béarn, Bigorre

The Pays Basque or Euskaleria, as it is called in its native tongue, is tucked away in the southwest corner of France, between the Atlantic coast and the Pyrenees. The origin of the Basques is unknown. Their language is like no other in Europe. It has been said that the devil tried to learn it for seven years and gave up in disgust. The language itself is primitive, and not suited to abstract thought. Perhaps that is why the Basques express themselves better through their songs and dances.

The Basques are a proud, independent people who have retained their own culture, even under centuries of French rule. Their architecture is unique, with asymetrical whitewashed houses, tiled roofs, wooden balconies, and timbers reminiscent of the Tudor style. The Pays Basque was once part of the kingdom of Navarre, when it was ruled by Ferdinand and Isabella. Today three of its seven provinces are in France. The remainder spill over into Spain.

The cooking of the Pays Basque still shows Spanish influence. Probably the most famous dish is *pipérade*, an omelette or scrambled eggs made with tomatoes, onions, and hot red peppers called *les piments d'Espelette* (named after the town of Espelette where they are grown).

Beans, potatoes, and cabbage appear in many dishes. Fruit is abundant, especially apples, which grow well in the cool breezes of the Atlantic. Corn is widely grown and made into various soups, porridges, fritters, breads, and cakes.

Bayonne is famous for its chocolate, which has been made here since the early seventeenth century. The first chocolate factories were started by Jews who were fleeing the Spanish Inquisition. Bayonne is also famous for the manufacture of weapons; Bayonne gave its name to the bayonnet.

Cheese has been made in the Pays Basque for four thousand years. The Basques claim their tradition of making cheese is the oldest surviving in the world. Basque cheese is generally made from ewe's milk and is called *Ardi–Gasna*—which means *fromage du pays* (local cheese). A mild cow's milk cheese, *Lou Palou*, is also made.

Irouleguy is the most famous wine, which Curnonsky claimed made girls dance. *Izarra* (literally, "star") is a liqueur made from various herbs and wild flowers, and is known for its digestive qualities. There are two kinds: yellow and green.

Béarn lies to the east of the Pays Basque, in the heart of the Pyrénées. The Béarnais are an equally independent people, with a reputation for gaiety and bravado. They, too, have their own language, a dialect of Gascon. The capital, Pau, is the birthplace of Henri of Navarre, who later became Henri IV of France.

The Béarnais like their food spicy, with plenty of onions, garlic, and shallots. Butter is the main cooking fat. Like most mountain people, they are soup-lovers. *Touli*, or *ouliat*, is an onion soup thickened with egg yolks and poured over slices of bread. If leeks and grated cheese are added it is called *soupe de berger*. Another soup is *cousinette*, a vegetable broth made with beet greens, spinach, lettuce, sorrel, and *cousine* (a wild member of the mallow family). Sometimes cousinette is thickened with cornmeal, in which case it is called *jerbilhou*.

The best-known cheese is *Ossau–Iraty*, made with ewe's milk, or a mixture of ewe's and cow's milk.

Several wines are produced: Jurançon, an amber-colored white wine that was a favorite of Henri of Navarre (there is also a red); and two wines from Vic Bilh: Madiran, a full-bodied red wine that is said to have tonic qualities; and Portet. Vic Bilh is also famous for its mustard made with white wine.

Bigorre is a land of snow-capped mountains, lakes, and forests.

The capital, Tarbes, has been a spa and center of market gardening since Roman times. Lourdes, in the north, is probably the most famous shrine in France, where millions flock each year in search of miracle cures.

The cooking of Bigorre overlaps with that of Béarn. *Toulia* is an onion soup similar to the ouliat of Béarn. Butter is also used for cooking.

The best-known cheeses are *Vic–en–Bigorre* and *Esbareich*, a soft ewe's milk cheese that matures into a hard grating cheese.

LOCAL SPECIALTIES

LE PIL–PIL BASQUE. A mixture of garlic and hot red peppers, pounded together and used for seasoning.

POTAGE BASQUE. Green bean and potato soup, garnished with olives and served with grated cheese on the side.

BARTXURI SALDA. Garlic soup with poached eggs, hot red peppers, and croutons.

PURÉE DE CIBOURE, or SOUPE LUZIENNE. Potato and haricot bean soup, with leeks, shallots, and olives.

POTAGE CRÈME DE MAÏS À LA TOMATE. Cream of cornmeal and tomato soup, thickened with egg yolks.

BROYE, or JERBILHOU. Cornmeal porridge, made with milk or vegetable broth.

OMELETTE À LA BIGOURDANE. An omelette with truffles topped with a wine sauce.

OEUFS MARITCHU. Scrambled eggs with artichokes and tomatoes.

TOMATES FARCIS DE BIDART. Tomatoes stuffed with onions and sweet peppers, topped with breadcrumbs and baked in the oven.

CÈPES À L'AIL. Cèpe mushrooms sautéed with garlic and hot red pepper.

ARBIGARAS. Turnip tops sautéed in olive oil with garlic and hot red pepper.

SAUCE GAZTE. A green mayonnaise made with spinach, sorrel, and hard-boiled egg yolks.

MILLHASSOU. Cornmeal flan flavored with orange flower water

ESCOTONS BÉARNAIS. Cornmeal fritters, sprinkled with sugar.

GÂTEAU BASQUE. A large pastry filled with crème patisserie, and sometimes cherry preserves.

ETCHE BISKOXA. A ring-shaped yeast cake with a prune filling.

LE RASIMAT. Walnut and raisin cake.

ARROUCHQUILLA. Sweet pastry filled with crème patisserie.

ROUSQUILLES D'OLORUN. Traditional anise-flavored cakes.

MOUCHOUS BASQUES. Red macaroons.

LE GALFOU or GARFOU. A pound cake. A specialty of Orthez.

MÉTURE DE POTIRON. Cornmeal pumpkin bread.

TOURON, or TTOURON. A kind of nougat made with ground almonds, pistachio nuts, and candied fruit, shaped into decorate loaves.

PÂTÉ DE CEDRAT. Citron fruit jellies. A specialty of Bayonne.

Languedoc, Roussillon

The name Languedoc means the language of *"oc,"* or *"yes,"* which once was spoken in most of southern France from the Alps to Bordeaux, as opposed to the language of *"oui"* that is spoken in northern France.

The people of the Languedoc are independent, with a strong feeling for their cultural heritage. In 121 BC Languedoc became part of the Roman province of Narbonensis. Later it was conquered by the Visigoths, the Franks, and the Arabs. In the twelfth century it became a stronghold of the Cathars, a heretical Christian sect who believed that the material world was created by the devil. In the thirteenth century a crusade, led by the notoriously cruel Simon de Montfort, was launched against the Cathars until they were finally wiped out at the end of the century.

The cooking of Languedoc is influenced by Arab and Roman cuisines. All kinds of beans, called *mounjetas* or *favots*, and lentils are used in cooking, especially in the north around Toulouse. Chestnuts are a staple in the Cévennes. Corn and buckwheat are grown in the Comté de Foix, and are made into porridges and pancakes called *pescajous* and *matefains*. In the south the cooking is based on olive oil and garlic, with plenty of tomatoes, eggplants, and green—rather than black—olives. À *la languedocienne* means with tomatoes, eggplant, and cèpe mushrooms, flavored with garlic. Truffles are gathered in the Garrigues, but they do not grow to the proportions of those in the Périgord.

Excellent fruit is grown, especially peaches, apricots, cherries, plums, and melons. Chestnuts, almonds, and pinenuts appear in many desserts. *Touron*, a kind of nougat, is made at Limoux. Toulouse is famous for its candied violets.

Goat cheese is produced in the mountains: *Pelardon*, which is usually preserved in olive oil with garlic and herbs, and *Fourme de Labro*, a blue cheese made in the Cévennes. *Foudjou* is a fromage fort made with a mixture of fresh and dried goat cheese, brandy, garlic, herbs, and plenty of pepper.

Languedoc produces a vast quantity of wine, mainly *vin ordinaire*, but there are some better-known wines: Tavel, Clairette du Languedoc, Blanquette–de–Limoux, Côtes du Rhône, and Côtaux du Languedoc.

Roussillon, the red land, was part of Spanish Catalonia until it became French in 1659. In the thirteenth century it had been part of the kingdom of Mallorca, which included the city of Montpelier, as well as the Balearic Islands, with Perpignan as its capital. The Catalan language is still spoken in Roussillon today. The Catalan influence is also reflected in the cooking, which is based on olive oil and garlic. *El pa y all* (slices of bread rubbed with garlic and sprinkled with olive oil) is often served as an hors-d'oeuvre, or even for breakfast. *All i oli* is an ancester of the Provençale *aïoli* (garlic mayonnaise), but without the egg yolks. Tomatoes and hot peppers are widely used in the cooking. Bitter oranges and saffron appear as additional flavorings.

The wide coastal plain of Roussillon has the sunniest climate in France, and produces fine early vegetables and exotic fruit such as jujubes and medlars. Tangerines, peaches, apricots, melons, cherries, and figs flourish.

Roussillon produces no cheese. Like Languedoc, this is wine country. The best-known wines are Banyuls (red and rosé), Côtes du Roussillon, Maury, and Rivessaltes.

LOCAL SPECIALTIES

SOUPE À L'AIL. Garlic soup thickened with a mixture of egg yolks and olive oil, poured over slices of bread.

POTAGE NÎMOISE. Vegetable soup with onions, tomatoes, carrots, leeks, potatoes, peas, herbs, and cream.

POTAGE NARBONNAISE. White bean soup with rice and sorrel.

OEUFS GARDIOLE. Fried eggplants, topped with fried egg, tomato, garlic, and herbs.

MATAFAN. A thick pancake made of wheat and buckwheat flour, topped with tomato sauce and Gruyère cheese, and gratinéed.

LES ORONGES FARCIS. Oronge-milk mushrooms topped with béchamel sauce, Gruyère cheese and breadcrumbs, and gratinéed.

HARICOTS FRAIS À L'OCCITANE. Fresh haricot beans simmered with olive oil, garlic, tomato, and herbs.

AUBERGINES À LA NÎMOISE. Eggplants stuffed with tomato, fennel, garlic, and breadcrumbs.

FABONADE. A stew of broad beans, onions, and herbs, thickened with egg yolks.

CARBASSOUS À LA CRÈME. Zucchini topped with béchamel sauce and breadcrumbs, gratinéed.

POMMES DE TERRE À LA LANGUEDOCIENNE. Potatoes simmered with onions, tomatoes, and green olives.

SOUFFLÉ ROUSSILLONNAIS. Peach soufflé.

CRÈME D'HOMÈRE. Baked custard made with egg, honey, and white wine.

LE PÉRAT. Fresh pears, dried figs, and prunes poached in red wine with cinnamon.

KALOUGA. A chocolate cake.

LE GÂTEAU DE MILLAS. Cornmeal cake flavored with orange flower water and lemon rind.

BUNYETES. Sweet fritters.

AMENLOUS. Almond pastries.

LES ESCALETOS. Sweet waffles.

LE GÂTIS. Brioche stuffed with fresh white cheese.

GALETOUS. Buckwheat pancakes.

Provence, Comté de Nice

The landscape of Provence is one of the most spectacular in Europe. Its breathtaking coastline is dotted with some of the most famous resorts in the world—St. Tropez, Cannes, Juan–les–Pins. To the north and east lie the wild, sun-baked mountains of Haute–Provence and the Alpes–Maritime. To the west is the rich alluvial plain of the Rhône Valley, which opens out into the salty marshlands of the Camargue in the south.

Provence has its own language and traditions. It has been invaded by almost every race around the Mediterranean. It was originally built by the Greeks and then the Romans, who called it their *Provincia*, hence its name. The Comté de Nice was annexed to France in 1860; before then it was part of the kingdom of Sardinia, which included Savoy and Piedmont.

Provence is a gourmnet's paradise. The cuisine is light and healthy, based on olive oil, garlic, and herbs. The growing season is virtually all year round. The cooking is imaginative, and distinct from both the cuisine of France and Italy. The climate is idyllic, but for the savage mistral that can hurl down the Rhône Valley at almost any time of the year. This fertile valley is the market garden of France, producing onions, garlic, tomatoes, eggplants, zucchini, sweet peppers, artichokes, Swiss chard, asparagus, and spinach in abundance. More than thirty varieties of olives are grown and superb olive oil is made. Black truffles are gathered around Carpentras, and many different kinds of wild mushrooms are found. Rice is cultivated in the Carmargue.

Vegetables play an important role in the cooking of Provence. They are stuffed, made into delicious gratins and *tians*, omelettes, savory pastries, and stews such as the well-known ratatouille made with eggplants, zucchini, sweet peppers, onions, and tomates.

The fruit is superlative, especially figs, peaches, cherries, strawberries, table grapes, watermelon, and the famous orange-fleshed melons of Cavaillon. Fresh fruit is usually served for dessert, but many traditional cakes and fritters, often made with honey and nuts, are made for festivals and religious holidays. *Les treize desserts* (the thirteen desserts)—almonds, walnuts, hazelnuts, dried figs, raisins, prunes, pears, apples, oranges, white nougat, black nougat, winter melon, and *pompe a l'huile* (a yeast cake with candied peel, raisins, and lemon rind)—are traditionally served at the end of the evening meal on Christmas Eve. *Marrons glacés* are made at Collobrières.

Provence produces few cheeses: *les brousses* are various mild fresh cheeses that are usually made from goat's milk, and are not unlike the Italian ricotta or the Corsican *Brocciu*. They are often used in cooking, or may be eaten fresh with salt or sugar. *Le Broussin* is a strong and piquant fromage fort, wrapped in chestnut leaves. If it is sprinkled with summer savory it is called *pebre d'ail*, or *poivre d'âne* (donkey's pepper), the local name for summer savory.

Châteauneuf–du–Pape is king of Provençal wines, followed by the amber Tavel wines. Noilly Prat, an important French Vermouth, is made in Marseilles. Various fruit ratafias and liqueurs are made.

LOCAL SPECIALTIES

AÏOLI, or AILLOLI. Garlic-flavored mayonnaise.

AIGO–BOUIDO. Garlic and herb soup poured over slices of bread.

LO SOUPO–PISTOU. Vegetable soup similar to the Italian minestrone, usually made with green and yellow French beans, potatoes, tomatoes, zucchini, pasta and *pistou* (garlic and basil sauce), served with grated cheese on the side.

LA FOURNADO, or SOUPE AU BÂTON. A thick soup or porridge made with chickpea flour.

BOUI–ABAISSO D'ÉSPINARC. Spinach soup with onion, potatoes, olive oil, saffron, garlic, and herbs, poured over slices of bread and served with poached eggs and grated cheese.

BARBOUÏADO DE CAPOUN. Scrambled eggs with cabbage, onion, and tomato.

BARBOUÏADO DE RABASSO. Scrambled eggs with truffles and Gruyère cheese.

TROUCHA, or TROUCHIA. A flat Swiss chard and spinach omelette.

LA SOCCA. A chickpea flour crêpe or galette, similar to *la cado* of Toulon.

BORSOTTI, or BOUSSOTOU. Ravioli stuffed with spinach, rice, egg, and grated cheese.

RAVIOLES DE COURGE. Pumpkin ravioli, usually served with walnut sauce. A Christmas specialty.

PASTA PISTOU. Fresh egg noodles with garlic and basil sauce.

TIAN À LA BOUSSOULENCA. Gratin of courgettes, rice, and bread soaked in milk and grated cheese.

BOUMIANO. Eggplant and tomato purée with Parmesan cheese, topped with breadcrumbs and gratinéed.

CASSOLO D'ESPINARC E DE CACHOFLE. A spinach and artichoke gratin.

BARBOUÏADO DE FAVO. Broad beans simmered in olive oil with artichokes and thyme.

BIGNET DE FLOUR DE COUGOURDETO. Zucchini flower fritters.

ROUSSIN D'ESPINARC. Sautéed spinach mixed with béchamel sauce, and garnished with sliced hard-boiled eggs.

SALADE CHAMPÊTRE, or SALADO CHAMPAN-ELLO. A salad of wild herbs.

PASTISSOUN DE CALENA. A yeast cake with almonds, raisins, grated lemon rind, anise seed, and orange flower water. A Christmas specialty.

TORTA DE BLEA. A sweet Swiss chard or spinach tart with raisins.

FOUGASSETTES. Little cakes flavored with saffron and orange flower water.

LOU CHICHI–FRÉGI. Small sweet fritters flavored with orange flower water.

GNOCCHI DE TRUFO. Potato dumplings.

Corsica

Napoleon said he would know Corsica with his eyes shut by the fragrance of her *maquis* or scrubland. Corsica lies on the crossroads between Spain and Italy, France and North Africa. This beautiful and mysterious island is virtually a mountain surrounded by the sea, with a thousand kilometers of rugged coastline.

Centuries of invasions by Etruscans, Carthaginians, Greeks, Romans, Ostrogoths, Saracens, Pisans, Lombards, Genoans, and the French have forced much of the population away from the narrow coastal plains up into the almost-inaccessible mountain villages. This isolation has made the Corsicans fiercely self-reliant, but dependent on their own families for survival. A Corsican respects his country, his elders, and above all, his family name.

In the Middle Ages wheat was an important staple, but when the island was under Genoan rule, wheat was so heavily taxed that the Corsicans stopped growing it and made their bread from chestnut flour instead. To this day chestnut flour is used in many of the local dishes.

Life in Corsica is simple and austere. Most villagers have their own *jardins potager* or vegetable gardens and although the selection of produce is limited, it is of the highest quality. Artichokes, eggplants, zucchini, sweet peppers, tomatoes, leeks, garlic, olives, and almonds are grown, as well as many unusual fruits: pomegranates, medlars, jujubes, arbutus berries, kumquats, oranges, citrons, cedrats, apricots, peaches, cherries, avocados, and wine and table grapes. The growing season is virtually year-round.

Corsican cooking is rustic and simple. Thick soups with vegetables and beans are often served for the evening meal, perhaps with some Brocciu cheese or a fried egg. Only a few of the dishes are reminiscent of Italy—gnocchi, canneloni, ravioli, *poulenda* (polenta) often made with chestnut flour instead of cornmeal. Many vegetable and herb fritters, savory pancakes, and pastries are made.

Corsican cheese is usually made with goat's or ewe's milk. The most famous cheese is *Brocciu*, which may be fresh or dried. The fresh cheese is often served as a dessert mixed with brandy and sprinkled with sugar.

Most Corsican wine is produced in the region of Ajaccio and Sartène. The rosé wines are best, with a high alcoholic content and a strong bouquet. Various fruit wines and liqueurs are also produced.

LOCAL SPECIALTIES

BRILLULI. Chestnut flour porridge.

MACAREDDA. Chestnut soup.

SOUPE DE CAMPILE. Onion and Swiss chard soup, thickened with Brocciu cheese and egg.

SOUPE AUX POIS CHICHES. Chickpea and pasta soup. An Easter specialty.

ARTICHAUTS AUX BROCCIU. Artichokes stuffed with Brocciu cheese.

BROUILLADE AUX ASPERGES SAUVAGES. Scrambled eggs with wild asparagus tips.

AUBERGINES À LA BONIFACIENNE. Eggplants stuffed with bread soaked in milk, eggs, and cheese.

LAMATA CASTAGNINA. A baked chestnut flour "pancake" topped with spinach and Brocciu cheese.

MULLADE. A rustic pancake made with flour and goat cheese.

OMELETTE AU BROCCIU À LA MENTHE.
Omelette filled with Brocciu cheese and mint.

PIVARUNTA. Sweet peppers stuffed with rice and herbs.

STORZAPRETI À LA BASTIASE. Spinach and Brocciu cheese gnocchi.

RAVIOLI AU FENOUIL À LA MENTHE. Ravioli stuffed with cheese, fennel and mint, served with tomato sauce and grated cheese on the side.

BASTELLE D'HERBES. Vegetable turnovers.

FRITELLE DE COURGETTES. Zucchini fritters.

TORTA CASTAGNINA. A chestnut flour tart with nuts and raisins, flavored with rum.

FIADONE. A simple cheesecake made with Brocciu cheese, eggs, sugar, and lemon rind.

PANETTE DOUCE. Sweet raisin bread. An Easter specialty.

FALCULELLE. Sweet cheese-filled pastries.

FRAPPE. Anise seed-flavored fritters.

PISTICCHINI. Chestnut soufflé.

FLAN À LA FARINE DE CHATAÎGNES. A kind of baked custard, thickened with chestnut flour.

NICCI. Chestnut-flour pancakes.

HORS D'OEUVRES AND SALADS

LES HORS-D'OEUVRES ET LES SALADES

Hors-d'oeuvres literally means "outside the main work." They are intended to stimulate the appetite while you are waiting for the main course. The custom of serving hors-d'oeuvres dates back to Roman times when herbs, lettuce, egg, cheese, and olives were often served at the start of a meal.

Hors-d'oeuvres can be very simple, such as steamed artichokes or asparagus served with a vinaigrette sauce. In the Languedoc fresh broad beans or tiny peas are simply served with a grinding of coarse salt with perhaps some country bread rubbed with garlic, and sprinkled with olive oil and a dash of wine vinegar. In Provence meals usually begin with fresh fruit such as melon or figs, or with a salad. A wide variety of salad greens and herbs are used: all kinds of lettuce, escarole, curly endive, tender young dandelion leaves, purslane, arugula, salad burnet, and lamb's lettuce, to name a few. There is even a salad made entirely of wild herbs from the fields called *salade champêtre*, or *salado champanello*.

Composed salads are made up of two or more cooked ingredients: most of the French provinces have their own favorite combinations. In the Lyonnais a typical composed salad might consist of dandelion leaves, beets, sliced onion, and hard-boiled egg. In the Perigord a composed salad might be made of cooked green beans, lettuce, sliced artichoke hearts, and chopped walnuts.

Good quality olive oil, preferably cold-pressed, and pure wine vinegar, or lemon juice, are essential for making good hors-d'oeuvres and salads. The type of oil and vinegar used varies from province to province. Extra-virgin olive oil and wine vinegar is essential in Provence and the Languedoc. In Normandy cider vinegar is preferred. Walnut or hazelnut oil is often used in Poitou, the Perigord, and Dauphiné. Many herb and fruit vinegars made in France are available in health food shops and gourmet delicatessens.

CRUDITÉS

Crudités are the simplest and most healthy way to start a meal. Almost any vegetable, sliced or cut into sticks, can be used: radishes, cherry tomatoes, scallions, small white mushrooms, celery, fennel bulb, sweet peppers, cucumbers, cauliflower, or broccoli florets.

Arrange a colorful selection of vegetables on a large serving platter, with a bowl of vinaigrette sauce or aïoli (see pages 104–105 and 108) on the side. Guests can dip the vegetables into the sauce of their choice.

ARTICHOKES

Catherine de Medici first introduced the artichoke to France when she married the Dauphin in 1533. She was so fond of artichokes, she is said to have eaten them until she burst.

Two main varieties are cultivated in France—the large round *gros camus* of Brittany, which is grown in the Leon and the Côte d'Emeraude, and the small purple variety called *macau* cultivated in Roussillon and Provence. When it is young and tender the purple variety may be eaten raw *au sel*—with a little salt.

Brittany

ARTICHOKES WITH BRETON SAUCE
(Artichauts sauce Bretonne froide)

Sauce bretonne can mean several things in Brittany, from a hot wine and cream sauce with mushrooms to this creamy vinaigrette sauce flavored with gherkin and capers.

4   large artichokes
¾   cup peanut or olive oil
¼   cup cider vinegar
3   tbsp. light cream
1   small gherkin, finely chopped
1   tsp. capers, roughly chopped
1   tbsp. fresh chives, chopped
    salt
    freshly ground black pepper

Trim the stems of the artichokes. Steam the vegetables for 1 to 1¹/₂ hours, or until the bottoms are tender when pierced with a sharp knife and the outer leaves pull away easily. Set aside to cool.

Mix the peanut oil and cider vinegar together in a small bowl. Stir in the cream, gherkin, capers and chives and mix well. Season with salt and black pepper to taste. Pour the sauce into 4 small pots. Arrange the artichokes on individual platters and serve with a pot of sauce on the side. *Serves 4.*

L y o n n a i s

STUFFED ARTICHOKES
(Artichauts Farcis)

In this recipe from Lyon artichokes are stuffed with a creamy béchamel sauce mixed with chopped hard-boiled egg, garlic, and parsley. Gruyère cheese is sprinkled over the top and the artichokes are briefly gratinéed in a hot oven.

4	globe artichokes
1¼	cups béchamel sauce (see page 99)
2	tbsp. light cream
2	hard-boiled eggs, finely chopped
2	garlic cloves, crushed
2	tbsp. fresh parsley, finely chopped
	salt
	freshly ground black pepper
½	cup Gruyère cheese, grated

Trim the stems of the artichokes. Steam the vegetables for 1 to 1¹/₂ hours, or until the bottoms are tender when pierced with a sharp knife and the outer leaves pull away easily. Set aside to cool slightly, then remove the inside leaves and hearts.

Prepare the béchamel sauce and stir in the cream. Remove from the heat, stir in the chopped hard-boiled eggs, garlic, and parsley, and season to taste with salt and black pepper. Arrange the artichokes side by side in a well-oiled shallow baking dish. Spoon the stuffing into the artichokes and sprinkle with Gruyère cheese. Bake in a preheated 400° F. oven for 10 minutes, or until the tops are golden. Serve at once. *Serves 4.*

Paris,   Ile-de-France

ASPARAGUS CHANTILLY
(Asperges au Chantilly)

Chantilly is usually sweetened whipped cream but in this dish it is a mixture of home-made mayonnaise and plain whipped cream.

 2 **pounds asparagus**
 1 **cup homemade mayonnaise (see page 107)**
 ½ **cup whipping cream**
     salt
     white pepper

Trim the ends of the asparagus and peel the stalks with a sharp knife or vegetable parer up to 3 inches from the tips. Steam the asparagus for 15 minutes or until tender. Chill thoroughly. Prepare the mayonnaise as directed on page (107). Whip the cream stiff and fold into the mayonnaise. Season to taste with salt and white pepper. Arrange the asparagus on individual plates and serve with chantilly sauce on the side. *Serves 6.*

Auvergne, Limousin

BLUE CHEESE
CANAPÉS

(Canapés au bleu)

These canapés are delicious with a glass of dry
red wine.

$^1/_2$ **pound Bleu d'Auvergne cheese**
$^1/_4$ **pound butter, softened**
 2 **tbsp. cognac or brandy**
 6 **slices whole wheat bread, toasted**

Blend the Bleu d'Auvergne cheese and butter together in a mixing
bowl. Add the cognac and mix well. Cut the toast into quarters
diagonally and spread with the cheese mixture. *Serves 6.*

Poitou, Charnete

BROCCOLI WITH WALNUT OIL
(Broccoli à l'huile de noix)

Walnut oil is widely used in France, especially in Poitou, Périgord and the Dauphiné. It has a distinctive flavor and makes a delicious salad dressing.

> 1   **pound broccoli**
> 6   **tbsp. walnut oil**
> 2   **tbsp. wine vinegar**
> 2   **garlic cloves, crushed**
>   **salt**
>   **freshly ground black pepper**

Trim the stalk of the broccoli and break the head into florets. Steam for 7 or 8 minutes or until the broccoli is tender but still firm. Place in a salad bowl.

Mix the walnut oil, wine vinegar, and garlic in a small bowl and season to taste with salt and black pepper. Pour over the warm broccoli, toss lightly, and serve at room temperature. *Serves 4.*

Auvergne, Limousin

CÈPE MUSHROOMS WITH TOMATOES, SHALLOTS, AND DRY WHITE WINE

(Cèpes "mode de Brive")

Cèpes are one of the most highly prized wild mushrooms in France. They are a member of the boletus family and are generally found in woodlands. They grow especially well in the volcanic soil of the Limousin. If unavailable, any other mushroom may be used instead.

1½	pounds cèpe mushrooms
3	tbsp. olive oil
1	celery stalk, diced
3	shallots, finely chopped
2	plum tomatoes, peeled, seeded, and chopped
½	cup dry white wine
	juice of ½ lemon
1	bay leaf
2	cloves
	pinch of thyme
	pinch of coriander seeds
	salt
	freshly ground black pepper

Wipe the cèpes with a damp cloth, peel the stalks, and cut into fairly thin slices. Heat the olive oil in a heavy-based saucepan and cook the celery and shallots over a moderate heat for 3 minutes. Add the cèpes and cook for 5 minutes. Add the chopped tomatoes, dry white wine, lemon juice, herbs, and spices, and season to taste with salt and black pepper. Bring to a boil, cover, and simmer until the sauce is reduced to a syrupy consistency. Transfer to a serving dish and serve cold. *Serves 4 to 6.*

Provence,   Comté   de   Nice

STUFFED EGGS WITH OLIVES AND CAPERS

(Oeufs farcis aux olives et aux capres)

8   Niçoise or similar black olives, pitted and
    finely chopped
1   tbsp. capers, chopped
3   tbsp. olive oil
4   hard-boiled eggs
    salt
    freshly ground black pepper
4   lettuce leaves

Place the olives, capers, and olive oil in a small bowl and mash well with a fork, or use a mortar and pestle if you have one. Cut the eggs in half lengthwise, remove the yolks and mash in a bowl. Add the olive mixture and blend well. Season with salt and black pepper to taste. Spoon the mixture back into the egg halves and serve on a bed of lettuce. *Serves 4.*

Provence, Comté de Nice

MARINATED FENNEL
WITH BLACK OLIVES
(*Lou fenouii en samoïra*)

Celery, mangetout peas, small white onions, carrots, and mushrooms may all be prepared in the same way.

3 fennel bulbs (about 1¼ to 1½ lbs.)
4 tbsp. olive oil
3 garlic cloves, peeled and cut in half
2 cups water
   juice of 1 lemon
1 bay leaf
   a sprig of thyme
4 peppercorns
   salt
12 Niçoise or similar black olives

Remove the stems and coarse outer leaves from the fennel bulbs. Trim the bases and cut into wedges. Heat the olive oil in a saucepan and cook the garlic for 1 minute. Add the water, lemon juice, bay leaf, thyme, and peppercorns and bring to a boil. Add the fennel and season with salt to taste. Simmer, uncovered, for 20 minutes. Remove the fennel with a slotted spoon to a serving dish. Raise the heat and reduce the cooking liquid by half. Remove the bay leaf. Pour over the fennel and garnish with black olives. Refrigerate for 2 or 3 hours before serving. *Serves 4 to 6.*

Burgundy

SMALL WHITE ONIONS SIMMERED WITH TOMATOES, SULTANAS, AND WHITE WINE

(Petits oignons à la bourguignonne)

1½   pounds small white onions
3   tbsp. sultanas (white raisins)
4   tbsp. olive oil
2   tbsp. white wine vinegar
2   canned plum tomatoes, forced through a
     sieve or puréed in a food processor
3   garlic cloves, crushed
1   bay leaf
     pinch of thyme
     pinch of sage
     salt
     freshly ground black pepper
¾   cup dry white wine

Peel the onions and place in a saucepan with the sultanas, olive oil, vinegar, puréed tomatoes, garlic, herbs, and salt and black pepper to taste. Pour in the wine and bring to a boil. Cover, and simmer for 45 to 50 minutes, or until the onions are tender and the sauce is reduced to a syrupy consistency. Transfer to a serving dish and serve cold. *Serves 4 to 6.*

Provence, Comté de Nice

SWEET PEPPERS WITH ONIONS AND CAPERS

(Pebroun au vinaigre)

6   sweet red peppers
2   medium onions, thinly sliced
4   tbsp. olive oil
2   tbsp. wine vinegar
2   tsp. capers
    salt
    freshly ground black pepper

Remove the ribs and seeds from the sweet peppers and cut peppers into strips. Heat the olive oil in a large frying pan and add the sweet peppers and onions. Cover and simmer for 30 minutes, or until the peppers are tender. There should be a little juice from the onions. If there is too much juice, raise the heat and cook until the excess is evaporated. Stir in the vinegar and capers and season with salt and black pepper to taste. Cook over a moderate heat for 5 minutes to blend the flavors. Transfer to a serving dish and chill. *Serves 6.*

Normandy

APPLE SALAD
WITH TARRAGON
(Salade de pommes)

This refreshing salad consists of diced apple in a creamy vinaigrette sauce made with walnut oil. If you like the salad may be garnished with chopped walnuts.

4 or 5   apples
    6   tbsp. walnut oil
    2   tbsp. cider vinegar
    2   tbsp. light cream
    1   tbsp. fresh parsley, finely chopped
    1   tsp. fresh tarragon leaves, chopped
         salt
         freshly ground black pepper

Peel, core, and dice the apples and place in a salad bowl. Combine the walnut oil, cider vinegar, cream, and herbs in a small bowl and mix well. Season to taste with salt and black pepper. Pour the dressing over the apples, toss lightly, and serve. *Serves 4.*

Burgundy

BEET SALAD
WITH MUSTARD
CREAM DRESSING

(Salade de betterave à la crème)

3 or 4	medium beets (about 1 lb.)
1	medium purple onion, thinly sliced
6	tbsp. walnut oil
2	tbsp. wine vinegar
1	tsp. Dijon mustard
2	tbsp. light cream
2	tbsp. fresh chives, chopped
	salt
	freshly ground black pepper

Wash and scrub the beets and pat them dry. Place on a baking sheet and bake at 350° F. for 45 minutes to 1 hour, or until the beets are tender. Remove the skins and set aside to cool. Place the walnut oil, wine vinegar, mustard, cream, and chives in a small bowl and mix well. Season with salt and black pepper to taste. Cut the beets into rounds about ¹/₈ inch thick. Place in a serving bowl with the sliced onion. Pour over the dressing, toss lightly, and serve at once. *Serves 4.*

Languedoc, Roussillon

BROAD BEAN AND PURSLANE SALAD
(Salade de fèves)

Purslane, or *pourpier* as it is called in France, is a pale green, slightly astringent salad green available in most Greek or Middle Eastern delicatessens.

6	ounces freshly shelled broad beans
1/2	bunch purslane
1/2	head of Boston lettuce
2	shallots, thinly sliced
12	Niçoise or similar black olives
	a handful of fresh mint, finely chopped
3	tbsp. olive oil
1	tbsp. wine vinegar
1/2	tsp. Dijon mustard
	salt
	freshly ground black pepper

Bring the beans to a boil in lightly salted water and cook, covered, for 45 to 50 minutes, or until tender. Drain, cool slightly, and place in a salad bowl.

Break the purslane and lettuce into bite-size pieces and add to the beans, shallots, black olives, and mint.

Make a vinaigrette sauce with the olive oil, vinegar, and mustard, and season to taste with salt and black pepper. Pour over the salad, toss lightly, and serve at once. *Serves 4.*

Normandy

CABBAGE AND APPLE SALAD WITH WHITE RAISINS, CALVADOS, AND CRÈME FRAÎCHE

(Salade de chou)

1/2	small white cabbage
2	apples, peeled, cored, and diced
1/4	cup raisins
1/3	cup crème fraîche (see page 110)
1	tbsp. lemon juice
1	tbsp. Calvados or brandy
1	tbsp. fresh chives
	salt
	freshly ground black pepper

Place the cabbage, apples, and raisins in a salad bowl, and mix well. Combine the cream, lemon juice, Calvados, and chives in a small bowl and blend well. Season to taste with salt and black pepper. Pour over the cabbage mixture, toss well, and serve at once. *Serves 4.*

Franche   Comté

COMTÉ CHEESE
SALAD
(Salade au Comté)

This salad consists of diced Comté cheese, lettuce, tomatoes, and shallots in a creamy vinaigrette sauce. Comté cheese, or Gruyère de Comté as it is sometimes called, is a smooth, hard cheese with a delicious, nutty flavor. If unavailable, Gruyère cheese may be used.

1	head of Boston lettuce
1¹/₂	cups (6 oz.) Comté or Gruyère cheese, diced
2	shallots, thinly sliced
¹/₂	tsp. Dijon mustard
1	tbsp. light cream
3	tbsp. olive oil
1	tbsp. wine vinegar
1	tbsp. fresh chives, chopped
	salt
	freshly ground black pepper

Break the lettuce into bite-size pieces and place in a salad bowl with the tomatoes, cheese, and shallots.

Mix the mustard and cream in a bowl. Blend in the olive oil, wine vinegar, and chives, and season to taste with salt and black pepper. Pour over the salad, toss lightly, and serve at once. *Serves 4.*

Savoie, Dauphiné

CURLY ENDIVE, LAMB'S LETTUCE, AND WALNUT SALAD
(Salade Dauphinoise)

Lamb's lettuce has several names in France: *mâché*, which comes from *mâcher* (to chew), *boursette*, from *bourse-à-berger*, meaning shepherd's purse, and *doucette*, for its slightly sweet taste.

- ½   **small curly endive**
- ¼   **pound lamb's lettuce**
- 1   **endive, trimmed and sliced**
- ¼   **cup walnuts, roughly chopped**
- 3   **tbsp. walnut oil**
- 1   **tbsp. wine vinegar**
- 1   **garlic clove, crushed**
-     **salt**
-     **freshly ground black pepper**

Break the curly endive and lamb's lettuce into bite-size pieces and place in a salad bowl with the endive and walnuts. Make a vinaigrette sauce with the walnut oil, wine vinegar, and garlic. Season to taste with salt and black pepper. Pour over the salad, toss lightly, and serve at once. *Serves 4.*

Poitou, Charente

LAMB'S LETTUCE, APPLE, AND WALNUT SALAD
(Salade de boursette aux noix)

- ½   pound lamb's lettuce
- 2   granny smith apples
- 2   ounces walnuts, roughly chopped
- 3   tbsp. walnut oil
- 1   tbsp. wine vinegar
- 1   tbsp. light cream
- 1   tbsp. fresh mint, chopped

Break the lamb's lettuce into bite-size pieces and place in a salad bowl. Peel, core, and dice apples. Add to the lettuce and walnuts.

Combine the walnut oil, vinegar, cream, and mint in a small bowl and mix well. Pour over the salad, toss lightly, and serve at once. *Serves 4.*

Auvergne, Limousin

HOT LENTIL SALAD

(Salade de lentilles)

The tiny greenish-black lentils from Le Puy are the most highly prized in France. If unavailable, small green lentils may be used instead.

1 cup Le Puy lentils
1 carrot, diced
1 small onion, stuck with 3 cloves
1 bay leaf
3 shallots, finely chopped
1 tbsp. wine vinegar
1 tsp. Dijon mustard
4 tbsp. olive oil
  salt
  freshly ground black pepper

Soak the lentils for 1 hour and drain. Place in a saucepan with the carrot, onion, cloves, and bay leaf. Cover with water, and bring to a boil. Cover, and simmer for 45 minutes to 1 hour, or until the lentils are tender. Drain and remove the bay leaf and cloves.

Place in a salad bowl with the shallots. Make a vinaigrette: mix the vinegar and mustard, then add the olive oil in a slow, steady stream, whisking constantly. Season to taste with salt and black pepper. Pour over the lentils, toss lightly, and serve at once. *Serves 4 to 6.*

Languedoc, Roussillon

MUSHROOM SALAD WITH BLACK OLIVES AND PARSLEY

(Les russules en salade)

Russule is a variety of mushroom with firm white flesh and a pleasant flavor that is found in many parts of France. If unavailable, small white mushrooms may be used.

- ³/₄ **pound russule or small white mushrooms**
- 2 **garlic cloves, crushed**
- 1 **tbsp. fresh parsley, finely chopped**
- 6 **tbsp. olive oil**
-    **juice of 1 lemon**
-    **salt**
-    **freshly ground black pepper**
- 12 **Niçoise or similar black olives**

Slice the mushrooms and place in a serving bowl. Combine the garlic, parsley, and olive oil and pour over the mushrooms. Cover with a plate and leave to marinate for 2 hours. Just before serving, add the lemon juice and season to taste with salt and black pepper. Toss lightly, and garnish with black olives. *Serves 4.*

Provence,   Comté   de   Nice

LOU MESCLUN
(Lou mesclun)

Mesclun, literally a "mixture," is a salad of at
least 7 different salad greens and herbs, usually
including arugula, wild chicory, lamb's lettuce,
cos or oak leaf lettuce, watercress, purslane,
dandelion leaves, salad burnet, radicchio, fennel, or chervil.

1/2	oak leaf lettuce
1/2	bunch watercress
1/4	head escarole
1/4	head radicchio (red chicory)
	a handful of arugula
	a handful of lamb's lettuce
	a handful of purslane
2	shallots, thinly sliced into rounds
6	tbsp. olive oil
2	tbsp. wine vinegar
2	garlic cloves
	salt
	freshly ground black pepper

Break the salad greens into bite-size pieces and place in a salad
bowl with the shallots. Make a vinaigrette with the olive oil, vinegar, mustard, and garlic, and season with salt and black pepper to
taste. Pour over the salad, toss lightly, and serve at once. *Serves 6.*

Lyonnais

DANDELION SALAD
WITH BEETS AND
HARD-BOILED EGGS
(Salade composé)

If dandelion leaves are unavailable, this salad is equally good made with arugula or lamb's lettuce, or a mixture of both.

¹/₂	pound young dandelion leaves
2	small beets, boiled and sliced
2	hard-boiled eggs, sliced
3	tbsp. olive oil
1	tbsp. wine vinegar
¹/₂	tsp. Dijon mustard
1	garlic clove, crushed
	salt
	freshly ground black pepper

Break the dandelion leaves into bite-size pieces. Place in a salad bowl with the sliced beets and boiled eggs. Make a vinaigrette sauce with the olive oil, vinegar, mustard, and garlic and season to taste with salt and black pepper. Pour over the salad, toss lightly, and serve at once. *Serves 4.*

Auvergne, Limousin

MIXED GREEN SALAD WITH BLUE CHEESE DRESSING
(La pastourelle)

The dressing for this salad is made with Bleu d'Auvergne cheese, a semi-hard blue cheese made from cow's milk. Although it is usually made with the same mold as Roquefort cheese, it is much less strong and has a creamier texture.

1/2	oak leaf lettuce
1/4	curly endive
1/4	pound lamb's lettuce
1 1/2	oz. Bleu d'Auvergne cheese
3	tbsp. walnut oil
1	tbsp. wine vinegar
2	tbsp. light cream
2	garlic cloves, crushed

Break the lettuce, curly endive, and lamb's lettuce into bite-size pieces and place in a salad bowl. Mash the blue cheese with a fork in a small bowl. Gradually blend in the remaining ingredients until the sauce is smooth and creamy. Pour over the salad, toss lightly, and serve at once. *Serves 4.*

Périgord, Quercy, Rouergue

MIXED GREEN SALAD WITH GREEN BEANS, ARTICHOKES, AND WALNUTS

(Salade composé)

¹/₄	pound green beans
¹/₂	head of Boston lettuce
¹/₂	bunch of watercress
2	artichoke bottoms, boiled and sliced
12	walnut halves, broken into small pieces
3	tbsp. walnut oil
1	tbsp. wine vinegar
1	garlic clove, crushed
	salt
	freshly ground black pepper

Trim the ends of the beans and steam for 15 minutes, or until tender. Cut into 2-inch lengths. Break the lettuce and watercress into bite-size pieces and place in a salad bowl with the beans, artichoke bottoms, and walnuts. Make a vinaigrette with the walnut oil, vinegar, and garlic and season to taste with salt and black pepper. Pour over the salad, toss lightly, and serve at once. *Serves 4.*

Alsace, Lorraine

POTATO SALAD WITH CAPERS AND MUSTARD CREAM DRESSING

(Grumbeeresalad)

This potato salad from Alsace is dressed with a mixture of mustard, cream, wine vinegar, capers, and chives.

1¹/₂	**pounds new potatoes**
2	**celery stalks, thinly sliced**
1	**small onion, finely chopped**
6	**tbsp. light cream**
1	**tbsp. wine vinegar**
¹/₂	**tsp. Dijon mustard**
1	**tsp. capers, roughly chopped**
3	**tbsp. fresh chives, chopped**
	salt
	freshly ground black pepper

Scrub the potatoes but do not peel. Bring to a boil in lightly salted water and simmer for 20 minutes or until tender. Drain, and peel while still warm. Cut into medium dice and place in a serving bowl with the celery and onion.

Mix the mustard, vinegar, and cream in a small bowl. Stir in the chives and season with salt and black pepper to taste. Pour over the potato salad and garnish with capers. Toss lightly, and serve at room temperature. *Serves 4.*

Anjou, Tourraine

ARTICHOKE AND POTATO SALAD
(Salade de pommes de terre et fonds d'artichauts)

This salad is usually dressed with a mixture of mayonnaise and *crème fraîche* or heavy cream, but I prefer to use yogurt instead.

3   artichoke bottoms, boiled and sliced
1   pound new potatoes, boiled and sliced
2   scallions, thinly sliced
3   tbsp. homemade mayonnaise (see page 107)
3   tbsp. yogurt
1   tbsp. fresh chives, chopped
    salt
    freshly ground black pepper
1   tsp. capers

Place the artichoke bottoms and potatoes in a salad bowl while they are still warm. Add the scallions.

In a small bowl mix the mayonnaise with the yogurt and chives. Season to taste with salt and black pepper. Pour over the vegetables and toss lightly. Garnish with capers and serve at room temperature. *Serves 4.*

Provence, Comté de Nice

PROVENÇALE POTATO SALAD

(Salade des pommes de terre à la Provençale)

This potato salad has a delicious Mediterranean flavor.

2 pounds new potatoes
4 shallots, finely chopped
4 medium tomatoes, cut into wedges
2 tbsp. fresh parsley, finely chopped
¼ cup Niçoise or similar black olives
6 tbsp. olive oil
2 tbsp. wine vinegar
2 garlic cloves, crushed
   salt
   freshly ground black pepper

Scrub the potatoes but do not peel. Bring to a boil in lightly salted water and simmer for 20 minutes or until tender. Drain and peel while still warm. Cut into medium dice and place in a serving bowl with the shallots, tomatoes, parsley, and black olives.

Make a vinaigrette sauce with the olive oil, vinegar, and garlic and season to taste with salt and black pepper. Pour over the potato salad, toss lightly, and serve at room temperature. *Serves 6.*

Bordeaux, Les Landes

PURSLANE AND ARUGULA SALAD
(Salade de pourpier)

¹/₂	bunch purslane
¹/₄	pound arugula
2	shallots, thinly sliced into rounds
2	hard-boiled eggs, sliced
3	tbsp. olive oil
1	tbsp. wine vinegar
1	garlic clove, crushed
	salt
	freshly ground black pepper

Break the purslane and arugula into bite-size pieces and place in a salad bowl with the shallots and boiled eggs. Make a vinaigrette sauce with the olive oil, vinegar, and garlic, and season to taste with salt and black pepper. Pour over the salad, toss lightly, and serve at once. *Serves 4.*

Languedoc, Roussillon

CATALAN RICE SALAD
(Salade de riz à la catalane)

Rice salads are especially good for buffets. Sliced scallions, artichoke hearts, radishes, and fennel are all possible additions.

    1   recipe rice pilaf, cooked (see page 232)
    1   sweet red pepper, diced
    2   medium tomatoes, cut into wedges
    1   celery stalk, cut into wedges
    1   purple onion, chopped
    1/4 cup mixed green and black olives, pitted and
        sliced
    1   ounce fresh cilantro, finely chopped
        a handful of fresh mint, finely chopped
    3   tbsp. olive oil
    1   tbsp. wine vinegar
    1   garlic clove, crushed
        salt
        freshly ground black pepper

Combine the rice, sweet pepper, tomatoes, celery, onion, olives, and herbs in a salad bowl.

Make a vinaigrette sauce with the olive oil, vinegar, and garlic and season to taste with salt and black pepper. Pour over the rice salad and toss lightly. Chill for 1 or 2 hours before serving. *Serves 4.*

Provence, Comté de Nice

ROASTED SWEET PEPPERS
(Poivrons grillés)

Use the best quality extra-virgin olive oil you can find.

> 4   red, green, or yellow sweet peppers
> 6   tbsp. olive oil
>   salt
>   freshly ground black pepper
> 16   Niçoise or similar black olives
> 1   tsp. capers

Roast the peppers under a hot grill until they are blackened all over. Wash under cold water and remove skins. Cut into quarters, lengthwise and remove the core, fibers, and seeds. Place on a serving platter, dribble over the olive oil and season to taste with salt and black pepper. Garnish with black olives and capers and let marinate for 1 hour before serving. *Serves 4.*

Provence,   Comté   de   Nice

SPINACH AND PEPPERMINT SALAD
(Salade d'espinousos)

The addition of peppermint leaves makes this a deliciously refreshing salad. If peppermint is unavailable, ordinary garden mint may be used.

   ½   **pound spinach**
       a handful of fresh peppermint leaves, roughly chopped
   3   **tbsp. olive oil**
   1   **tbsp. wine vinegar**
   1   **garlic clove, crushed**
       salt
       freshly ground black pepper

Break the spinach into bite-size pieces and place in a salad bowl with peppermint leaves.

Make a vinaigrette sauce with the olive oil, vinegar, and garlic and season to taste with salt and black pepper. Pour over the salad, toss lightly, and serve at once. *Serves 4.*

SAUCES

LES SAUCES

French sauces date back to the Middle Ages, when sauces were sold by *sauciers* (sauce cooks) in the streets of Paris. At that time sauces were heavily seasoned with spices and thickened with bread-crumbs or ground almonds. It was not until the seventeenth century that more refined sauces thickened with flour were invented. The great sauces of haute cuisine were not created until the eighteenth or nineteenth century, when Talleyrand claimed: "England has 3 sauces and 360 religions, whereas France has 3 religions and 360 sauces."

The ingredients used in sauces vary around France. In Normandy sauces are based on butter and cream; cider vinegar often appears in salad dressings. In Provence sauces are based on olive oil, garlic, and herbs. Mustard appears in many sauces in Burgundy. Walnut oil is often used in salad dressings in Dauphiné, Périgord, Poitou, and some parts of central France.

Paris, Ile-de-France

BÉCHAMEL SAUCE
(Sauce béchamel)

This classic white sauce is named after Louis de Béchameil, Marquis de Nointel, a wealthy financier who bought himself the post of *Maître d'hôtel* to Louis XIV. Originally béchamel sauce was made with stock and enriched with cream, instead of milk, which is used today.

4 tbsp. butter
3 tbsp. flour
2 cups hot milk
1/2 tsp. salt
   pinch of white pepper
   pinch of freshly grated nutmeg

Melt the butter in a heavy-bottomed pan. Stir in the flour and cook for 1 minute without browning. Pour in a little hot milk and stir vigorously with a wooden spoon until the mixture is free of lumps. Gradually add more milk until all the milk is incorporated and the sauce is very smooth and creamy. Season with salt, pepper, and nutmeg and simmer for 1 or 2 more minutes. *Makes about 1 pint.*

Paris, Ile-de-France

MORNAY SAUCE
(Sauce Mornay)

This sauce is based on béchamel sauce, with the addition of Gruyère cheese and cream. It is often used for vegetables prepared au gratin. Sometimes the sauce is enriched with 1 or 2 egg yolks instead of cream.

> 1   recipe béchamel sauce (see page 99)
> 2   tbsp. light cream
>   pinch of cayenne pepper
> ¹/₃ cup Gruyère cheese, grated

Prepare the béchamel sauce as directed on page 99 and stir in the cream. Season with cayenne pepper. Remove from the heat and stir in the Gruyère cheese. *Makes about 1 pint.*

Paris, Ile-de-France

MUSHROOM SAUCE

(Sauce duxelles)

Duxelles is a mixture of chopped shallots and mushrooms that is often added to sauces and stuffings. It is generally thought that duxelles was invented by La Varenne, chef to the Marquis d'Uxelles, and author of *Le Cuisinier Francois* (1651). However, it is sometimes claimed that duxelles comes from the town of Uxel in the Côtes du Nord in Brittany.

> 2   tbsp. butter
> ¹/₄ cup finely minced shallots
>   salt
>   freshly ground black pepper
>   pinch of freshly grated nutmeg
> 1   cup béchamel sauce (see page 99)

Heat the butter in a heavy frying pan and cook the shallots over a moderate heat for 5 minutes or until they start to turn golden. Add the mushrooms and cook over a fairly high heat until they are tender and any liquid from the mushrooms has evaporated. Season to taste with salt, black pepper, and nutmeg. Add the hot béchamel sauce and simmer for 2 or 3 minutes. Serve hot. *Makes about 2 cups.*

Paris, Ile-de-France

ONION SAUCE

(Sauce soubise)

This sauce was invented by the Maréchal de Soubise at his Hôtel de Soubise in Paris. Like so many aristocrats of the seventeenth and eighteenth century, he loved to cook.

> 3 **tbsp. butter**
> 1 **pound onions, finely chopped**
> 2 **tbsp. flour**
> 1 **tbsp. wine vinegar**
> 1¹/₂ **cups hot broth or water**
>   **a grating of nutmeg**
>   **salt**
>   **white pepper**
> 2 **tbsp. light cream**

Heat the butter in a heavy-bottomed pan and cook the onions over a moderate heat for 5 minutes, or until they are translucent. Stir in the flour and cook for 1 or 2 minutes without browning. Gradually add the vinegar mixed with the hot stock, stirring constantly with a wooden spoon, until the sauce is thickened. Simmer for 2 or 3 minutes. Stir in the cream and serve hot. *Makes about 3 cups.*

Provence, Comté de Nice

TOMATO SAUCE
(Sauce tomate)

If fresh plum tomatoes are unavailable, canned
plum tomatoes may be used.

- 3 tbsp. olive oil
- 3 garlic cloves, finely chopped
- 1 tbsp. fresh parsley, finely chopped
- 1 tbsp. fresh basil, chopped
- 1½ pounds ripe plum tomatoes, peeled, seeded, and chopped
- ½ bay leaf
- pinch of thyme
- salt
- freshly ground pepper

Heat the olive oil in a large frying pan and cook the garlic, parsley,
and basil for 1 minute. Add the chopped tomatoes, bay leaf, and
thyme, and season to taste with salt and black pepper. Cook,
uncovered, over a moderate heat for 15 minutes, or until the sauce
starts to thicken, mashing the tomatoes gently with a fork as they
cook.

For a smoother sauce, after cooking remove the bay leaf and force
through a sieve, or purée in a food processor. Return to the pan and
bring to a boil. Simmer for a few minutes or until the sauce is slightly thickened. *Makes about 2½ cups.*

Provence, Comté de Nice

BASIL SAUCE
(Pistou à l'huile)

Pistou is a garlicky basil sauce related to Italian pesto. Only fresh basil should be used.

- 1/4 **pound fresh basil**
- 6 **tbsp. olive oil**
- 4 **garlic cloves, crushed**
  salt
  freshly ground black pepper

Place the basil, olive oil, and garlic in a blender and mix slowly until the ingredients are chopped. Blend at high speed until the mixture is smooth. Season to taste with salt and black pepper. *Makes about 3/4 cup.*

All France

VINAIGRETTE SAUCE
(Sauce vinaigrette)

Vinaigrette sauce is usually made in the proportions of 1 tablespoon of wine vinegar to 3 tablespoons of oil. The quality of the sauce depends on the quality of the oil and vinegar used. Extra virgin olive oil and pure wine vinegar are best. 1 or 2 teaspoons of fresh herbs such as parsley, chives, basil, mint or oregano may be added for additional flavoring if you like.

2   garlic cloves, crushed
6   tbsp. extra virgin olive oil
2   tbsp. wine vinegar
    salt
    freshly ground black pepper

Combine all the ingredients with seasoning to taste in a small glass jar. Screw the cap on firmly and shake well until the ingredients have blended and the vinaigrette sauce is slightly thickened. *Makes ½ cup.*

P r o v e n c e ,   C o m t é   d e   N i c e

C I T R O N E T T E
(La citronette)

This delicious salad dressing is made with olive oil, lemon juice, mustard, cream, and herbs.

6   tbsp. extra virgin olive oil
    juice of 1 small lemon
1   tsp. Dijon mustard
1   tbsp. fresh chives, finely chopped
    salt
    freshly ground black pepper
2   tbsp. light cream

Combine the olive oil, lemon juice, mustard, chives, and seasoning to taste in a small glass jar. Screw the cap on firmly and shake vigorously until all the ingredients have blended and the sauce is slightly thickened. Pour into a small bowl and stir in the cream. *Makes about ⅔ cup.*

Alsace, Lorraine

LORRAINE VINAIGRETTE SAUCE
(Verdure Lorraine)

This is a simple vinaigrette sauce enriched with chopped hard-boiled egg and herbs.

6 tbsp. extra virgin olive oil
2 tbsp. wine vinegar
2 garlic cloves
1 tbsp. fresh parsley, finely chopped
1 tbsp. fresh chives, chopped
   a few leaves fresh tarragon
1 hard-boiled egg, finely chopped

Make a vinaigrette sauce with the olive oil, vinegar, and garlic and season to taste with salt and black pepper. Add the herbs and chopped hard-boiled egg and mix well. *Makes about ³⁄4 cup.*

All France

MAYONNAISE
(Mayonnaise)

Mayonnaise was probably invented in 1756 after the siege of Port Mahon in Minorca. There is some controversy over the origins of the word "mayonnaise," which may be a corruption of *moyeunaise*, which derives from the old French *moyeu* (egg yolk). Others believe it stems from magnonaise, a derivation of *manier* (to stir).

2	egg yolks
about 2	tbsp. wine vinegar or lemon juice
	pinch of white pepper
1½	cups sunflowerseed or olive oil, or a combination of both
1	tbsp. boiling water

Place the egg yolks in a mixing bowl with a few drops of vinegar. Add salt and white pepper to taste. Very slowly beat in the oil, drop by drop, with a wire whisk. Beat constantly. When the mixture becomes very thick, thin it with a few drops of vinegar. Once the oil is used up, gradually beat in the boiling water. This will improve the consistency and help to prevent the mayonnaise from separating. *Makes about 1½ cups.*

Provence,   Comté   de   Nice

AÏOLI
(Aïoli)

Aïoli—often called the "butter"—of Provence, is a garlicky mayonnaise. It is usually served as a dip surrounded by a selection of raw vegetables (crudités), or cooked vegetables such as artichoke hearts, potatoes, haricot or green beans.

> 8 garlic cloves, crushed
> 1 egg yolk
>   salt
>   cayenne pepper
> ³/₄ cup olive oil
> 1 tbsp. boiling water

Place the garlic cloves, egg yolk, salt, and cayenne pepper to taste in a bowl and beat with a wire whisk until slightly thickened. Very slowly beat in the oil, drop by drop, as for mayonnaise. Once the oil is used up, gradually beat in the boiling water. This will improve the consistency and help to prevent the aïoli from separating. *Makes about ¾ cup.*

Burgundy

DIJONAISE SAUCE
(Sauce Dijonaise)

Mayonnaise can also be made with hard-boiled egg yolks like this sauce from Dijon. If you like, the hard-boiled egg whites may be

sieved and added to the sauce, which gives it
a nice lightness.

> 2 **hard-boiled egg yolks**
> 2 **tsp. Dijon mustard**
> **salt**
> **freshly ground black pepper**
> ½ **cup olive or sunflowerseed oil**
> **lemon juice to taste**

Mash the egg yolks with the mustard in a bowl until they are very
smooth and creamy. Season with salt and black pepper to taste.
Very slowly beat in the oil, drop by drop, with a wire whisk. Beat
constantly. When the mixture becomes very thick, thin it with a few
drops of lemon juice. Once the oil is used up, correct the seasoning.
Makes about ½ cup.

B u r g u n d y

M U S T A R D   C R E A M
S A U C E
(Sauce moutarde à la crème)

This sauce makes an especially good salad
dressing for celeriac, cabbage, and beets.

> 3 **tbsp. Dijon mustard**
> 6 **tbsp. light cream**
> 2 **tsp. lemon juice or to taste**
> **salt**
> **freshly ground black pepper**

Blend the mustard and cream together in a bowl. Add the lemon
juice and season to taste with salt and black pepper. *Makes about*
⅔ cup.

All France

CRÈME FRAÎCHE
(Crème fraîche)

Crème fraîche is widely used in French cooking, especially in soups and sauces. It has a
very high butterfat content (up to 60 percent)
which enables it to be boiled down to half of its
original volume without any risk of curdling.
It also contains lactic acid and other ferments
that are added after pasteurization, which
gives it its characteristic, slightly sour taste.
Crème fraîche can easily be made at home in a
similar way to yogurt.

> 1   **cup heavy cream**
> 3   **tbsp. whole milk yogurt**

Stir the cream and yogurt together in a small saucepan and heat
gently to 77° F. Pour into a glass jar and partially cover. Set in a
warm place for 6 to 8 hours until the cream is thickened. Stir lightly, cover and refrigerate. Crème fraîche will keep up to 2 weeks in
the refrigerator. *Makes about 1 cup.*

SOUPS

LES SOUPES ET LES POTAGES

Andre Dumas called France a *nation soupière*. Soup has always had an important place in the French diet. In the past soup was eaten three or even four times a day, especially in the poorer regions of France. *Soupe* originally meant the slices of bread dipped into the *potage* or contents of the pot. Even today a soupe, as opposed to a potage, is usually served with croutons or poured over slices of bread. The evening meal or *souper*—the equivalent of the English "supper"—is derived from "soupe."

An enormous variety of soups are made in France. Normandy is famous for its creamy vegetable soups. Beer soup is a specialty of Flanders, Alsace, and Lorraine. Onion soups called *tourin* or *ouliat* are made all over southwest France. Various garlic soups appear in Languedoc and Provence. In the Languedoc there was once a *ceremonie d'aillade* where garlic soup, dark with black pepper, was served to young couples on their wedding night. The *soupo-pistou* of Provence and the *soupe des herbes* of Corsica are both relatives of the Italian minestrone.

Paris, Ile-de-France

CARROT SOUP
(Potage Crécy)

There is some controversy over the origins of the name *"potage Crécy."* Sometimes it is said that it originated in Picardy, at the small village of Crécy–en–Pontheiu, famous for the battle of Crécy (1346). However, it probably originated at Crécy–en–Brie in the Ile–de–France, which has long been famous for its fine carrots.

2 tbsp. butter
2 leeks, thinly sliced (white part only)
1 pound carrots, diced
3 medium potatoes, peeled and diced
5 cups water
1/2 cup light cream
salt
freshly ground black pepper

Heat the butter in a large pot and cook the leeks over a moderate heat for 5 minutes. Add the carrots and potatoes and 5 cups of water. Bring to a boil, cover, and simmer for 45 minutes. Force through a sieve, or purée in a blender. Return to the pot and heat thoroughly. Stir in the cream and season to taste with salt and black pepper. Serve hot. *Serves 6.*

Picardy, Flanders, Artois

CARROT AND RICE SOUP
(Potage Crécy à la Picarde)

4	tbsp. butter
³/₄	pound carrots
1	medium onion, chopped
1	small turnip, diced
1	celery stalk, thinly sliced
4	cups water
¹/₄	cup long grain rice
	salt
	freshly ground black pepper

Heat half of the butter in a large pot and cook the carrots, onion, turnip, and celery over a moderate heat for 5 minutes. Add the water and bring to a boil. Cover, and simmer for 30 minutes. Raise the heat, and when the soup is boiling, pour in the rice. Cook for 15 to 20 minutes or until the rice is tender but still firm. Force through a sieve or purée in a blender. Return to the pot and heat thoroughly. Stir in the remaining butter and season to taste with salt and black pepper. Serve hot. *Serves 3 to 4.*

Brittany

CAULIFLOWER SOUP
(Potage aux choufleurs)

A specialty of Roscoff.

1	medium cauliflower, broken into florets
1/2	pound potatoes, peeled and quartered
3	cups broth or water
2	cups milk
3	tbsp. butter
1/4	tsp. freshly grated nutmeg
	salt
	freshly ground black pepper

Bring the cauliflower and potatoes to boil in the water and milk. Cover, and simmer for 30 minutes or until tender. Force through a sieve or purée in a blender. Return to the pot. Heat thoroughly. Stir in the butter and season with nutmeg, salt, and black pepper to taste. Serve hot. *Serves 4.*

Provence ,   Comté   de   Nice

ZUCCHINI AND
RICE SOUP
(La soupa de courgourda)

This soup may be made with zucchini or
pumpkin.

2	tbsp. olive oil
1¹/₄	pounds zucchini
2	medium onions, chopped
2	garlic cloves, finely chopped
5	cups water
1	bay leaf
2	tbsp. fresh parsley, finely chopped
	pinch of thyme
¹/₄	cup long grain rice
1	cup freshly grated Parmesan cheese

Trim the ends of the zucchini and cut into slices ¹/₂-inch thick. Heat
the olive oil in a large pot and cook the onions and garlic over a
moderate heat for 3 minutes. Add the zucchini and stir well. Add
the water and herbs and bring to a boil. Cover, and simmer for 30
minutes. Force through a sieve or purée in a blender. Return to the
pot and season to taste with salt and black pepper. Raise the heat,
and when the soup is boiling pour in the rice. Cook for 18 to 20
minutes or until the rice is tender but still firm. Serve at once with
grated cheese on the side. *Serves 4.*

Auvergne, Limousin

CREAM OF CHESTNUT SOUP

(Soupe aux marrons)

This soup from the Auvergne is sometimes called *cousinat*. It is usually served with slices of rye bread and perhaps some grated Cantal cheese on the side.

1   **pound chestnuts**
2   **tbsp. butter**
1   **large onion, chopped**
1   **leek, thinly sliced (white part only)**
1   **celery stalk, thinly sliced**
4   **cups broth or water**
1/2 **cup light cream**

With a sharp knife, cut a small cross into the base of the chestnut shells. Cook the chestnuts in plenty of boiling water for 10 minutes. Slip off the shells and remove the brown skins with a sharp knife.

Heat the butter in a large pot and cook the onion, leek, and celery over a gentle heat for 10 minutes, or until the vegetables are soft but not brown. Add the peeled chestnuts and the broth, and bring to a boil. Cover, and simmer for 45 minutes. Force through a sieve or purée in a blender. Return to the pot. Heat thoroughly. Stir in the cream and serve hot. *Serves 4.*

Corsica

CORSICAN HERB SOUP
(Soupe des herbes)

For this soup choose at least 3 or 4 of the following fresh herbs: parsley, mint, sorrel, borage, oregano, marjoram, dandelion, chives,
chervil, fennel, basil, and coriander.

1/4	**pound dried borlotti or cranberry beans**
6	**cups water**
3	**tbsp. olive oil**
2	**medium onions, chopped**
1	**leek, thinly sliced**
3	**garlic cloves, finely chopped**
3	**medium potatoes, peeled and diced**
4	**canned plum tomatoes, forced through a sieve or pureed in a food processor**
1	**bay leaf**
1/4	**pound fresh herbs, roughly chopped**
	salt
	freshly ground black pepper

Soak the beans overnight and drain. Place in a saucepan with 3
cups of water. Bring to a boil, cover, and simmer for 1¹/₂ to 2 hours
or until the beans are tender. Drain and discard the cooking liquid.

Heat the olive oil in a large saucepan and cook the onions, leek,
garlic, and potatoes over a moderate heat for 2 minutes. Add the
puréed tomatoes and cook for 2 more minutes. Add the beans, bay
leaf, and 3 cups of water. Bring to a boil, cover, and simmer for 40
minutes. Add the fresh herbs and season with salt and black pepper to taste. Simmer for 20 minutes and serve hot. *Serves 4.*

Provence, Comté de Nice

GARDEN VEGETABLE SOUP
(Soupe d'ourteto)

Ourteto means garden in the Provençal language.

        4   tbsp. olive oil
        1   medium onion, chopped
        2   garlic cloves, finely chpped
        3   leeks, thinly sliced
        2   celery ribs, thinly sliced
      3/4   pound spinach, shredded
      1/4   pound sorrel, shredded
        4   cups water
            salt
            freshly ground black pepper
        4   slices of whole wheat bread
      1/2   cup freshly grated Parmesan cheese

Heat the olive oil in a large pot and cook the onion, garlic, leek, and celery over a moderate heat for 5 minutes. Add the spinach, sorrel, and water and season with salt and black pepper to taste. Bring to a boil and simmer for 30 minutes. Place one slice of bread in each of the individual serving bowls. Pour over the soup and serve with grated cheese on the side. If you prefer the soup may be strained before serving. *Serves 4.*

Provence, Comté de Nice

GARLIC SOUP
(Aigo-bouido)

Aigo-bouido literally means "boiled water." It is one of the oldest traditional soups in Provence, and is probably the easiest to prepare. It consists of garlic cloves, herbs, and olive oil, simmered in water for 15 minutes, then poured over slices of bread. There are more sophisticated versions—some recipes include slices of Gruyère cheese or poached eggs. In Marseilles the soup is usually thickened with egg yolks and flavored with dried orange peel and fennel.

> 4 cups water
> 8 garlic cloves, crushed
> 2 tbsp. olive oil
> 2 bay leaves
> 4 sage leaves
> a pinch of thyme
> freshly ground coarse sea salt
> freshly ground black pepper
> 4 slices of French bread
> 1/2 cup Gruyère cheese, grated

Place the garlic cloves, olive oil, bay leaves, sage, thyme, water, and seasoning to taste in a saucepan. Bring to a boil, cover, and simmer for 15 minutes. Remove the bay leaf. Place the slices of bread in individual bowls and sprinkle with cheese. Pour over the hot soup and serve at once. *Serves 4.*

Normandy

GREEN BEAN SOUP
(Soupe aux haricots verts)

- ¹/₂ pound green beans
- 2 medium potatoes, peeled and diced
- a handful of sorrel, shredded
- 4 cups water
- 2 tbsp. light cream
- 2 tbsp. butter
- salt
- freshly ground black pepper
- 4 slices whole wheat bread, cut into croutons and dried in a 375° F. oven

Trim the ends of the green beans and cut into 2-inch lengths. Place in a pot with the potatoes, sorrel, and water. Bring to a boil, cover, and simmer for 30 minutes. Force through a sieve, or purée in a blender. Return to the pot and stir in the cream. Season with salt and black pepper to taste. Heat thoroughly and stir in the butter just before serving. Serve hot with croutons. *Serves 4.*

Savoie, Dauphiné

GREEN SOUP WITH RICE
(Soupe verte)

Almost any salad green can be used to make this soup: watercress, lamb's lettuce, purslane, all kinds of lettuce, spinach, or Swiss chard.

2	tbsp. butter
2	leeks, thinly sliced
¼	pound spinach, shredded
	a handful of sorrel, shredded
3 or 4	lettuce leaves, shredded
1	medium potato, peeled and diced
5	cups stock of water
½	cup long grain rice
½	cup light cream
	salt
	freshly ground black pepper

Heat the butter in a large pot and cook the leeks over a moderate heat for 5 minutes. Add the spinach, sorrel, lettuce, potato, and stock. Bring to a boil, cover, and simmer for 30 minutes. Force through a sieve or purée in a blender. Return to the pot and season to taste with salt and black pepper. Raise the heat, and when the soup is boiling, pour in the rice. Cook for 18 to 20 minutes, or until the rice is tender but still firm. Stir in the cream and serve hot. *Serves 4.*

Auvergne,   Limousin

AUVERGNE LENTIL SOUP
(Soupe auvergnate)

Auvergne is famous for its tiny greenish-black lentils from Le Puy, which are used to make this soup. If unavailable, small green lentils may be used instead.

$^1/_4$ pound Le Puy lentils
5 cups water
$^1/_2$ pound potatoes, peeled and quartered
2 large onions, sliced
2 garlic cloves, chopped
1 bay leaf
   pinch of cloves
3 tbsp. butter
   salt
   freshly ground black pepper
4 slices of rye bread, cut into croutons and dried in a 375° F. oven

Soak the lentils for 1 hour and drain. Place in a large pot with 5 cups of water. Add the potatoes, onions, garlic, bay leaf, and cloves and bring to a boil. Cover, and simmer for 1$^1/_2$ hours or until the lentils are tender. Force through a sieve or purée in a blender. Return to the pot and heat the soup thoroughly. Add a little more water if the soup is too thick. Stir in the butter and season to taste with salt and black pepper. Serve hot with croutons. *Serves 4.*

Provence, Comté de Nice

PROVENÇAL LENTIL SOUP
(Soupe de lentilles)

This warming winter soup makes a perfect meal in itself. Serve it with slices of whole wheat bread and a mixed salad on the side.

1 cup small green lentils
3 tbsp. olive oil
2 garlic cloves, finely chopped
1 medium onion, finely chopped
1 leek, thinly sliced
1/2 cup canned plum tomatoes, forced through a sieve or puréed in a food processor
5 cups water
1/2 pound new potatoes
salt
freshly ground black pepper

Soak the lentils for 1 hour and drain. Heat the olive oil in a large pot and cook the garlic, onion and leek over a moderate heat for 5 minutes. Add the tomatoes and bay leaf and cook 5 minutes. Add the lentils and water and bring to a boil. Cover, and simmer for 1½ hours or until the lentils are tender. Add the potatoes and cook for 20 minutes, or until the potatoes are tender, adding a little more water if the soup is too thick. Season with salt and black pepper to taste and serve hot. *Serves 4.*

Paris, Ile–de–France

MUSHROOM VELOUTÉ
(Potage velouté de champignons)

This classic mushroom soup from Paris is sometimes called *Pierre–le–Grand*.

1   pound small white mushrooms
2   tbsp. butter
2   tbsp. flour
4   cups hot stock or water
2   egg yolks
¹/₂   cup light cream
¹/₄   tsp. freshly grated nutmeg
     salt
     freshly ground black pepper

Trim the stems of the mushrooms and slice thinly. Heat the butter in a large pot and cook the mushrooms over a moderate heat for 5 minutes. Stir in the flour and cook for 1 minute. Gradually add the hot stock, stirring constantly until the soup is slightly thickened. Simmer for 30 minutes. Force through a sieve or purée in a blender, and return to the pot.

Beat the egg yolks and cream together in a bowl. Add a ladleful of hot soup into the egg and cream mixture, then stir it back into the soup. Season with nutmeg and salt and black pepper to taste. Heat gently to just below the simmering point. Do not boil or the soup will curdle. Serve hot. *Serves 4.*

Paris, Ile-de-France

MONTMARTRE ONION SOUP
(Soupe à l'oignon Montmartroise)

This is a delicious creamy onion soup flavored with white wine.

3	tbsp. olive oil
2	large onions, thinly sliced
2	tbsp. flour
½	cup dry white wine
5	cups hot stock or water
2	egg yolks
2	tbsp. light cream
	a grating of nutmeg
	salt
	freshly ground black pepper
4	slices of whole wheat bread cut into croutons and dried in a 375° F. oven

Heat the olive oil in a large pot and cook the onions over a moderate heat for 5 to 7 minutes or until they are softened and starting to turn golden. Stir in the flour and cook gently for 1 minute without browning. Gradually pour in the wine, stirring constantly, then pour in the hot stock. Bring to a boil, cover, and simmer for 30 minutes. The soup will be slightly thickened.

Beat the egg yolks and cream together in a bowl. Add a ladleful of hot soup into the egg and cream mixture, then stir it back into the soup. Season with nutmeg and salt and black pepper to taste. Heat thoroughly, but do not boil or the soup will curdle. Serve hot with croutons. *Serves 4.*

Provence ,   Comté   de   Nice

La   Soupo-Pistou
(La soupo–pistou)

La soupo–pistou originated in Genoa. It is a mixed vegetable soup made with fresh or dried haricot beans, zucchini, green beans, potatoes, and tomatoes. *Pistou*—a garlic and basil sauce—is stirred in at the end of cooking. The pistou is never cooked.

- ¹/₂ **cup dried white beans**
- 6 **cups water**
- ¹/₂ **pound green beans, cut into 1-inch lengths**
- 2 **medium potatoes, peeled and diced**
- 2 **zucchini, trimmed and sliced**
- 3 **peeled plum tomatoes, forced through a sieve or puréed in a food processor**
- **salt**
- **freshly ground black pepper**
- ¹/₂ **cup vermicelli, broken into 1-inch lengths**
- ¹/₂ **cup *pistou* sauce (see page 104)**
- 1 **cup freshly grated Parmesan cheese**

Soak the dry beans overnight and drain. Bring to a boil in 2 cups of water. Cover, and simmer for 1 to 1¹/₂ hours or until tender. Drain and discard the cooking liquid.

Place the green beans, potatoes, zucchini, and puréed tomatoes in a large pot with the cooked beans and 4 cups of water. Bring to a boil, cover, and simmer for 45 minutes. Season with salt and black pepper to taste. Raise the heat. When the soup is boiling add the vermicelli and cook for 15 minutes, or until it is tender but still firm. Remove from the heat and stir in the pistou sauce. Serve at once with grated cheese on the side. *Serves 4 to 6.*

Picardy,   Flanders,   Artois

PUMPKIN AND LEEK SOUP
(Soupe au potiron)

1   small pumpkin, about 2 pounds
4   tbsp. butter
1   large onion, chopped
2   leeks (white part only), thinly sliced
2   cups water
2   cups milk
    salt
    freshly ground black pepper

Slice the pumpkin. Cut off the skin and remove the seeds and fibers. Dice the flesh.

Heat half of the butter in a large pot. Add the onion and leeks and cook over a moderate heat for 2 or 3 minutes. Add the water and milk and bring to a boil. Cover, and simmer for 30 minutes or until the pumpkin is tender. Force through a sieve or purée in a blender. Return to the pot and heat thoroughly. Stir in the remaining butter and season with salt and black pepper to taste. Serve hot. *Serves 4.*

Provence, Comté de Nice

PURSLANE SOUP
(Soupe de pourpier)

Purslane, called *boutoulaigo* in the Provençal language, grows wild in much of Provence. The leaves are slightly smaller than the cultivated variety, with a similar, slightly acidic taste. It is available in most Greek and Middle Eastern delicatessens.

1/2	pound purslane
2	tbsp. olive oil
2	garlic cloves, finely chopped
2	leeks, thinly sliced
1	pound potatoes, peeled and diced
6	cups water
2	egg yolks
3	tbsp. light cream
	salt
	freshly ground black pepper
6	slices of whole wheat bread, cut into croutons and dried in a 375° F. oven

Trim the stalks of the purslane and cut into 2-inch lengths. Heat the olive oil in a large pot and cook the garlic and leeks over a moderate heat for 5 minutes. Add the potatoes, purslane, and water and bring to a boil. Cover, and simmer for 30 minutes. Force through a sieve or purée in a blender.

Beat the egg yolks and cream together in a bowl and gradually add a ladleful of soup. Mix well together and pour back into the soup. Season with salt and black pepper to taste. Heat thoroughly. Do not boil or the soup will curdle. Serve hot with croutons. *Serves 6.*

Languedoc, Roussillon

SPLIT PEA AND
VEGETABLE SOUP
(La soupe Nîmoise)

1	cup split peas
5¹/₂	cups water
4	tbsp. olive oil
1	leek, thinly sliced
2	carrots, diced
2	white cabbage leaves, shredded
1	turnip
2	medium potatoes, peeled and diced
	salt
	freshly ground black pepper
2	tbsp. fresh chives, finely chopped
4 to 6	slices of whole wheat bread, cut into croutons, and dried in a 375° F. oven

Soak the split peas for 2 hours and drain. Bring to a boil in 4 cups of water, and simmer for 1¹/₂ hours or until the peas are tender. Force through a sieve or purée in a blender.

Meanwhile heat the olive oil in a large pot and cook the leek, carrots, turnip, and cabbage over a gentle heat for 15 minutes or until the vegetables are tender but not brown. Add the split peas purée, diced potatoes, and the remaining water and season to taste with salt and black pepper. Bring to a boil, cover, and simmer for 20 minutes or until the potatoes are tender. Sprinkle with chives, and serve hot with croutons. *Serves 4 to 6.*

Bordeaux, Les Landes

TOMATO SOUP
(Tourin à la tomate)

Tourin or *tourain* is an onion soup made all over southwest France. Sometimes an egg is added, in which case it is called a *tourin blanchi*. Some recipes, like the one below, include tomatoes.

```
4   tbsp. olive oil
2   large onions, thinly sliced
3   garlic cloves, finely chopped
2   pounds ripe plum tomatoes, peeled, seeded
    and chopped
1   bay leaf
5   cups water
    salt
    freshly ground black pepper
1/4 cup vermicelli, broken into 1-inch lengths
2   tbsp. fresh chives, finely chopped
1/2 cup freshly grated Parmesan or Gruyère cheese
```

Heat the olive oil in a large pot and cook the onion and garlic over a moderate heat for 5 minutes or until the onions are translucent. Add the tomatoes and bay leaf and cook for 5 minutes. Pour in the water and season with salt and black pepper to taste. Bring to a boil, cover, and simmer for 30 minutes or until the vegetables are tender. Force through a sieve or purée in a blender and return to the pot. Increase the heat; when the soup is boiling drop in the vermicelli and cook until it is tender but still firm. Sprinkle with chives and serve at once, with grated cheese on the side. *Serves 4 to 6.*

Normandy

VEGETABLE SOUP WITH FLAGEOLET BEANS
(Soupe Normande)

The flageolet bean is a variety of haricot bean that stays green. Sometimes it is called *chevrier* after the man who originated it.

    2 tbsp. butter
    1 leek, thinly sliced
    1 celery rib, diced
    2 medium potatoes, peeled and diced
    ½ small green cabbage, shredded
    1½ cups fresh flageolet beans, if available, or
    1½ cups well-drained canned flageolet beans
    4 cups water
    3 tbsp. light cream
       salt
       freshly ground black pepper
    4 slices of whole wheat bread, cut into croutons
       and dried in a 375° F. oven

Heat the butter in a large saucepan and cook the leek, celery, and potatoes over a moderate heat for 3 minutes. Add the cabbage, flageolet beans, and water and bring to a boil. Cover, and simmer for 1 hour, or until the beans are very tender. Force through a sieve or purée in a blender. Return to the pot and stir in the cream and season with salt and black pepper to taste. Serve hot with croutons. *Serves 4.*

Paris, Ile–de–France

WATERCRESS SOUP
(Potage cressonière)

This soup is sometimes called *potage santé* or "health soup."

1   **bunch watercress**
1   **leek**
2   **tbsp. butter**
1   **pound potatoes, peeled and quartered**
6   **cups water**
3   **tbsp. light cream**
     salt
     freshly ground black pepper

Trim the stalks of the watercress and cut into 2-inch lengths. Trim away the root ends of the leek and cut in half lengthwise. Carefully wash away any dirt that collects between the leaves. Cut into 2-inch lengths; use the whole leek, including the green parts. Heat the butter in a large pot and cook the watercress and leek over a moderate heat for 5 minutes. Add the potatoes and water and bring to a boil. Cover, and simmer for 30 minutes. Force through a sieve or purée in a blender. Return to the saucepan and heat thoroughly. Stir in the cream and season with salt and black pepper to taste. Serve hot. *Serves 6.*

EGGS

LES OEUFS

Eggs have been a symbol of fertility since ancient times. They were also thought to have magical powers. The Romans used to break the shells after eating eggs to prevent them being used to make spells. In France eggs were generally thought to bring good fortune. In the seventeenth century it was customary for a bride to break an egg when she entered her new home.

Eggs are prepared in hundreds of ways in France. They are boiled, poached, fried, baked *en cocotte* (in a small ovenproof dish), scrambled, or made into omelettes, soufflés, and flans. Egg dishes are usually eaten for lunch or supper, rarely for breakfast. Soufflés are often served before the main course as an *entrée*. Although entrée literally means 'beginning' it was originally the third course of a formal meal. First came the hors d'oeuvres or soup, followed by the second course—called *le relevé* (the removed), which in turn was followed by the entrée and then the main course. In most French restaurants today an entrée simply means a light main course. Other recipes for entrées such as quiches, croquettes, stuffed vegetables, and various cheese dishes can be found in other chapters of this book.

Scrambled Eggs
(Les oeufs brouillés)

Scrambled eggs are very quick and easy to prepare. The French pay great attention not to overcook the eggs. Sometimes they are prepared in a *bain-marie*, which helps to prevent from overcooking and becoming dry.

To cook scrambled eggs, beat the eggs lightly and season with salt and black pepper to taste. Melt a little butter in a heavy pan and pour in the eggs. Cook over a gentle heat, stirring constantly with a wooden spoon until the eggs have reached the desired creamy consistency. Remove from the heat and serve at once. Some cooks stir in a tablespoon or two of cream when the eggs start to thicken.

Savoie, Dauphiné

SCRAMBLED EGGS
WITH MUSHROOMS
(Brouillade aux mousserons)

1/2 **pound small white mushrooms**
2 **tbsp. butter**
1 **tbsp. parsley, finely chopped**
4 **eggs**
   salt
   freshly ground black pepper
2 **tbsp. light cream**

Trim the ends of the mushrooms and slice them thinly. Heat the butter in a heavy pan and cook the parsley for 1 minute, then add the mushrooms. Cook over moderate heat for 5 minutes or until they are tender and the juices have evaporated. Beat the eggs lightly and season with salt and black pepper to taste. Pour the eggs over the mushrooms and cook over gentle heat, stirring constantly, until they start to thicken. Add the cream and continue to cook until the eggs have reached a creamy consistency. Do not overcook or the eggs will become dry. *Serves 2.*

P a y s   B a s q u e , B é a r n ,   B i g o r r e

SCRAMBLED EGGS WITH PEPPERS, ONIONS, AND TOMATOES
(Pipérade)

In the Pays Basque *pipérade* is made with a special variety of red pepper called *le piment d'Espelette*, named after the town of Espelette where it is grown. Sometimes the peppers are called *enragés* (enraged) because of their strong, hot taste. Pipérade is also made *en mourterade*, like a flat omelette.

3   sweet red peppers
3   tbsp. olive oil
1   large onion, thinly sliced
2   garlic cloves, finely chopped
1/2 fresh red chili pepper, seeded and finely chopped
3/4 pound tomatoes, peeled, seeded, and chopped
8   eggs
     salt
     freshly ground black pepper

Roast the peppers under a hot grill until the skins are blackened all over. Wash under cold water and remove the skins. Cut the peppers into strips.

Heat the olive oil in a heavy pan and cook the onion, garlic, and chili pepper over moderate heat for 5 minutes or until the onion is translucent. Add the sweet peppers and tomatoes and cook over moderate heat for 15 to 20 minutes or until the peppers are tender and the liquid from the tomatoes has evaporated.

Beat the eggs lightly and season with salt to taste. Pour over the sweet-pepper mixture and cook over gentle heat, stirring constantly, until the eggs have reached a creamy consistency. Serve at once. *Serves 4.*

Languedoc, Roussillon

SCRAMBLED EGGS WITH ZUCCHINI
(*Brouillade aux courgettes*)

- 1 pound zucchini
- 2 tbsp. olive oil
- 2 shallots, finely chopped
- 4 eggs
- salt
- freshly ground black pepper
- 2 tbsp. butter

Trim the ends of the zucchini and cut into thick rounds. Heat the olive oil in a heavy frying pan and cook the shallots over a moderate heat for 2 minutes. Add the zucchini and cook over fairly high heat until they are golden on both sides. Let cool slightly.

Beat the eggs lightly and season with salt and black pepper to taste. Stir in the zucchini mixture. Heat the butter in a heavy saucepan and pour in the egg mixture. Cook over gentle heat, stirring constantly until the eggs have reached a creamy consistency. Serve at once. *Serves 2.*

Omelettes
(Les omelettes)

"On ne fait pas des omelettes sans casser des oeufs."

—an old French saying*

In France there are two kinds of omelettes: the rolled omelette and the flat omelette. Both are very versatile and easy to prepare. Almost any vegetable can be added to an omelette. Most of the French provinces have their own specialties: *omelette savoyarde, omelette niçarde,* or *omelette lyonnaise.*

Rolled Omelette

To make a rolled omelette you will need a heavy iron frying pan. It is a good idea to keep a pan especially for omelettes. Always use very fresh eggs, preferably free range. Beat the eggs lightly, just enough to mix the yolks with the whites. Heat the pan so that the butter foams as soon as it is put in. Tilt the pan so the whole surface is coated with butter and then pour in the eggs. Let the eggs cook for about 10 seconds to set the bottom, then tilt the pan away from you and gently push the eggs toward the center of the pan. Now tilt the pan towards you so the unset eggs cover the space you have made. Repeat a couple of times until the eggs are evenly cooked. With a fork, carefully roll the omelette up away from you and slide it onto a serving plate. Serve at once.

Flat Omelette

Flat omelettes are made in a similar way to rolled omelettes, but instead of rolling they are turned and cooked on the other side like a pancake. If you like you can place the omelette under a hot grill for 20 seconds to set the top before turning and cooking the other side.

*You cannot make an omelette without breaking eggs.

Paris, Ile–De–France

CHEESE OMELETTE WITH CREAM
(Omelette au fromage à la crème)

This omelette is usually made with crème fraîche but I prefer to use sour cream instead.

> 4   eggs
>   a grating of nutmeg
>   salt
>   freshly ground black pepper
> ¹/₄ cup crème fraîche or sour cream
> ¹/₄ cup (2 oz.) Gruyère cheese, grated

Beat the eggs lightly and season with nutmeg, salt, and pepper to taste. Heat the butter in a heavy frying pan and follow the directions for rolled omelette on page 137. Just before rolling, spoon the crème fraîche over the center of the omelette and sprinkle over the grated cheese. Roll the omelette up and place in a preheated 400° F. oven for 2 or 3 minutes and serve at once. *Serves 2.*

Savoie, Dauphiné

SORRELL OMELETTE
(Omelette à l'oseille)

Variations of this classic omelette are made all over France. The acidic taste of sorrel goes particularly well with eggs.

a handful of fresh sorrel, finely shredded
3 **tbsp. butter**
4 **eggs**
   salt
   freshly ground black pepper

Heat 1 tablespoon of butter in a heavy frying pan and cook the sorrel over moderate heat for 5 minutes or until it is reduced to a purée. Beat the egg lightly and add the sorrel purée. Season with salt and pepper to taste. Heat the remaining butter in the same frying pan and pour in the egg mixture. Follow the directions for rolled omelette on page 137. *Serves 2.*

Provence,   Comté   de   Nice

FRESH TOMATO
OMELETTE
WITH BASIL
(Oumeleto ei poumo d'amour)

A specialty of Marseilles. The tomato is called the "apple of love" in the Provençal language because it once had the reputation of being an aphrodisiac.

4 **medium tomatoes**
4 **eggs**
2 **tbsp. fresh basil, chopped**
   salt
   freshly ground black pepper
2 **tbsp. olive oil**

Peel and slice the tomatoes. Beat the eggs lightly and add the tomatoes and basil. Season with salt and black pepper to taste. Heat the olive oil in a heavy frying pan and pour in the egg and tomato mixture. Follow the directions for rolled omelette on page 137. *Serves 2.*

Poitou, Charente

CÈPE OMELETTE
(Omelette aux cèpes)

In this omelette from Poitou, cèpes are sautéed in a mixture of butter and walnut oil before they are added to the eggs, which gives the omelette its distinctive flavor. If fresh cèpes are unavailable any other mushroom may be used instead.

¹/₂	pound cèpe or any other mushroom
2	tbsp. butter
1	tbsp. walnut oil
2	shallots, finely chopped
2	tbsp. fresh parsley, finely chopped
4	eggs
2	tbsp. light cream
	salt
	freshly ground black pepper

Wipe the cèpes clean with a damp cloth. Trim the stems and cut into thin slices. Heat 1 tablespoon butter and the walnut oil in a heavy frying pan and cook the shallots and parsley for 2 minutes. Add the cèpes and cook over a moderate heat for 8 to 10 minutes, or until they are tender. Beat the eggs and cream together and season with salt and black pepper to taste. Add the cèpe mixture and follow the directions for flat omelette on page 137. *Serves 2.*

Provence,   Comté   de   Nice

EGGPLANT AND
TOMATO OMELETTE
(Omelette à l'arlésienne)

If you like, two or three tablespoons of freshly
grated Parmesan cheese may be added to the
eggs before they are cooked.

1   **medium eggplant (about ¹/₂ lb.)**
¹/₄ **cup olive oil**
¹/₂ **pound ripe plum tomatoes, peeled, seeded, and
     chopped**
4   **eggs**
     salt
     freshly ground black pepper

Peel the eggplant and cut into ¹/₂-inch cubes. Heat 3 tablespoons of
olive oil in a heavy frying pan and cook the eggplant over moderate heat until they are golden on both sides. Meanwhile heat the
remaining olive oil in a separate frying pan and cook the tomatoes
over moderate heat for 5 minutes or until they are softened. Beat
the eggs lightly in a bowl and add the tomatoes. Season with salt
and black pepper to taste. Pour over the eggplant and follow the
directions for flat omelette on page 137. *Serves 2.*

Corsica

ZUCCHINI AND POTATO OMELETTE
(Omelette corse aux légumes)

2   medium zucchini
3   tbsp. olive oil
1/4   pound new potatoes, peeled, boiled, and
      sliced
4   eggs
      salt
      freshly ground black pepper

Trim the ends of the zucchini and cut into thin rounds. Heat the olive oil in a heavy frying pan and cook the zucchini and potatoes over a fairly high heat for 5 to 7 minutes or until the vegetables are golden on both sides. Beat the eggs lightly and season with salt and pepper to taste. Pour over the vegetables and follow the directions for flat omelette on page 137. *Serves 2.*

Poitou, Charente

POTATO AND HERB OMELETTE
(Omelette aux herbes)

This omelette is sometimes called *omelette du printemps* or "springtime omelette."

3   tbsp. butter
4   scallions, thinly sliced
    a handful of sorrel, shredded
2   tbsp. fresh chives, chopped
2   tbsp. parsley, finely chopped
1/4 pound new potatoes, boiled and sliced
4   eggs
2   tbsp. cream
    salt
    freshly ground black pepper

Heat the butter in a heavy frying pan and cook the scallions, herbs, and sorrel over a moderate heat for 3 minutes. Add the potatoes and cook for 5 minutes. Beat the eggs lightly with the cream and season with salt and pepper to taste. Pour over the potato and herb mixture and follow the directions for flat omelette on page 137. *Serves* 2.

Pays Basque, Béarn, Bigorre

MUSTARD OMELETTE
(Omelette à la moutarde)

This unique omelette is a specialty of Vic–bilh in Béarn, where a delicious whole grain mustard made with white wine called *moutarde de Lembeye* is produced. Serve it with a green salad on the side.

2 **eggs, separated**
2 **tsp. whole grain mustard with white wine**
   salt
   freshly ground black pepper
1 **tbsp. butter**

Beat the egg yolks with the mustard and season lightly with salt and pepper. Beat the egg whites stiff and fold into the egg yolk mixture.

Heat the butter in a heavy frying pan and, when it starts foaming, pour in the egg mixture. Cook over moderate heat for 1 or 2 minutes or until the underside is lightly browned. Place under a hot grill for about 30 seconds or until the omelette is nicely puffed. Fold in two and serve at once. *Serves 1.*

Corsica

ONION AND MINT OMELETTE
(Omelette aux oignons à la menthe)

3   tbsp. olive oil
2   large onions, thinly sliced
    a handful of fresh mint, finely chopped
4   eggs
    salt
    freshly ground black pepper

Heat the olive oil in a heavy frying pan and cook the onions and mint over moderate heat for 5 to 7 minutes, or until the onions start to turn golden. Beat the eggs lightly and season with salt and pepper to taste. Pour over the onion mixture and follow the directions for flat omelette on page 137. *Serves 2.*

Savoie, Dauphiné

POTATO AND CHEESE OMELETTE
(Omelette Savoyarde)

3   tbsp. butter
1   leek (white part only), thinly sliced
1/2   pound potatoes, peeled and diced
4   eggs
1/2   cup Beaufort or Gruyère cheese, diced
      salt
      freshly ground black pepper

Heat the butter in a heavy frying pan and cook the leek over moderate heat for 3 minutes. Add the diced potatoes and continue to cook for 8 to 10 minutes or until they are tender. Beat the eggs lightly and stir in the cheese. Season with salt and pepper to taste. Pour over the potato mixture and follow the directions for flat omelette on page 137. *Serves 2.*

Soufflés
(Les soufflés)

Soufflés were invented about two hundred years ago with the advent of draft-free stoves. Before 1795 most cooking was done over hot coals or in a primitive brick oven with no adjustable heat.

"Soufflé" literally means "puffed up," which aptly describes it. Soufflés are usually made with an ingredient such as cheese or puréed vegetables, combined with a sauce and egg yolks, and the addition of stiffly beaten whites. However some soufflés omit the sauce. This produces a very light, less creamy soufflé.

Soufflés can be made in one large ovenproof mould or dish, or in individual dishes or *cassolettes.* Serve soufflés immediately—they begin to deflate as soon as you take them out of the oven.

Auvergne, Limousin

CANTAL CHEESE SOUFFLÉ
(Soufflé au Cantal)

Cantal cheese is a semi-hard cheese made from cow's milk. It has a pale creamy color and a greyish crust flecked with gold. Cantal *vieux* (aged over 6 months) is best for cooking. If unavailable, Gruyère or cheddar cheese may be used instead.

3	tbsp. butter
4	tbsp. butter
9	oz hot milk
1/4	tsp. nutmeg, freshly grated
	salt
	freshly ground black pepper
3/4	cup Cantal cheese, grated
4	egg yolks
5	egg white

Follow the directions on page 99 and prepare a thick béchamel sauce with the butter, flour, and hot milk. Season with nutmeg, salt, and pepper to taste. Remove from the heat and stir in the cheese. Let cool slightly, then add the egg yolks one at a time, mixing well after each addition. Beat the egg whites stiff and fold a quarter of the egg whites into the sauce. Blend well and lightly fold in the remaining egg whites.

Pour in a well buttered 2^{1}/2-pint soufflé dish, place in the center of a preheated 400° F. oven, and reduce the heat immediately to 375° F. Bake for 25 to 30 minutes or until the soufflé is well risen and the center is done. Serve at once. *Serves 4.*

B o r d e a u x ,   L e s   L a n d e s

P U M P K I N   S O U F F L É
(Soufflé au potiron)

This soufflé from Les Landes is called *bouhe de cuye* in the local patois.

1¼	pounds pumpkin
3	tbsp. butter
3	tbsp. flour
½	cup hot milk or broth
¼	tsp. nutmeg, freshly grated
	salt
	freshly ground black pepper
½	cup Gruyère cheese, grated
3	egg yolks
4	egg whites

Peel the pumpkin and scrape away the seeds and fibers. Cut into chunks and steam for 12 to 15 minutes or until tender. Force through a sieve or purée in a food processor.

Follow the directions on page 99 and prepare a thick béchamel sauce with the butter, flour, and hot milk. Season with nutmeg, salt, and pepper to taste. Remove from the heat and stir in the cheese. Let cool slightly. Add the egg yolks one at a time and then add the pumpkin purée. Blend well. Beat the egg whites stiff and fold in a quarter of the egg whites into the sauce. Blend well and lightly fold in the remaining egg whites. Pour into a well-buttered 2-pint soufflé dish. Place in the center of a preheated 400° F. oven and reduce the heat immediately to 375° F. Bake for 20 to 25 minutes or until the soufflé is well risen and the center is done. Serve at once. *Serves 2 to 4.*

Paris, Ile-de-France

GREEN BEAN SOUFFLÉ
(Soufflé aux haricots verts)

In this recipe the green beans are not combined with the soufflé mixture. Instead the
soufflé is baked on top of the green beans.
Asparagus tips or peas are often prepared the
same way.

1	pound green beans
2	tbsp. butter
3	tbsp. flour
3/4	cup hot milk
	a grating of nutmeg
	salt
	freshly ground black pepper
1/2	cup Gruyère cheese, grated
3	eggs, separated

Trim the ends of the green beans and steam for 10 minutes or until
they are tender. Place in the bottom of a well buttered 2-pint soufflé
dish.

Follow the directions on page 99 and prepare a thick béchamel
sauce with the butter, flour, and hot milk. Season with nutmeg, salt,
and pepper to taste. Remove from the heat and stir in the cheese,
Let cool slightly. Add the egg yolks one at a time and mix well after
each addition. Beat the egg whites stiff and fold in a quarter of the
egg whites into the sauce. Blend well and lightly fold in the remaining egg whites. Pour over the green beans, place in a preheated
400° F. oven, and reduce the heat immediately to 375° F. Bake for 20
to 25 minutes or until the soufflé is well risen and the center is
done. Serve at once. *Serves 3 to 4.*

Languedoc, Roussillon

ZUCCHINI SOUFFLÉ
(Soufflé aux courgettes)

This soufflé is made without a béchamel sauce, which gives it a very light texture.

1½ **pounds zucchini**
3 **tbsp. olive oil**
¾ **Gruyère cheese, freshly grated**
3 **eggs, separated**
salt
freshly ground black pepper

Trim the ends of the zucchini and cut them into thin rounds. Heat the olive oil in a large frying pan and cook the zucchini over high heat until they are just starting to turn golden. Drain away any excess oil. Force through a sieve or purée in a food processor. Add the cheese and egg yolks and mix well. Season with salt and pepper to taste. Beat the egg whites stiff and fold a quarter of the egg whites into the zucchini mixture. Blend well and lightly fold in the remaining egg whites. Pour in a well buttered soufflé dish, place in the center of a preheated 400° F. oven, and immediately reduce the heat to 375° F. Bake for 20 to 25 minutes or until the soufflé is well risen and the center is done. Serve at once. *Serves 3 to 4.*

Poitou, Charente

SPINACH SOUFFLÉ
(Soufflé aux épinards)

This soufflé is also made without a béchamel sauce.

    ¹/₂   **pound spinach**
    1   **tbsp. butter**
    ¹/₃   **cup Parmesan cheese, freshly grated**
       a grating of nutmeg
       salt
       freshly ground black pepper
    3   **eggs, separated**

Wash the spinach and cook in a covered saucepan over moderate heat for 5 minutes. The water clinging to the leaves is sufficient to prevent scorching. Stir in the butter and season with nutmeg, salt, and pepper to taste. Simmer for 1 minute. Drain and chop finely. Stir in the Parmesan cheese. Add the egg yolks one at a time and mix well after each addition. Beat the egg whites stiff and fold a quarter of the egg whites into the spinach mixture. Blend well and lightly fold in the remaining egg whites.

Pour into a well-buttered 2-pint soufflé dish. Place in the center of a preheated 400° F. oven and immediately reduce the heat to 375° F. Bake for 20 to 25 minutes or until the soufflé is well risen and the center is done. Serve at once. *Serves 2 to 3.*

CHEESE

LES FROMAGES

"Un dessert sans fromage est une belle à qu'il manque un oeil."
—Brillat-Savarin.*

The word fromage (cheese) derives from the Greek *formos*, which were wicker baskets used to drain cheese. Cheese was known to the Sumerians in 4000 BC, the ancient Egyptians and the Chaldeans. Cheese was mentioned in the Bible. When the Romans came to Gaul, Cantal cheese was already being produced in the Auvergne. There are several thousand types of cheese made in the world today, and more than five hundred are made in France.

Cheese may be fermented or fresh. There are two kinds of fermented cheese: the soft cheese such as Brie, *Livarot*, and Camembert; and the hard cheeses such as Cantal or Roquefort. Some cheeses, such as *Emmental*, Gruyère, and *Port Salut* are made with scalded curds.

Cheese is widely used in French cooking. It is made into various dips and spreads such as *la cervelle de canut* of the Lyonnais, or *bibbelkäse* of Alsace. Cheese is made into fritters, croquettes, soufflés, flans, and all kinds of pastries and turnovers. Various cheese fondues are made, especially in Savoie, Franche Comté, and the Auvergne, with white wine, milk, or even water. Sometimes whole eggs or egg yolks are included.

Fromage blanc appears in many French recipes. It is an unsalted, fresh cheese that is similar to a fairly liquid curd cheese. Sometimes 'fromage blanc' needs to be well drained before it is used in cooking, in which case it will be closer to the consistency of curd cheese. Cream cheese is not a suitable substitute as it tends to separate in cooking.

*"A dessert without cheese is like a beautiful woman with only one eye."

Cheese plays an important part in the French meal. It appears after the main course and before the dessert—sometimes instead of the dessert. It is usually served with wine, but in some parts of northern France it may be served with beer, cider, or Calvados. In Mâcon, in Burgundy, cheese was once served with every meal. Sometimes it was the whole meal—with, of course, some bread and wine. It should be remembered that in France, as Raymond Oliver wrote in *The French at Table*, "the person who chooses and buys his own bread, wine and cheese, however humble his social status, is behaving like a true gastronome."

Lyonnais

LA CERVELLE DE CANUT
(La cervelle de canut)

La cervelle de canut (literally, "silk weaver's brains") is a simple cheese spread flavored with herbs that was a favorite snack of the silk weavers of Lyon in the nineteenth century. It was also called *claqueret,* which derives from *claquer* (to beat). Serve it with slices of whole-wheat bread or with potatoes baked in their jackets.

³/₄ **pound white farmer's cheese**
¹/₂ **cup light cream**
  2 **shallots, finely chopped**
  1 **tbsp. fresh chives, chopped**
  1 **tbsp. fresh parsley, finely chopped**
  1 **tbsp. fresh tarragon, chopped**
  1 **tbsp. olive oil**
  2 **tsp. wine vinegar**
    salt
    freshly ground black pepper

In a mixing bowl beat the farmer's cheese with the cream until it is very smooth. Stir in the shallots, herbs, olive oil, and vinegar. Season with salt and pepper to taste. Refrigerate for at least 8 hours before serving. *Serves 6.*

Savoie, Dauphiné

OLD-FASHIONED CHEESE FONDUE
(Fondue du siecle dernier)

Cheese fondue—the well-known dish of cheese melted in wine—was hardly known in France before the Second World War. Before then "fondue" was usually made with milk, like the Italian *fonduta*, or with eggs and cream, like this adaptation of a nineteenth-century recipe from Savoy.

> 3 eggs
> 1 cup light cream
> 2 tbsp. milk
> 1 cup (4 oz.) Comté or Gruyère cheese,
>   thinly sliced
>   a grating of nutmeg
>   pinch of salt
>   pinch of white pepper
> 2 tbsp. butter
> 4 slices whole-wheat toast, cut into
>   fingers

Beat the eggs, cream, and flour together in a bowl. Add the cheese, and season with nutmeg, salt, and white pepper. Melt the butter in a heavy pan and pour in the egg mixture. Cook over gentle heat, stirring constantly with a wooden spoon, until the mixture is thickened and very smooth and creamy. Serve at once with fingers of whole-wheat toast. *Serves 4.*

Franche   Comté

COMTÉ CHEESE CROQUETTES
(Croquettes de Comté)

If Comté cheese is unavailable Gruyère cheese may be used instead.

> ½   **pound Comté cheese**
> **whole-wheat flour seasoned with salt and cayenne pepper**
> 2   **eggs, beaten**
> **whole-wheat breadcrumbs**
> **oil for deep-frying**

Remove the rind from the Comté cheese and cut into ½-inch cubes. Dust all over with the seasoned flour, then dip a few at a time into the beaten egg. Roll in breadcrumbs and fry in hot (360° F.) oil until golden on both sides. Drain on a paper towel and serve at once. *Serves 4.*

Franche   Comté

CHEESE MERINGUES
(Délicieuses au fromage)

Délicieuses are not literally meringues, but very light deep-fried cheese fritters.

> 3   **egg whites**
> **salt**
> 1½   **cups (6 oz.) Comté or Gruyère cheese, grated**
> **pinch of cayenne pepper**
> **whole-wheat breadcrumbs for dusting**
> **oil for deep frying**

Beat the egg whites with the salt until stiff. Gradually fold in the grated cheese and the cayenne pepper. Drop by small spoonfuls into hot (360° F.) and fry until golden all over. Drain on a paper towel and serve at once. *Serves 3.*

Paris, Ile–de–France

BREAD AND CHEESE PUDDING
(Pain perdu au fromage)

Pain perdu is usually a breakfast or dessert dish. This recipe, however, is a kind of savory bread and butter pudding.

2¼   **cups milk**
3   **eggs**
  a grating of nutmeg
  salt
  freshly ground black pepper
4   **tbsp. butter**
7   **slices (7 oz.) silced whole-wheat bread**
1   **cup (4 oz.) Gruyère cheese, grated**

Bring the milk to just below the simmer and set aside to cool slightly.

Beat the eggs together in a large bowl and slowly add the warm milk. Season with nutmeg, salt, and black pepper to taste. Butter the slices of bread and arrange in the bottom of a well-buttered, shallow baking dish. Pour over the egg and milk mixture and let stand for 10 minutes. Sprinkle with the grated cheese and bake in a preheated 375° F. oven for 20 to 25 minutes or until the pudding is set and the top is golden. *Serves 4 to 6.*

Alsace, Lorraine

CHEESE RAMEKIN
(Ramequin messin)

The name 'ramekin' derives from the Flemish
rammeken (literally "light cream"). A *ramequin*
can mean several things in France, from a kind
of Welsh rarebit to a cheese tart. It can also
refer to the small soufflé dish in which a
ramekin is sometimes baked. The following
recipe from Lorraine is a cross between a very
light cheese soufflé and a *gougère*—the well-
known cheese puff pastry from Burgundy.

> 1   cup plus 2 tbsp. milk
> 3   tbsp. flour
> ³/₄   cup (3 oz.) Gruyère cheese
> 3   eggs, separated
> ¹/₄   tsp. nutmeg, freshly grated
>   salt
>   freshly ground black pepper

Bring the milk to a boil in a heavy saucepan and remove from heat.
Add the flour and cheese, stirring constantly with a wooden spoon
until the cheese is melted. Return to the stove and cook gently, stirring constantly, until the mixture is very smooth and thick and no
longer sticks to the sides of the pan. Remove from heat and let cool
slightly. Add the egg yolks one at a time, blending well after each
addition. Season with nutmeg, salt, and pepper to taste. Beat the
egg whites stiff and fold into the mixture. Turn into a well-buttered
1¹/₂-pint soufflé dish and bake in a preheated 375° F. oven for 20
to 25 minutes or until the ramekin in nicely puffed and the top is
golden. Serve at once. *Serves 3 to 4.*

MAIN COURSES

Pies and Tarts
(Les tourtes et les tartes)

Pies and tarts make elegant and colorful main courses for both special occasions and family meals. The French are great lovers of pies and tarts and each province has its own specialties. There are many names for tarts in France, such as quiche, flamiche, tourte, tarte, croustade, and flan. The quiche originally comes from Alsace. The name derives from *kueche*, which means "pie" in the Alsatian dialect. In the past bread dough was used, but it has now been replaced by *pâte brisée* (shortcrust pastry).

Tartes are usually open-faced, and tourtes are double-crusted. Tartes are sometimes called "flans" which can be confusing, as a flan can also be made without a pastry case. The word "tourte" is thought to derive from the Latin word *turtus* meaning "round."

SHORTCRUST PASTRY

(*Pâte brisée*)

Pâte brisée is suitable for most open-faced tarts and quiches. Always make pastry well in advance as it needs time to rest before use. If you are in a hurry 30 minutes is sufficient, but for best results allow 1 to 2 hours.

1³/₄	cup whole wheat pastry or unbleached white flour
¹/₄	tsp. salt
¹/₄	pound chilled unsalted butter, cut into very small cubes
about 4	tbsp. iced water

Combine the flour, salt, and butter in a mixing bowl. Rub the butter into the flour with your fingertips, until the mixture resembles coarse breadcrumbs. Working very quickly, sprinkle in enough ice water to form a soft ball of dough. The dough should not be sticky. Wrap in wax paper and refrigerate for 1 to 2 hours before rolling. Makes enough for a 9- or 10-inch pie shell.

Rolling out the dough:

Place the dough on a lightly floured work surface and knead it briefly. Roll out into a circle about 12 inches in diameter and ¹/₈ inch thick. (Any extra dough can be used for tartlets.) Carefully roll the dough around the rolling pin and unroll it onto a well-buttered pie plate. Trim away any excess dough and flute the edges with a fork. Prick the bottom in a few places. Cover the dough with a sheet of aluminum foil and fill with dried beans or aluminum pie pellets. This keeps the pie from puffing up while baking.

*For a partially
baked pie shell:*

Preheat the oven to 400° F. and bake the pastry for 8 to 10 minutes. The pastry should have shrunk away from the sides of the pie plate. Remove from the oven and carefully remove the foil and beans or pellets.

*For a fully-
baked pie
shell:*

Return to the oven. Prick the bottom again and bake for another 8 to 10 minutes, until the pastry is very light brown.

S H O R T C R U S T P A S T R Y   W I T H   E G G
(Pâte brisée à l'oeuf)

3	cups whole wheat pastry or unbleached white flour
1/2	tsp. salt
6	ounces chilled unsalted butter, cut into very small cubes
2	eggs, well beaten and refrigerated
about 2	tbsp. iced water

Combine the flour, salt, and butter in a mixing bowl. Rub the butter into the flour with your fingertips, until the mixture resembles coarse breadcrumbs. Mix the iced water with the beaten egg and sprinkle over the mixture. Working very quickly, form into a soft ball. The exact amount of water depends on the dryness of the flour used. Wrap in wax paper and refrigerate for 1 to 2 hours before rolling. *Makes enough for 1 double-crusted 9- or 10-inch pie shell.*

Franche Comté

COMTÉ CHEESE
TART
(Flan Comtois)

Comté cheese, or Gruyère de Comté as it is
sometimes called, is one of the finest and most
popular cheeses of France. It is usually made
from raw cow's milk and has a smooth texture
and a deliciously nutty flavor. If unavailable,
Gruyère cheese may be used instead.

      2   cups milk
      4   eggs
      1   cup Comté cheese, grated
    ¹/₄   tsp. freshly grated nutmeg
          salt
          freshly ground black pepper
          a 9-inch partially baked pie shell
          (see pages 160–161)

Bring the milk to just below simmer in a saucepan, and set aside to
cool. Beat the eggs in a large mixing bowl and slowly add the hot
milk in a thin stream. Add the grated cheese and nutmeg, and season to taste with salt and black pepper. Pour into the partially
baked pie shell and bake in a preheated 375° F. oven for 30 minutes
or until the tart is lightly browned and puffed. *Serves 4 to 6.*

Picardy, Flanders, Artois

LEEK PIE
(Flamiche aux poireaux)

Flamiche, or *flamique,* means "pie" or "cake" in Flemish. It is made all over northeast France. Leeks are the favorite filling, but other vegetables, especially onions, pumpkin, or carrots are also used. Flamiche is also made in Burgundy.

Shortcrust Pastry with Egg:

3	cups whole wheat or unbleached white flour
¹/₂	tsp. salt
6	ounces chilled unsalted butter, cut into very small cubes
2	eggs, well beaten and refrigerated
about 2	tbsp. iced water
1	egg, beaten (for glaze)

Filling:

2	pounds leeks
3	tbsp. butter
2	egg yolks
¹/₄	cup light cream
¹/₄	tsp. cinnamon
¹/₄	tsp. freshly grated nutmeg
	pinch of cloves
	salt
	freshly ground black pepper

Prepare the shortcrust pastry with egg as directed on page 161.

To make the filling, trim the root ends of the leeks. Cut lengthwise into halves and wash away any dirt that collects between the leaves. Cut into 1-inch lengths. Heat the butter in a large saucepan and add the leeks. Cover, and cook gently for 15 to 20 minutes, or until the leeks are very soft. Remove from the heat. Beat the egg yolks and cream together in a large mixing bowl. Stir in the leeks and mix well. Add the cinnamon, nutmeg, and cloves and season with salt and black pepper to taste. Set aside.

Remove the dough from the refrigerator and place on a lightly floured work surface. Knead it briefly. Divide into two parts, one slightly larger than the other. Roll the larger part into a circle about 12 inches in diameter and ⅛ inch thick. Carefully roll the dough around the rolling pin and unroll it onto a well-buttered pie plate. Trim away any excess dough. Prick the bottom all over with a fork and pour in the leek filling. Brush the edges with a little of the beaten egg.

For the top crust, roll out the remaining dough into a circle 11 inches in diameter and ⅛ inch thick. Place on top of the pie and trim away any excess dough. Press around the edges with your fingers or a fork to seal in the filling. Brush the top with the remaining beaten egg and cut a few slits to allow any steam to escape during baking. Bake in a preheated 375° F. oven for 45 to 55 minutes or until the top is golden. *Serves 6.*

Provence, Comté de Nice

MUSHROOM AND SHALLOT TART

(Tarte aux champignons et aux échalotes)

A similar tart is made in Poitou, but with walnut oil instead of olive oil.

> 1 **pound small white mushrooms**
> 3 **tbsp. olive oil**
> 6 **shallots, finely chopped**
> **juice of 1 lemon**
> 3 **eggs**
> 1¹/₂ **cups light cream**
> **salt**
> **freshly ground black pepper**
> **a 9-inch partially baked pie shell**
> **(see pages 160–161)**

Wash the mushrooms quickly under cold water and pat dry with a paper towel. Trim the stems and slice the mushrooms fairly thinly. Rub them all over with lemon juice. Heat the butter in a large frying pan and cook the shallots over a moderate heat for 3 minutes. Add the mushrooms and cook for 5 minutes or until they are tender. Raise the heat if necessary to evaporate any liquid from the mushrooms. Beat the eggs and cream together in a bowl. Stir in the mushroom and shallot mixture and season with salt and black pepper to taste. Pour into the partially baked pie shell and bake in a preheated 375° F. oven for 30 minutes or until the tart is lightly browned and puffed. *Serves 4 to 6.*

Alsace, Lorraine

ONION TART

(Tarte à l'oignon)

This delicious creamy onion tart from Alsace is sometimes called *zewelwaïa* or *zewelmaïa*.

1¹/₂	**pounds onions**
4	**tbsp. butter**
2	**tbsp. flour**
1	**egg**
2	**egg yolks**
1¹/₄	**cups light cream**
¹/₄	**tsp. freshly grated nutmeg**
	salt
	freshly ground black pepper
	a 9-inch partially baked pie shell
	(see pages 160–161)

Peel the onions and slice them thinly. Heat the butter in a large frying pan and add the onions. Cover, and cook gently for 25 to 30 minutes, or until they are very soft. Do not brown. Stir in the flour and continue to cook for 2 or 3 minutes. Set aside to cool slightly.

Beat the egg, egg yolks, and cream together in a bowl. Stir in the onions and season with nutmeg, salt, and black pepper to taste. Pour into the partially baked pie shell and bake in a preheated 375° F. oven for 30 minutes or until the tart is lightly browned and puffed. *Serves 4 to 6.*

Picardy,   Flanders,   Artois

Spinach, Onion, and Fromage Frais Tart

(Croustarde à l'djotte de nivelles)

This is an adaptation of a recipe from Picardy.
It may also be made with *fromage blanc,* a fresh
white cheese with the consistency of a fairly
liquid curd cheese.

½   pound spinach or spinach beet
2   tbsp. butter
1   medium onion, finely chopped
1¼ cup *fromage frais* (or 1 cup curd cheese
     mixed with 2 or 3 tbsp. of milk)
¼   cup whipping cream
2   eggs, lightly beaten
2   tbsp. flour
¼   tsp. freshly grated nutmeg
     salt
     freshly ground black pepper
     a 9-inch partially baked pie shell
     (see pages 160–161)

Wash the spinach carefully and cook in a covered saucepan over a
moderate heat for 5 minutes or until it is tender. The water clinging
to the leaves is sufficient to prevent scorching. Drain, squeeze dry,
and chop it coarsely. Heat the butter in a heavy frying pan and cook
the onion over a moderate heat for 5 minutes or until it is translucent. Set aside to cool slightly.

Combine the fromage frais, whipping cream, the eggs, and flour in
a large bowl and mix well together. Stir in the spinach and onion
and season with nutmeg and salt and black pepper to taste. Pour
into the partially baked pie shell and bake in a preheated 375° F.
oven for 30 minutes or until the top is lightly browned and puffed.
Serves 4 to 6.

Bourbonnais, Ninervais

POTATO AND
ONION PIE
(Truffat)

Potato pies are made all over central France, especially in the Bourbonnais, where potatoes are nicknamed the "truffles of the poor."

Shortcrust Pastry with Egg:

3	cups whole wheat pastry or unbleached white flour
1/2	tsp. salt
6	ounces chilled unsalted butter, cut into small cubes
2	eggs, well beaten and refrigerated
about 2	tbsp. iced water
1	egg beaten with 1 tablespoon of water (for glaze)

Filling:

1 1/4	pounds potatoes
1	medium onion, finely chopped
2	tbsp. butter or oil
	salt
	freshly ground black pepper
3/4	cup heavy cream

Prepare the shortcrust pastry with egg as directed on page (161).

For the filling, boil the potatoes in lightly salted water for 10 minutes or until they are half cooked. Drain, and cut into thin slices. Heat the butter in a large frying pan and cook the onion over moderate heat for 5 minutes or until it is translucent. Add the sliced potatoes and cook for a further 2 minutes. Set aside to cool slightly.

Remove the dough from the refrigerator and place on a lightly floured work surface. Knead briefly. Divide into two parts, one slightly larger than the other. Roll the larger part into a circle about 12 inches in diameter and $1/8$ inch thick. Carefully roll the dough around the rolling pin and unroll it onto a well-buttered pie plate. Trim away any excess dough. Prick the bottom all over with a fork and fill the pie with the potato mixture. Brush the edges with a little of the beaten egg yolk.

For the top crust, roll out the remaining dough into a circle 11 inches in diameter and $1/8$ inch thick. Place on top of the pie and trim away any excess dough. Press around the edges with your fingers or a fork to seal in the filling. Brush the top with the remaining beaten egg and cut a hole about $3/4$ inch in diameter in the center of the pie. Bake in a preheated 350° F. oven for 40 to 50 minutes or until the top is lightly browned. Pour the cream into the hole in the crust and bake for a further 5 minutes. *Serves 6.*

Picardy, Flanders, Artois

PUMPKIN AND ONION PIE
(Tourte au potiron)

This 2-crust pie from Picardy is filled with a mixture of puréed pumpkin, fried onion, egg, and spice.

Shortcrust Pastry with Egg:

3	cups whole-wheat pastry or unbleached white flour
1/2	tsp. salt
6	ounces chilled unsalted butter, cut into very small cubes
2	eggs, well beaten and refrigerated
about 2	tbsp. iced water
1	egg, beaten (for glaze)

Filling:

1¼	pounds pumpkin
1	large onion, finely chopped
1	egg, beaten
1/4	tsp. cinnamon
1/4	tsp. ground cloves
1/4	freshly grated nutmeg
	salt
	freshly ground black pepper

Prepare the shortcrust pastry with egg as directed on page 161.

To make the filling, peel the pumpkin, remove the seeds and fibers, and cut into large dice. Steam for 15 minutes or until tender. Force through a sieve or purée in a food processor. Heat the butter in a frying pan and cook the onion gently for 15 to 20 minutes, or until it is very soft. Combine the pumpkin purée, onion, beaten egg, and spices in a bowl and mix well. Season to taste with salt and black pepper.

Remove the dough from the refrigerator and place on a lightly floured work surface. Knead it briefly. Divide into two parts, one slightly larger than the other. Roll the larger part into a circle about 12 inches in diameter and $1/8$ inch thick. Carefully roll the dough around the rolling pin and unroll it onto a well-buttered pie plate. Trim away any excess dough. Prick the bottom all over with a fork and pour in the pumpkin filling. Brush the edges with a little of the beaten egg.

For the top crust, roll out the remaining dough into a circle 11 inches in diameter and $1/8$ inch thick. Place on top of the pie and trim away any excess dough. Press around the edges with your fingers or a fork to seal in the filling. Brush the top with the remaining beaten egg and cut a few slits to allow any steam to escape during baking. Bake in a preheated 375° F. oven for 45 to 55 minutes or until the top is lightly browned. *Serves 6.*

Burgundy

SPINACH TART
(Tarte aux épinards)

This is a classic spinach tart made with eggs and cream.

2 pounds spinach
2 tbsp. butter
2 eggs
1 cup light cream
1/4 tsp. freshly grated nutmeg
salt
freshly ground black pepper
a 9-inch partially baked pie shell
(see pages 160–161)
1/2 cup Gruyère cheese, grated

Wash the spinach carefully and cook in a covered saucepan over a moderate heat for 5 minutes. The water clinging to the leaves is sufficient to prevent scorching. Drain, squeeze dry, and chop coarsely.

Heat the butter in a large frying pan, cook the spinach gently for 2 minutes, and set aside.

Beat the eggs and cream together in a bowl. Stir in the spinach and mix well. Season with nutmeg and salt and black pepper to taste. Pour into the partially baked pie shell and sprinkle the grated cheese over the top. Bake in a preheated 375° F. oven for 30 minutes or until the top is lightly browned and puffed. *Serves 4 to 6.*

Provence, Comté de Nice

SWISS CHARD TART WITH CURRANTS AND PARMESAN

(Tarte aux bettes a la Niçoise)

This tart, a specialty of Nice, originally comes from Italy. Sometimes it is made with Gouda instead of Parmesan cheese.

2   pounds of Swiss chard
2   tbsp. olive oil
3/4 cup freshly grated Parmesan cheese
3   tbsp. currants
2   eggs
     salt
     freshly ground black pepper
     a 9-inch partially baked pie shell
     (see pages 160–161)

Wash the Swiss chard and cook in a covered saucepan over a moderate heat for 5 minutes or until tender. The water clinging to the leaves is sufficient to prevent scorching.

Heat the olive oil in a large frying pan, cook the Swiss chard gently for 2 minutes, and set aside.

Combine the beaten eggs, Parmesan cheese, Swiss chard and currants in a bowl and mix well. Season to taste with salt and black pepper. Pour into the partially baked pie shell and bake in a preheated 375° F. oven for 30 minutes or until the top is lightly browned and puffed. *Serves 4 to 6.*

Provence, Comté de Nice

SWISS CHARD, ONION, AND TOMATO TART
(Tarte aux bettes)

This tart, another specialty of Nice, is filled with layers of Swiss chard, sautéed onions and tomatoes, and slices of Gruyère cheese. Fresh tomatoes are best for this recipe.

1 pound Swiss chard
4 tbsp. olive oil
1 large onion, thinly sliced
3 garlic cloves, finely chopped
³/₄ pound ripe tomatoes, peeled, seeded, and chopped
   pinch of thyme
   salt
   freshly ground black pepper
   a grating of nutmeg
1 cup (4 oz.) Gruyère cheese, thinly sliced
   a 9-inch partially baked pie shell
   (see pages 160–161)

Wash the Swiss chard and remove the stalks. Roll the leaves up and cut into 1-inch strips. Unroll, and cut each strip into 2-inch lengths. Heat half of the olive oil in a large sauce pan and add the Swiss chard. Cook, covered, over a moderate heat for 5 minutes, or until tender, stirring occasionally so the chard cooks evenly. Set aside.

Heat the remaining olive oil in a heavy frying pan and cook the onions and garlic gently for 15 minutes or until the onions are soft but not brown. Add the tomatoes and thyme and cook over a moderate heat for 10 to 15 minutes or until the tomatoes are tender and any excess liquid has evaporated. Season with salt and black pepper to taste. Set aside.

Spread the Swiss chard mixture over the partially baked pie shell and sprinkle with a grating of nutmeg. Arrange half of the slices of Gruyère cheese over the top. Spoon over the onion and tomato mixture and top with the remaining slices of Gruyère cheese. Bake in a preheated 375° F. oven for 35 to 40 minutes or until the top is golden. *Serves 4 to 6.*

Gratins and Tians
(Les gratins et les tians)

Vegetable gratins make delicious and attractive main courses. "Gratin" refers to the crust that is formed when a dish is browned in the oven or under a grill. This crust is usually made with breadcrumbs or grated cheese, such as Gruyère, Parmesan, or Cantal. Almost and vegetable can be made into a gratin, but asparagus, cauliflower, broccoli, cabbage, pumpkin, potatoes, zucchini, and green leafy vegetables are especially good. Potato gratins may be found in the chapter on potatoes.

A gratin dish is generally oval or round and made of enamelled cast-iron or earthenware. It is always shallow, which allows the dish to cook quickly and form a large crust.

A *tian* is a traditional Provençal dish that usually consists of puréed or chopped vegetables, such as spinach, Swiss chard, eggplant, or zucchini. Sometimes beaten egg, cream, tomatoes, or rice are added. The tian is then topped with breadcrumbs or grated cheese and browned in the oven. The dish is named after the large earthenware dish in which it is cooked.

Paris, Ile–de–France

ASPARAGUS GRATIN
(Asperges au gratin)

   1   pound asparagus
   2   cups béchamel sauce (see page 99)
 ½   cup Gruyère cheese, grated
   2   tbsp. whole wheat breadcrumbs
   2   tbsp. freshly grated Parmesan cheese
   2   tbsp. butter

Trim the ends of the asparagus and remove any fibrous parts from the lower stalks. Steam for 15 to 20 minutes or until tender.

Meanwhile prepare the béchamel sauce as directed on page 99. Remove from the heat and stir in the Gruyère cheese. Pour some of the sauce into the bottom of a shallow baking dish. Arrange the asparagus on top in one layer and pour over the remaining sauce. Mix the breadcrumbs and Parmesan cheese and sprinkle over the top. Dot with the butter. Bake in a preheated 375° F. oven for 25 minutes or until the top is golden. *Serves 2 to 4.*

Auvergne, Limousin

CABBAGE GRATIN

(Choux à la crème, gratinée)

This creamy gratin from the Auvergne is usually made with young tender green cabbages such as "spring greens." It is equally good made with Swiss chard, beet greens, or spinach.

1   medium green cabbage
2   cups béchamel sauce (see page 99)
1/2   cup light cream
1/2   cup Gruyère cheese, grated
1/4   cup whole wheat breadcrumbs
2   tbsp. butter

Remove the outer leaves of the cabbage and cut away the stalk. Cut into quarters and blanch for 5 minutes in lightly salted water. Drain thoroughly and chop coarsely. Drain away any excess liquid from the cabbage.

Prepare the béchamel sauce as directed on page 99 and stir in the cream. Heat thoroughly. Remove from the heat and stir in the cheese. Add to the chopped cabbage and mix well. Pour into a well-buttered shallow baking dish. Sprinkle the breadcrumbs over the top and dot with butter. Bake in a preheated 375° F. oven for 25 minutes or until the top is golden. *Serves 4.*

Picardy, Flanders, Artois

CAULIFLOWER GRATIN
(Choufleur au gratin)

1	medium cauliflower
4	tbsp. butter
1	small onion, finely chopped
3	tbsp. flour
2	cups hot milk
3	tbsp. light cream
1	bay leaf
½	tsp. salt
	a pinch of cayenne pepper
½	cup Gruyère cheese, grated

Cut away the stem of the cauliflower and break the head into florets. Steam for 8 minutes or until just tender.

Melt the butter in a heavy-based saucepan and cook the onion over a moderate heat for 5 minutes or until translucent. Stir in the flour and cook for 1 minute without browning. Pour in a little hot milk and stir vigorously with a wooden spoon until the mixture is thick and free of lumps. Gradually add more milk until all the milk is incorporated and the sauce is very smooth and creamy. Simmer for 5 minutes. Stir in the cream and season with salt and cayenne pepper. Simmer for 2 or 3 more minutes then remove from the heat.

Pour some of the sauce into the bottom of a shallow baking dish. Cover with the cauliflower and pour over the remaining sauce. Sprinkle cheese over the top and bake in a preheated 375° F. oven for 25 to 30 minutes or until the top is golden. *Serves 4.*

Auvergne, Limousin

CHESTNUT AND POTATO GRATIN
(Le gratin Auvergnat)

Chestnuts were once a staple food of the people of the Auvergne and Limousin. The chestnut tree was once called *"l'arbre à pain"* (the bread tree), as chestnut flour was used to make bread and porridge. If fresh chestnuts are unavailable, ¹/₂ pound of dried chestnuts, soaked overnight and boiled until tender, may be used instead.

1	**pound potatoes**
1	**pound chestnuts**
¹/₂	**cup light cream**
about ¹/₂	**cup milk**
	salt
	freshly ground black pepper
¹/₄	**cup Cantal cheese, grated**
3	**tbsp. whole wheat breadcrumbs**
2	**tbsp. butter**

Bring the potatoes to boil in lightly salted water for 20 minutes or until they are tender. Mash with a potato ricer and mix with half of the cream and enough of the hot milk to make a smooth purée. The exact amount of milk will depend on the type of potatoes used.

Pierce the chestnut shells with a sharp knife and boil for 10 minutes in plenty of lightly salted water. Drain 2 or 3 at a time and peel away the shells and inner skins while the chestnuts are hot. (When cold they are difficult to peel.) When all the chestnuts are peeled, return to the pan of water and continue to cook for 30 minutes or until the chestnuts are soft. Drain and mash with a potato ricer.

Mix with the remaining cream and enough milk to make a purée that is similar in consistency to the potatoes. Combine the two purées and blend well together. Season with salt and black pepper to taste. Transfer to a well-buttered shallow baking dish. Combine the cheese with the breadcrumbs and sprinkle over the top. Dot with butter and bake at 375° F. for 30 minutes or until the top is golden. *Serves 6.*

Picardy,   Flanders,   Artois

ENDIVE GRATIN
(Endives au gratin)

6   **large heads of endive**
2   **tbsp. butter**
     juice of ½ lemon
2   **tsp. sugar**
     salt
     freshly ground black pepper
2   **cups béchamel sauce (see page 99)**
1   **cup (4 oz.) Gruyère cheese, grated**

Trim the ends of the endive and cut away any discolored edges. Cut in half lengthwise and steam for 7 minutes or until just tender.

Heat the butter in a large frying pan and add the endive. Sprinkle with lemon juice and sugar and season to taste with salt and black pepper. Cover, and cook over a gentle heat for 8 to 10 minutes, or until the endives are tender and any liquid has evaporated. Prepare the béchamel sauce and pour a little into the bottom of a shallow baking dish. Arrange the endives on top in one layer. Pour over the remaining béchamel sauce and sprinkle the cheese over the top. Bake in a preheated 375° F. oven for 25 minutes or until the top is golden. *Serves 3 to 4.*

Provence, Comté de Nice

ZUCCHINI, RICE, AND TOMATO GRATIN

(Courgettes à la Nicoise)

This gratin consists of layers of sautéed zucchini, rice, tomato sauce, and grated cheese, baked in the oven until the top is golden.

2	pounds zucchini
	salt
about ⅓	cup olive oil
1	cup long grain rice
2	tbsp. butter
½	small onion, finely chopped
1½	cups boiling stock or water
	salt
	freshly ground black pepper
2	cups tomato sauce (see page 103)
1	cup freshly grated Parmesan cheese

Trim the ends of the zucchini and cut lengthwise into slices about ⅛ inch thick. Sprinkle with salt and set in a colander for 30 minutes to release their excess moisture. Wash off the salt and pat dry with a paper towel. Fry in hot oil until golden on both sides. Drain on a paper towel.

Meanwhile prepare a rice pilaf with the rice, butter, onion, and stock as directed on page 232. Season with salt and black pepper to taste. Arrange a layer of sautéed zucchini in the bottom of a well-oiled shallow baking dish. Cover with a layer of rice pilaf. Spoon over a little tomato sauce and sprinkle with grated cheese over the top. Repeat the layers ending with grated cheese. Bake in a preheated 400° F. oven for 15 to 20 minutes or until the top is golden. *Serves 4.*

Provence, Comté de Nice

ZUCCHINI, SPINACH, AND RICE GRATIN
(Tian à la boussoulenca)

This dish is a specialty of Nice.

À la boussoulenca means "gypsy style" in the Provençal language.

4	medium zucchini
3	tbsp. olive oil
1	medium onion, finely chopped
2	garlic cloves, finely chopped
1/2	pound Swiss chard or spinach
1/4	cup long grain rice
3	eggs, beaten
1	tbsp. fresh basil, chopped
1	tbsp. fresh parsley, finely chopped
1	cup freshly grated Parmesan cheese
	salt
	freshly ground black pepper

Trim the ends of the zucchini and chop coarsely. Heat the olive oil in a large frying pan and cook the onion and garlic over a fairly high heat for 5 minutes, or until the onion starts to turn golden. Add the chopped zucchini and cook for 5 minutes, stirring occasionally so the vegetables cook evenly.

Meanwhile wash the Swiss chard and remove the stalks. Cook in a covered saucepan over moderate heat for 5 minutes. The water clinging to the leaves is sufficient to prevent scorching. Drain and chop coarsely.

Cook the rice in plenty of lightly salted water for 12 minutes, rinse under cold water, and drain well.

In a large mixing bowl combine the zucchini mixture, the Swiss chard, and the rice. Stir in the eggs, basil, parsley, and half of the cheese. Mix well, and season to taste with salt and black pepper. Pour into a well-oiled shallow baking dish and sprinkle the remaining cheese over the top. Bake in a preheated 350° F. oven for 30 minutes, or until the top is golden and the tian is nicely puffed. *Serves 4 to 6.*

Provence, Comté de Nice

LA PARMESANE
(La parmesane)

Many delicious eggplant gratins are made in Provence. This one consists of layers of sautéed eggplant, béchamel sauce and Parmesan cheese.

> 2 or 3   **medium eggplants (1½ to 1¾ lbs.)**
> about ¾   **cup olive oil**
> 2   **cups béchamel sauce (see page 99)**
> 1   **cup freshly grated Parmesan cheese**

Trim the ends of the eggplant but do not peel them. Cut into round slices ⅛ inch thick, sprinkle with salt, and set in a colander for 1 hour to release the bitter juices. Wash off the salt and pat dry with a paper towel. Fry in hot oil until golden on both sides. Drain on a paper towel.

Arrange a layer of fried eggplant on the bottom of a shallow baking dish. Spoon some béchamel sauce over the top and sprinkle with cheese. Repeat the layers until all the ingredients are used up, ending with the cheese. Bake in a preheated 350° F. oven for 30 minutes or until the top is golden. *Serves 4.*

Provence, Comté de Nice

EGGPLANT GRATIN
(Aubergines Saint Loup)

In this recipe sautéed eggplant are layered with Parmesan cheese, and a mixture of tomato sauce and beaten egg. The dish is then topped with breadcrumbs and browned in the oven.

3 or 4	medium eggplants (about 2 lbs.)
about 1	cup olive oil
1	cup tomato sauce (see page 103)
2	eggs
1	cup freshly grated Parmesan cheese
	salt
	freshly ground black pepper
3	tbsp. whole wheat breadcrumbs

Trim the ends of the eggplant, but do not peel them. Cut into rounds ⅛ inch thick. Sprinkle with salt and set in a colander for 1 hour to release the bitter juices. Wash off the salt and pat dry with a paper towel. Fry in hot oil until golden on both sides. Drain on a paper towel.

Beat the eggs lightly in a mixing bowl and add the the tomato sauce and half of the cheese. Blend well together.

Arrange a layer of fried eggplant on the bottom of a well-oiled shallow baking dish. Spoon some of the tomato sauce and egg mixture over the top and sprinkle with grated cheese. Repeat the layers until all the ingredients are used up, ending with the cheese. Sprinkle the top with breadcrumbs and dribble with 2 tablespoons of olive oil. Bake in a preheated 350° F. oven for 30 minutes or until the top is golden. *Serves 4.*

Languedoc, Roussillon

EGGPLANT, ONION, AND TOMATO TIAN
(Le tian Nîmois)

A specialty of Nîmes.

2	medium eggplant (about 1¹/₂ lbs.)
	whole wheat flour for dusting
about ³/₄	cup olive oil
2	large onions, thinly sliced
6	plum tomatoes, peeled and thinly sliced
3	garlic cloves, finely chopped
2	tbsp. fresh parsley, finely chopped
2	tbsp. fresh basil, chopped
	salt
	freshly ground black pepper
1¹/₂	cups (6 oz.) Gruyère cheese, grated

Trim the ends of the eggplant, but do not peel them. Cut into rounds ¹/₈ inch thick, sprinkle with salt and set in a colander for 1 hour to release the bitter juices. Wash off the salt and pat the slices dry with a paper towel. Meanwhile heat 3 tablespoons of olive oil in a large frying pan, add the onions, and cook over a moderate heat for 8 minutes or until they start to turn golden. Set aside.

Dip the eggplant slices in the whole wheat flour and fry in hot oil until they are golden on both sides. Arrange a layer of eggplant in the bottom of a well-oiled shallow baking dish. Cover with a layer of fried onions and then a layer of sliced tomato. Sprinkle with a little chopped garlic, herbs, and grated cheese. Repeat the layers until all the ingredients are used up, ending with a layer of grated cheese. Bake in a preheated 350° F. oven for 30 minutes or until the top is golden. *Serves 4.*

Savoie, Dauphiné

PUMPKIN GRATIN
(La courge au gratin)

2	pounds pumpkin
6	tbsp. butter
$^1/_2$	cup milk
2	eggs
$^1/_2$	cup Gruyère cheese, grated
$^1/_4$	tsp. freshly grated nutmeg
	salt
	freshly ground black pepper
3	tbsp. whole wheat breadcrumbs

Peel the pumpkin, remove the seeds and fibers, and cut into large dice. Steam for 15 minutes or until tender. Mash with a potato ricer, or force through a sieve. Add 4 tablespoons of butter, the milk, 1 whole egg and 1 yolk, and half of the cheese; blend well. Season with nutmeg, salt, and black pepper to taste. Beat the remaining egg white stiff and fold into the pumpkin mixture. Pour into a well-buttered shallow baking dish. Mix the remaining cheese with the breadcrumbs and sprinkle over the top. Dot with the remaining butter. Bake in a preheated 350° F. oven for 30 minutes or until the top is golden. *Serves 4.*

Savoie, Dauphiné

SPINACH GRATIN
(Gratin d'épinards)

3	pounds spinach
3	tbsp. olive oil
¹/₄	tsp. freshly grated nutmeg
	salt
	freshly ground black pepper
2	cups béchamel sauce (see page 99)
3	tbsp. light cream
2	eggs, beaten
3	tbsp. whole wheat breadcrumbs

Wash the spinach carefully and cook in a covered saucepan over a moderate heat for 5 minutes. The water clinging to the leaves is sufficient to prevent scorching. Drain well and chop finely.

Heat 2 tablespoons olive oil in a large frying pan and add the spinach and nutmeg, and season with salt and black pepper to taste. Simmer for 2 or 3 minutes.

Meanwhile, prepare the béchamel sauce and stir in the cream. Remove from the heat and stir in the spinach. Add the eggs and mix well together. Pour into a well-oiled shallow baking dish. Sprinkle the breadcrumbs over the top and drizzle with the remaining olive oil. Bake in a preheated 350° F. oven for 25 to 30 minutes or until the top is golden. *Serves 4.*

Fritters and Croquettes
(Les beignets et les croquettes)

Fritters have been made in France since the Middle Ages, especially for religious holidays and festive occasions. All kinds of vegetables can be used—eggplant, cauliflower, broccoli, artichoke bottoms— even green leafy vegetables such as spinach and sorrel.

Croquettes are small cylinders of food that are dipped in egg and breadcrumbs and deep-fried. A light vegetable oil, such as peanut, soy, or corn oil, is best for deep-frying. Fill a deep-fryer or heavy saucepan no more than half way with oil. Heat the oil to 360° F. before adding the fritters or croquettes. (If you do not have a cooking thermometer, drop a morsel of bread into the hot oil, and when it is golden the oil is ready to be used.) Do not overcrowd the fritters when cooking, as they need space to puff up.

All   France

FRYING BATTER
(Pâté à frire)

1³/₄	cups whole wheat or unbleached white flour
¹/₂	tsp. salt
2	tbsp. olive oil
about 1¹/₄	cups water
2	egg whites

Place the flour and salt in a large bowl. Gradually mix in the olive oil and enough water to make a smooth batter the consistency of light cream. Let it rest for 1 hour. Just before using beat the egg whites stiff and fold into the batter. *Makes about 3½ cups.*

Picardy,   Flanders,   Artois

FRYING BATTER
WITH BEER
(Pâté à frire à la bière)

2	cups whole wheat or unbleached white flour
	pinch of salt
2	eggs, separated
2	tbsp. butter, melted
1/2	cup beer
about 3/4	cup water

Place the flour and salt in a large bowl. Make a well in the center and begin to work in the egg yolks and melted butter. Gradually add the beer and enough water to form a smooth batter the consistency of light cream. Let rest for 1 hour. Just before using, beat the egg whites stiff and fold into the batter. *Makes about 4 cups.*

Languedoc, Roussillon

GYPSY STYLE
EGGPLANT
FRITTERS
(Aubergines à la gitane)

These fritters are very simple to prepare. Slices
of eggplant are dipped into beaten egg mixed
with grated cheese and a dash of chili pepper,
then dipped into flour and deep-fried.

  2 **medium eggplant (about 1¼ lbs.)**
  3 **eggs**
 ½ **cup freshly grated Parmesan or Gruyère
      cheese
      salt**
  2 **pinches of chili pepper
      whole wheat flour for dusting
      oil for deep-frying**

Trim the ends of the eggplants but do not peel. Cut into rounds ½
inch thick. Beat the eggs with the cheese and season with salt and
chili pepper to taste. Dip the eggplant slices into the egg mixture
and then into flour. Deep-fry in hot oil until they are golden on both
sides. Drain on a paper towel and serve at once. *Serves 4.*

Brittany

CAULIFLOWER
FRITTERS
(Beignets de choufleur)

1	small cauliflower
¼	cup dry white wine
¼	cup peanut or olive oil
1	tbsp. lemon juice
	pinch of thyme
	salt
	freshly ground black pepper
	frying batter (see page 189)

Cut away the stalk of the cauliflower and break into florets. Steam for 6 or 7 minutes or until just tender but still retains its crispness. Mix the wine, oil, lemon juice, and thyme in a bowl and season with salt and black pepper to taste. Add the cauliflower florets and marinate for 1 hour, turning from time to time. Remove with a slotted spoon and dip the florets into batter. Deep-fry in hot oil until golden on both sides. Drain on a paper towel and serve at once. *Serves 4.*

Picardy, Flanders, Artois

ENDIVE FRITTERS
(Fritot d'endives)

Brussels sprouts may be prepared the same way.

8 **Belgian endives**
¹/₃ **cup olive oil**
   juice of 1 lemon
   salt
   freshly ground black pepper
1 **recipe frying batter with beer (see page 190)**
   oil for deep frying

Trim the ends of the endives and cut away any discolored edges. Cut lengthwise into halves and steam for 7 or 8 minutes or until just tender. Squeeze out any excess moisture. Mix the olive oil and lemon juice and season with salt and black pepper to taste. Add the endives and allow to marinate for 1 hour. Remove with a slotted spoon and dip in the batter. Deep-fry in hot oil until golden on both sides. Drain on a paper towel and serve at once. *Serves 4.*

Poitou, Charente

SORREL FRITTERS

(Beignets de feuilles d'oseille)

Sorrel leaves make delicious fritters. Spinach or arugula may be prepared the same way.

1   **cup whole wheat or unbleached white flour**
    pinch of salt
1   **egg, separated**
1   **tbsp. peanut or olive oil**
1   **tbsp. cognac or brandy**
½   **cup milk**
    about 20 sorrel leaves
    oil for deep frying

Place the flour and salt in a large bowl. Make a well in the center and begin to work in the egg yolk, peanut oil and cognac. Gradually add the milk to form a smooth batter the consistency of light cream. Let rest for 1 hour.

Wash the sorrel leaves and trim away the stalks. Pat dry with a paper towel. Beat the egg white stiff and fold into the batter. Dip about 5 leaves into the batter and fry in hot oil until golden on both sides. Repeat until all the leaves are used. Serve at once. *Serves 2 to 4.*

Bordeaux, Les Landes

SWEETCORN FRITTERS
(Beignets de maïs)

> 1½ cups sweet corn kernels, or 2 or 3
>   ears of sweet corn
> 2 eggs plus 1 egg white
> 3 tbsp. whole wheat flour
>   salt
>   freshly ground black pepper
> about ¼ cup olive oil (for frying)

If using ears of corn remove the husks and silky threads, and cut off the kernels with a sharp knife. Place the corn in a small amount of lightly salted water and bring to a boil. Cover and simmer for 5 minutes or until the corn is just tender. Drain well.

Mix the whole eggs with the flour in a bowl until smooth. Add the corn and season with salt and black pepper to taste. Beat the egg white stiff and fold into the corn mixture.

Heat 2 or 3 tablespoons of olive oil in a heavy frying pan and drop in spoonfuls of the mixture. Fry until golden on both sides. Drain on a paper towel and serve at once. *Serves 4.*

Paris, Ile – de – France

POTATO CROQUETTES
(Croquettes de pommes de terre)

Potato croquettes are made all over France. Sometimes a little freshly grated Parmesan cheese is added. In Périgord ground walnuts are often included.

1¼   **pounds potatoes**
2   **egg yolks**
¼   **tsp. freshly grated nutmeg**
   salt
   freshly ground black pepper
1   **egg, beaten**
   whole wheat breadcrumbs
   oil for deep frying

Peel the potatoes and bring to a boil in lightly salted water for 20 minutes or until tender. Force through a sieve into a saucepan and cook over a gentle heat for 2 or 3 minutes to evaporate any excess moisture. Remove from the heat and beat in 2 egg yolks. Season with nutmeg, salt, and pepper to taste. Allow the mixture to cool completely. Shape into cylinders 1½ inches long and 1 inch in diameter. Dip in the beaten egg, then roll in breadcrumbs. Deep-fry in hot oil until crisp and golden. Drain on a paper towel and serve at once. *Serves 4.*

Savoie, Dauphiné

SPINACH AND POTATO CROQUETTES

(Croquettes de pommes de terre aux épinards)

¹/₂   **pound spinach**
1¹/₂   **pounds potatoes**
1   **small egg plus 1 yolk**
¹/₂   **cup whole wheat flour**
¹/₄   **tsp. freshly grated nutmeg**
   salt
   freshly ground black pepper
   whole wheat flour for dusting
   oil for deep frying

Wash the spinach carefully and cook in a covered saucepan for 5 minutes or until tender. The water clinging to the leaves is sufficient to prevent scorching. Squeeze dry and chop fine. Boil the potatoes in lightly salted water for 20 minutes or until they are tender. Force through a sieve or mash with a potato ricer into a saucepan and cook over a gentle heat for 2 or 3 minutes to evaporate any excess moisture. Place in a mixing bowl with the chopped spinach, the egg and egg yolk, and mix well together. Blend in the whole wheat flour and season with nutmeg and salt and black pepper to taste. Form into cylinders 1¹/₂ inches long and 1 inch in diameter. Roll in flour and deep-fry in hot oil until golden. Drain on a paper towel and serve at once. *Serves 6.*

Auvergne, Limousin

LENTIL CROQUETTES
(Croquettes de lentilles)

If Le Puy lentils are unavailable, small green
lentils may be used instead

1   cup Le Puy lentils
1   egg yolk
1   tbsp. butter
2   garlic cloves, crushed
2   tbsp. parsley, finely chopped
    salt
    freshly ground black pepper
    whole wheat flour for dusting
1   egg, beaten
    whole wheat breadcrumbs

Soak the lentils for 1 hour and drain. Place in a saucepan and cover
with water. Bring to a boil, cover, and simmer for $1^1/_4$ to $1^1/_2$ hours
or until the lentils are tender. Drain thoroughly.

Place in a bowl and add the egg yolk, butter, garlic, and parsley.
Mix well and season with salt and black pepper to taste. Shape into
cylinders 2 inches long and 1 inch in diameter. Roll in flour, dip in
beaten egg, then roll in breadcrumbs. Fry in hot oil until crisp and
golden. *Serves 4.*

Stuffed Vegetables
(Les légumes farcis)

Stuffed vegetables make delicious main courses, hors-d'oeuvres, or side vegetables, depending on their size and the quantity used. In Provence in the summer months a selection of stuffed vegetables are often served as a main course, especially for Sunday lunch or festive occasions.

The most popular vegetables for stuffing are eggplant, sweet peppers, tomatoes, zucchini, and mushrooms. Stuffings are generally based on rice or breadcrumbs, with the addition of beaten egg, grated cheese, or ground nuts.

Périgord,   Quercy,   Rouergue

STUFFED EGGPLANT WITH MUSHROOMS AND WALNUTS

(Aubergines farcis aux noix)

A specialty of Périgord.

4	small eggplants (about 5 oz. each)
1/2	cup olive oil
2	shallots, finely chopped
2	garlic cloves, finely chopped
2	tbsp. fresh parsley, finely chopped in a blender or food processor
1/4	pound mushrooms, chopped
	salt
	freshly ground black pepper
1/4	cup walnuts, finely chopped in a blender
1/2	cup whole wheat breadcrumbs

Place the eggplants whole into a saucepan of boiling water and simmer for 5 minutes. Remove and cut in half lengthwise. Scoop out the pulp, taking care not to damage the skins, to leave a shell about 1/8 inch thick. Chop the pulp coarsely.

Heat 3 tablespoons of olive oil in a large frying pan and cook the shells over a moderate heat for 5 minutes, or until they start to turn golden. Remove and place side by side in a well-oiled shallow baking dish. Set aside.

Heat another 3 tablespoons of olive oil in the same frying pan and cook the shallots, garlic, and parsley for 2 minutes. Add the mushrooms and chopped eggplant. Cover, and cook gently for 10 to 15 minutes, or until the vegetables are tender. Season with salt and black pepper to taste.

Remove from the heat and stir in the walnuts and half of the bread-crumbs. Fill the eggplant shells with the mixture. Sprinkle the remaining breadcrumbs over the top and dribble over the remaining olive oil. Bake in a preheated 350° F. oven for 25 to 30 minutes or until the tops are golden. *Serves 4.*

Provence, Comté de Nice

STUFFED EGGPLANT WITH OLIVES AND CAPERS
(Merinjana farcit)

This dish is equally good as an hors-d'oeuvre or side vegetables. If you are serving it as a main course choose a high-protein first course or end your meal like the French—with some cheese and a glass of red wine.

- 3   medium eggplants (about ¹/₂ lb. each)
- ¹/₂   cup olive oil
- 1   small onion, finely chopped
- 3   garlic cloves, finely chopped
- 1   cup whole wheat breadcrumbs
- ¹/₂   cup parsley, finely chopped
- ¹/₃   cup Niçoise or similar black olives, pitted and chopped
- 2   tsp. capers, roughly chopped
      salt
      freshly ground black pepper

Place the whole eggplants in a saucepan of boiling water and simmer for 5 minutes. Remove and cut lengthwise in half. Scoop out the pulp, taking care not to damage the skins, to leave a shell about ¹/₈ inch thick. Chop the pulp coarsely.

Heat 3 tablespoons of olive oil in a frying pan and cook the shells, cut side down over a moderate heat for 5 minutes or until they start to turn golden. Remove and place side by side in a well-oiled shallow baking dish. Set aside.

Heat 4 tablespoons of olive oil in the same frying pan and cook the onion and garlic over a moderate heat for 5 minutes or until the onions are translucent. Add the chopped eggplant. Cover, and cook gently for 10 to 15 minutes, or until the eggplant are tender. Remove from the heat and stir in ³/₄ cup of breadcrumbs, the parsley, olives, and capers. Season to taste with salt and black pepper.

Fill the eggplant shells with the mixture. Sprinkle the remaining breadcrumbs over the top and drizzle with the remaining olive oil. Bake in a preheated 350° F. oven for 25 to 30 minutes or until the tops are golden. *Serves 4 to 6.*

Savoie, Dauphiné

ZUCCHINI STUFFED WITH RICE AND TOMATOES
(Courgettes farcis à la Savoyarde)

about 2¹/₂	cups vegetable broth or water
6	medium zucchini
2	tbsp. olive oil
1	garlic clove, finely chopped
1	small onion, finely chopped
3	ripe plum tomatoes, peeled, seeded, and chopped
1	cup arborio rice
2	tbsp. butter
1¹/₂	cups freshly grated Parmesan or Gruyère cheese
	salt
	freshly ground black pepper
2	cups tomato sauce (see page 103)

Bring the broth to boil in a saucepan and keep just below the simmering point.

Trim the ends of the zucchini and cut in half lengthwise. Scoop out
the flesh with a melon-baller, leaving a shell about ¼ inch thick.
Steam the hollowed out shells for 10 minutes or until they are
almost tender.

Heat the olive oil in a heavy-based saucepan and cook the garlic
and onion over a moderate heat for 5 minutes, or until the onion is
translucent. Add the chopped tomatoes and cook for another 5
minutes. Stir in the rice and add a ladleful of hot broth. Cook, stirring constantly, until the liquid has almost evaporated. Repeat until
the rice is tender but still firm. This will take about 25 minutes. Five
minutes before the end of cooking stir in the butter and season with
salt and black pepper to taste.

Stuff the zucchini shells with the rice and sprinkle grated cheese
over the top. Arrange side by side on a well-oiled shallow baking
dish and bake in a preheated 375° F. oven for 20 to 25 minutes or
until the tops are golden. *Serves 6.*

Poitou, Charente

CÈPE MUSHROOMS STUFFED WITH WALNUTS AND MARJORAM
(Cèpes farcis)

Some cèpes have large bulbous stems and almost no cap. For this recipe choose the variety with a wide cap. If unavailable any large mushroom may be used instead.

6 to 8	cèpes or any other large mushroom
¹/₄	cup walnut oil
4	shallots, finely chopped
¹/₂	cup fresh parsley, finely chopped
1	tsp. fresh marjoram, chopped (or ¹/₄ tsp. dry)
³/₄	cup whole wheat breadcrumbs
¹/₄	cup walnuts, finely ground in a blender
	salt
	freshly ground black pepper

Wash the cèpes carefully and wipe dry. Remove the stems and chop the stems finely. Place the caps on a well-oiled shallow baking dish and brush lightly with walnut oil. Bake in a preheated 350° F. oven for 10 minutes or until they are slightly tender. Remove from the oven and set aside.

Heat 2 tablespoons of walnut oil in a frying pan and cook the shallots over a moderate heat for 2 minutes. Add the mushroom stems and cook for 5 minutes or until tender. Stir in the parsley and marjoram and cook for 2 minutes. Remove from the heat and stir in ¹/₂ cup breadcrumbs and the chopped walnuts. Mix well and season to taste with salt and black pepper. Stuff the cèpes with the mixture. Sprinkle with remaining breadcrumbs and drizzle with remaining walnut oil. Bake in a preheated 375° F. oven for 20 minutes or until the tops are golden. *Serves 3 to 4.*

Picardy, Flanders, Artois

MUSHROOMS STUFFED WITH SPINACH AND SORREL

(Roses du nord farcis)

8	large mushrooms
2	pounds spinach
2	tbsp. peanut or olive oil
4	tbsp. butter
6	shallots, finely chopped
1	cup sorrel leaves, finely shredded
$1/4$	cup heavy cream
$1/4$	tsp. freshly grated nutmeg
	salt
	freshly ground black pepper
1	cup whole wheat breadcrumbs
$1/2$	cup Gruyère cheese, grated

Wash the mushrooms carefully and wipe dry. Remove the stems and chop them finely. Brush the mushroom caps lightly with peanut oil and bake in a preheated 350° F. oven for 10 minutes or until the mushrooms are slightly tender. Remove from the oven and arrange side by side on a well-oiled shallow baking dish.

Wash the spinach carefully and cook in a covered pan over a moderate heat for 5 minutes, or until tender. The water clinging to the leaves is sufficient to prevent scorching. Drain well and chop coarsely.

Heat 2 tablespoons of butter in a large frying pan and cook the shallots over a moderate heat for 2 minutes. Add the chopped mushroom stems and shredded sorrel and continue to cook for 5 minutes or until the vegetables are tender. Stir in the spinach and cream and simmer for 2 or 3 minutes. Season with nutmeg and salt and black pepper to taste.

Stuff the mushroom caps with the mixture. Combine the bread-crumbs with the grated cheese and sprinkle over the top. Dot with the remaining butter and bake in a preheated 375° F. oven for 15 to 20 minutes or until the tops are golden. *Serves 4.*

P r o v e n c e ,   C o m t é   d e   N i c e

PROVENÇAL
STUFFED
VEGETABLES
(Les farcis Provençaux au maigre)

In Provence stuffed vegetables are traditionally served for Sunday lunch, buffets, and picnics. They usually consist of a colorful selection of vegetables such as eggplant, zucchini, sweet peppers, onions, and tomatoes. It is difficult to be precise about the exact number of vegetables as it depends on their size.

    1   recipe rice pilaf (see page 232)
    3   medium eggplants
    3   sweet red peppers
  1/3   cup olive oil
    3   zucchini
    3   large onions
    3   large tomatoes
    1   pound spinach
    3   garlic cloves, finely chopped
    2   tbsp. fresh parsley, finely chopped
  1/4   pound mushrooms, roughly chopped
    2   eggs, beaten
    1   cup freshly grated Parmesan cheese
        salt
        freshly ground black pepper

Prepare the rice pilaf as directed on page 232.

To prepare the vegetable shells, brush the eggplant and sweet peppers lightly with olive oil and place in a well-oiled baking sheet. Bake in a preheated 350° F. oven for 10 minutes. Remove from the oven and set aside to cool slightly. Cut the eggplant in half, lengthwise, and scoop out the flesh, taking care not to damage the skins; leave the shells about $1/8$ inch thick.

Cut off the tops of the sweet peppers and carefully scoop out the fibers and seeds. Trim the zucchini and cut in half lengthwise. Scoop out the pulp with a melon-baller, leaving the shells about $1/8$ inch thick. Cut the tomatoes in half crosswise and scoop out most of the pulp and seeds, leaving the shells about $1/4$ inch thick. Peel the onions and drop in a saucepan of boiling water. Simmer for 5 minutes, drain, and cut in half crosswise. Scoop out the centers to leave the shells about $1/2$ inch thick.

To prepare the filling, chop all the vegetable pulp and combine in a bowl. Wash the spinach carefully and cook in a covered saucepan over a moderate heat for 5 minutes or until tender. The water clinging to the leaves is sufficient to prevent scorching. Drain well, and chop coarsely. Heat 2 tablespoons of olive oil in a large frying pan and cook the eggplant and zucchini shells over a moderate heat on both sides until tender and starting to turn golden. Remove and set aside. In the same frying pan heat 3 more tablespoons of olive oil and cook the garlic and parsley for 1 minute. Add the mushrooms and chopped vegetable pulp. Cover and cook over gentle heat, stirring occasionally, until the vegetables are tender.

Remove from the heat and stir in the rice, spinach, beaten eggs, and half of the cheese. Mix well and season to taste with salt and pepper. Spoon the filling into the prepared vegetable shells and sprinkle the remaining cheese over the top.

Arrange the stuffed vegetables side by side on one or two well-oiled baking sheets and bake in a preheated 350° F. oven for 30 minutes or until the tops are golden. Serve hot or cold. *Serves 6.*

Languedoc, Roussillon

CATALAN STUFFED PEPPERS
(Poivrons farcis à la Catalane)

This dish has a Spanish influence. The peppers are stuffed with rice, pine nuts, currants, green olives, and capers, and flavored with saffron and herbs. If you like, the peppers may be served with a tomato sauce on the side.

8 to 10	sweet red peppers
1/4	cup olive oil
1	medium onion, finely chopped
2	tbsp. fresh cilantro, finely chopped
2	tbsp. fresh parsley, finely chopped
1	cup long grain rice
2	tbsp. currants
2	tbsp. pine nuts
1/4	cup green olives, pitted and sliced
2	tsp. capers, roughly chopped
2 1/2	cups boiling water
1/4	tsp. powdered saffron, dissolved in 1 tbsp.of the boiling water
	salt
	freshly ground black pepper

Brush the peppers lightly with olive oil and place on a well-oiled baking sheet. Bake in a preheated 350° F. oven for 10 minutes. Remove from the oven and let cool slightly. Cut off the tops and reserve. Remove the pith and seeds.

Heat 2 tablespoons of olive oil in a heavy saucepan and cook the onion, coriander, and parsley for 3 minutes. Add the rice and cook for 1 minute, so each grain is coated with oil. Add the currants, pine nuts, green olives, and capers and stir well. Add 2 cups of the boiling water and the saffron in liquid and season with salt and black pepper to taste. Cover, and simmer for 18 to 20 minutes, or until the rice is tender but still firm. Stuff the peppers with the mixture and place the reserved caps on top.

Arrange side by side in a well-oiled shallow baking dish and pour in $1/2$ cup of boiling water and the remaining olive oil. Bake in a preheated 350° F. oven for 40 to 50 minutes, or until the peppers are tender. *Serves 4 to 5.*

Crêpes and Galettes
(Les crêpes et les galettes)

Crêpes and galettes make delicious breakfasts, main courses, and desserts. They can be served plain with a squeeze of lemon juice and a dusting of sugar, or they can be filled with vegetables, with or without a sauce, cheese, or scrambled eggs. In Brittany, where crêpes originated, they are usually made with wheat flour and are sweetened. Galettes, or *gaoffs* as they are sometimes called, are made with buckwheat flour and usually have a savory filling.

Traditionally crêpes are served in France on Mardi Gras (Shrove Tuesday), *Chandeleur* (Candlemas Day, Feb. 2), and New Year's Day, when there is an old custom of tossing a crêpe in the air while holding a coin in your hand. If you catch the crêpe without dropping the coin, you will have good fortune that year.

A l l   F r a n c e

CRÊPE BATTER
(Pâté à crêpe)

For best results, use a heavy cast iron or steel pan. In France crêpe pans are usually very shallow with a curved lip, which enables crêpes to slide out easily after cooking. To keep crêpes warm, place them between two soup plates and set on top of a saucepan of simmering water.

1¾   **cups whole wheat or plain white flour**
      pinch of salt
3   **eggs**
1¾   **cups milk (or half milk, half water)**
2   **tbsp. olive oil**

Place the flour and salt in a bowl. Make a well in the center and drop in the eggs. Mix well with a wooden spoon. Gradually add the water, beating constantly, to form a smooth batter the consistency of thin cream. Let stand for 1 hour before using.

Heat a little olive oil in a 6-inch heavy frying pan. When it is hot, pour in 2 tablespoons of batter. Quickly tilt the pan in all directions so the batter evenly covers the pan. Cook for 1 minute on each side. Slide the crêpe on to a soup plate and keep it warm as described above. Lightly oil the pan again and repeat until all the batter is used up. *Makes enough for 15 crêpes.*

Franche Comté

CHEESE CRÊPES, GRATINÉE
(Crêpes au fromage, gratinées)

2¹/₂   pints béchamel sauce (see page 99)
3   tbsp. light cream
2   cups (¹/₂ lb.) Comté or Gruyère cheese, grated
15   crêpes (see pages 210–211)

Prepare the béchamel sauce as directed on page 99. Stir in the cream and simmer for 1 or 2 minutes. Remove from the heat and stir in half of the Comté cheese. Spoon a little sauce into each crêpe and roll up. Arrange the crêpes side by side in a well-oiled shallow baking dish. Cover with the remaining sauce and sprinkle over the remaining cheese. Bake in a preheated 400° F. oven for 15 minutes or until the crêpes are heated through and the tops are golden. *Serves 4 to 5.*

Picardy, Flanders, Artois

ENDIVES CRÊPES GRATIN

(Crêpes aux endives, gratinées)

In this recipe crêpes are wrapped around heads of chicory, topped with a béchamel sauce and grated cheese, and gratinéed in a hot oven.

8   Belgian endives
8   crêpes (see pages 210–211)
2   cups béchamel sauce (see page 99)
1   cup Gruyère cheese, grated

Trim the ends of the endives and cut away any discolored leaves. Steam for 8 minutes or until they are tender. Place each endive on a crêpe and roll up.

Prepare the béchamel sauce as directed on page 99. Spoon a little sauce into the bottom of a well-oiled shallow baking dish. Arrange the stuffed crêpes side by side on top. Cover with the remaining sauce. Bake in a preheated 400° F. oven for 15 minutes or until the crêpes are heated through and the tops are golden. *Serves 4.*

Languedoc, Roussillon

MATAFANS
(Matafans)

In Savoy *matafans* or *matefaims* are thick potato pancakes, but these *matafans* from the Comté de Foix are pancakes made with a mixture of buckwheat and wheat flour, topped with fried onions, tomato sauce, and cheese, and gratinéed in the oven.

Pancake batter:	1	cup whole wheat or unbleached white flour
	¼	cup buckwheat flour
		pinch of salt
	2	eggs
	¾	cup milk
	½	cup water
	1 or 2	tbsp. olive oil (for frying)
Topping:	2	tbsp. olive oil
	2	medium onions, thinly sliced
	2	cups tomato sauce (see page 103)
	1	cup Gruyère cheese, grated

For the pancake batter:
Combine the whole wheat and buckwheat flour and salt in a bowl. Make a well in the center and begin to work in the eggs. Gradually add the milk and enough water to form a smooth batter the consistency of thin cream. Let stand for 1 hour.

Heat the olive oil in a 6-inch heavy frying pan. When it is hot, pour in 2 tablespoons of batter. Quickly tilt the pan in all directions so the batter evenly covers the pan. Cook for about 1 minute on each side. Lightly oil the pan again and repeat until all the batter is used up. Roll up the pancakes and arrange side by side in a well-oiled shallow baking dish. Set aside.

For the topping:
Heat 2 tablespoons of olive oil in a heavy frying pan and cook the onions over a moderate heat for 5 to 7 minutes or until they start to turn golden. Sprinkle a little fried onion over each rolled pancake and spoon a little tomato sauce over the top. Sprinkle the cheese. Bake in a preheated 400° F. oven for 15 minutes, or until the pancakes are heated through and the tops are golden. *Serves 4 to 5.*

B r i t t a n y

B U C K W H E A T
G A L E T T E S
(Gaoffs)

Galettes, or *gaoffs* as they are called in the Côtes du Nord, were once a staple food in Brittany, when they were eaten instead of bread. They are still very popular, and *crêperies* where they are made can be found all over Brittany.

Galettes are traditionally made without eggs, but I find that the addition of 1 or 2 eggs helps to prevent the batter from sticking.

Once cooked, the galettes may be filled with the filling of your choice, or simply spread with a little soft butter and a sprinkling of pepper and served hot.

1 ½   cup buckwheat flour
¾   cup whole wheat flour
pinch of salt
2   eggs
1   tbsp. butter, melted
about 2½   cups water
1 or 2   tbsp. oil (for frying)

Combine the buckwheat flour, whole wheat flour and salt in a bowl. Make a well in the center and begin to work in the eggs, melted butter, and salt. Gradually add the water, beating constantly, to form a smooth batter the consistency of thick cream. Let stand for 1 to 2 hours before using.

Heat a little oil in a 9-inch frying pan. When it is hot pour in a few tablespoons of batter. Quickly tilt the pan in all directions so the batter evenly covers the pan. Cook for about 1 or 2 minutes on each side. Slide onto a soup plate and keep warm as directed on page 210.

Lightly oil the pan again and repeat until all the batter is used up. *Makes enough for 12 galettes.*

Cheese filling: ½   tsp. butter
2   tbsp. grated Gruyère cheese
freshly ground black pepper

Spread the butter over the galette while it is still in the pan. Sprinkle with grated cheese and black pepper to taste. Cook for a few seconds to melt the cheese, then fold the galette in four like an envelope. Serve hot.

Spinach filling: 1   pound spinach
1   tbsp. butter
¼   tsp. freshly grated nutmeg
salt
freshly ground black pepper
3   tbsp. light cream

Wash the spinach carefully and cook in a covered saucepan over moderate heat for 5 minutes. The water clinging to the leaves is sufficient to prevent scorching. Drain well, and chop finely.

Heat the butter in a saucepan and add the spinach. Season with nutmeg and salt and black pepper to taste. Cook over moderate heat for 2 or 3 minutes. Stir in the cream and simmer for 1 or 2 more minutes.

Spoon a little filling into the center of the galettes and fold in four like an envelope. Serve hot. *Makes enough for 6 galettes.*

Mushroom filling:	2	**tbsp. butter**
	3	**shallots, finely chopped**
	1	**small onion, finely chopped**
	1	**pound mushrooms, thinly sliced**
	1	**tbsp. flour**
	3/4	**cup hot milk**
		salt
		freshly ground black pepper

Heat the butter in a saucepan and cook the shallots and onion over a moderate heat for 5 minutes, or until translucent. Add the mushrooms and cook for 5 minutes or until tender. Stir in the flour and cook for 1 more minute. Gradually pour in the hot milk, stirring constantly, and simmer for 5 minutes until the sauce is thickened. Season with salt and pepper to taste.

Spoon a little filling into the center of each galette and fold in four like an envelope. Serve hot. *Makes enough for 6 galettes.*

L y o n n a i s

POTATO CRÊPES
(*Crêpes vonnassiennes*)

Crêpes vonnassiennes are little pancakes made with puréed potatoes, eggs, milk, cream, and flour.

1	pound potatoes
¼	cup flour
4	eggs
¾	cup hot milk
3	tbsp. crème fraîche (see page 110) or heavy cream
	a grating of nutmeg
	salt
	freshly ground black pepper
about ¼	cup olive oil

Prepare the crème fraîche (see page 110).

Bring the potatoes to boil in plenty of lightly salted water. Cook for 20 minutes, or until tender. Drain and peel when they are cool enough to handle. Force through a sieve into a mixing bowl. Add the flour, eggs, hot milk, and cream and blend well together. The mixture should have the consistency of thick cream. Season with nutmeg and salt and black pepper to taste.

Heat a little of the olive oil in a heavy frying pan and drop in tablespoons of the mixture, to form rounds about 3 inches in diameter. Fry on both sides until golden.

Repeat until all the ingredients are used. Serve at once. *Serves 4.*

Potatoes
(Les pommes de terre)

The potato originated in the Andes in South America. It was first brought to Europe by the Spaniards in the middle of the sixteenth century. At first it was thought to be poisonous—even to cause leprosy. It took another two hundred years to be accepted as a food throughout France. It was Antoine–Auguste Parmentier, a military pharmacist, who championed the potato as a solution to the recurring famine in France. He persuaded Louis XVI of its virtues. Parmentier is said to have held a court dinner at which every course—soup, entrée, *entremets,* salad, dessert, biscuits, and even the bread—was made of potatoes. Today any dish with the suffix *parmentier* always includes potatoes.

The French have become great lovers of potatoes. Hundreds of potato recipes have been created all over France. Potatoes are boiled, baked, sautéed, deep-fried, puréed, stuffed, or made into pies, puddings, gratins, soufflés, pancakes, croquettes, dumplings, and salads.

Potatoes are one of the most important crops in the world. They are very rich in vitamins and minerals, especially vitamin C and iron. According to recent research in the United States, it is possible to survive on a diet of potatoes and whole milk.

Savoie, Dauphiné

FARÇON
(Farçon)

Farçon, or *farcement*, is a potato pudding from Savoy that may be sweetened or salted. Each village or hamlet has its own recipe—usually a closely guarded secret. It may be made with either grated or puréed potatoes. Some recipes include cabbages, turnips, or onions; others are made with raisins, prunes, or dried pears. In the past it was usually made for Sunday lunch, when the lady of the house would take it to the local baker to cook while she attended mass. Baking was long and slow. The longer it is cooked the better it is.

> 2   **pounds potatoes**
> ½   **cup hot milk**
> ¼   **cup light cream**
> 6   **tbsp. butter**
> 3   **eggs, beaten**
> 2   **tsp. sugar**
> 2   **tbsp. fresh chervil, finely chopped**
> ½   **cup raisins**
>   **a grating of nutmeg**
>   **salt**
>   **freshly ground black pepper**

Bring the potatoes to boil in lightly salted water for 20 minutes or until tender. Force through a sieve or mash with a potato ricer. Add the hot milk, 4 tablespoons butter, and the cream and mix well. Gradually add the beaten egg, sugar, and chervil and blend well. Stir in the raisins and season with nutmeg, salt, and black pepper to taste. Turn into a well-oiled shallow baking dish and dot with the remaining butter. Bake in a preheated 350° F. oven for 50 to 60 minutes or until the top is golden. *Serves 4 to 6.*

Savoie, Dauphiné

POTATO PIE
WITH ONIONS
AND GRUYÈRE
(Farcement)

This version of *farçon* or *farcement* is made with grated potatoes, sautéed onion, Gruyère cheese, and eggs. It makes a delicious lunch or supper dish with a green salad on the side.

2	tbsp. olive oil
1	medium onion, chopped
1½	pounds potatoes
2	eggs
¼	cup Gruyère cheese, grated
	salt
	freshly ground black pepper
2	tbsp. butter

Heat the olive oil in a heavy frying pan and cook the onion over gentle heat for 10 minutes or until it is softened but not browned.

Peel the potatoes and grate them coarsely into a mixing bowl. Add the onion, eggs, and cheese; mix well. Season with salt and black pepper to taste. Transfer to a well-oiled shallow baking dish and dot with butter. Bake in a preheated 350° F. oven for 40 to 50 minutes or until the top is nicely browned. *Serves 3 to 4.*

Périgord, Quercy, Rouergue

A L I G O T
(Aligot)

Aligot is the most famous dish of the Rouergue. It is made of a mixture of puréed potatoes, butter, milk, and cheese. It is beaten with a wooden spoon over low heat until the cheese melts and forms long threads when the spoon is raised.

Tomme fraîche de Cantal—also known as *tomme d'Aligot*—a mild unmatured cheese that is widely used in the cooking of the Rouergue and the Auvergne, is generally used to make aligot. If it is unavailable, Mozzarella makes a good substitute.

1½ pounds potatoes, peeled and quartered
½ cup hot milk
3 tbsp. butter
2 garlic cloves, crushed
   salt
   freshly ground black pepper
¾ pound tomme fraîche de Cantal or
   Mozzarella cheese, thinly sliced

Bring the potatoes to boil in lightly salted water and cook for 20 minutes or until tender. Force through a sieve into a heavy-based saucepan. Add the hot milk, butter, and garlic and mix well to form a smooth purée. Season with salt and black pepper to taste. Add the cheese and cook over a gentle heat, beating vigorously with a wooden spoon. If the mixture is too stiff, add a little more hot milk. The aligot is ready when it makes long stringy threads as it falls from the spoon. Serve at once. *Serves 4 to 6.*

Lyonnais

POTATO GRATIN
(Gratin de pommes de terre)

This potato gratin consists of layers of sliced potatoes, onions, and grated cheese, topped with a mixture of milk and vegetable broth, and browned in the oven

- 2 **pounds potatoes**
- 2 **medium onions, thinly sliced**
- 1 **cup hot milk**
- $^3/_4$ **cup hot vegetable broth or water**
  salt
  freshly ground black pepper
- 2 **cups ($^1/_2$ lb.) Gruyère cheese, grated**

Peel the potatoes and slice them thinly. Arrange a layer of potatoes in the bottom of a well-oiled shallow baking dish. Cover with a layer of sliced onions, then a layer of grated cheese. Mix the hot milk and broth together and pour some of the liquid over the vegetables. Season with salt and black pepper to taste.

Repeat the layers until all the ingredients are used, ending with the grated cheese. Bake in a preheated 350° F. oven for $1^1/_2$ to $1^3/_4$ hours or until the potatoes are tender and the top is golden. *Serves 4 to 6.*

Provence, Comté de Nice

BROCCOLI AND POTATO GRATIN

(Gratin de broccoli et pommes de terre)

1	pound potatoes
1	head (about ³/₄ lb.) of broccoli
3	garlic cloves, crushed
2	tbsp. fresh parsley, finely chopped
2	tbsp. olive oil
¹/₂	cup hot milk
¹/₄	cup light cream
1	cup Gruyère cheese, grated
¹/₄	tsp. freshly grated nutmeg
	salt
	freshly ground black pepper

Peel the potatoes and bring to a boil in lightly salted water for 20 minutes or until tender. Drain, and force through a sieve or mash with a potato ricer.

Trim the stalks of the broccoli. Break the heads into florets and cut the stalks into 2-inch lengths. Steam for 8 minutes or until just tender. Force through a sieve or purée in a food processor.

Heat the olive oil in a small saucepan, and cook the garlic and parsley over moderate heat for 1 minute. Add the hot milk and bring to just below simmer. Remove from the heat.

Combine the potato and broccoli purées in a large bowl and add the hot milk mixture, the cream, and half of the Gruyère cheese. Mix well. Season with nutmeg, salt, and black pepper to taste. Transfer to a well-oiled shallow baking dish and sprinkle the remaining cheese over the top. Bake in a preheated 375° F. oven for 30 minutes or until the top is nicely browned. *Serves 4 to 6.*

Savoie, Dauphiné

POTATO AND MUSHROOM GRATIN
(Gratin de pommes de terres au morilles)

Morilles or morel mushrooms are highly prized in France. They are found in springtime on the edge of woods and are distinguished by their black honeycombed caps. If unavailable any other mushroom may be used instead.

2	tbsp. butter
2	garlic cloves
2	tbsp. parsley, finely chopped
1/2	pound morel (or any other) mushrooms, thinly sliced
1 1/2	pounds potatoes
1	medium onion, finely chopped
	salt
	freshly ground black pepper
1	tsp. flour
3/4	cup light cream
1	cup milk, scalded

Heat the butter in a heavy frying pan and cook the garlic and parsley for 1 minute. Add the mushrooms and cook over a moderate heat for 5 minutes or until they are tender.

Peel the potatoes and slice them thinly. Arrange a layer of potatoes in the bottom of a well-oiled shallow baking dish. Top with a layer of the mushroom mixture and sprinkle with a little chopped onion. Season with salt and pepper to taste.

Repeat the layers until all the vegetables are used.

Mix the flour with the cream, then add the hot milk. Pour over the gratin. Dot with the remaining butter. Bake in a preheated 350° F. oven for 1¹/₂ to 1³/₄ hours or until the potatoes are tender and the top is golden. *Serves 4.*

Provence,   Comté   de   Nice

POTATO AND TOMATO GRATIN
(Gratin de pommes de terre Provençal)

1¹/₂	pounds potatoes, peeled
¹/₃	cup olive oil
1	large onion, thinly sliced
2	garlic cloves, finely chopped
1	pound tomatoes, peeled and thinly sliced
2	tbsp. fresh basil, chopped
	salt
	freshly ground black pepper
1¹/₂	cups Gruyère cheese, grated

Boil the potatoes in lightly salted water for 15 minutes or until almost tender. Drain and slice ¹/₈ inch thick. Heat 2 tablespoons of olive oil in a frying pan and cook the onion over a moderate heat for 5 to 7 minutes or until it starts to turn golden.

Arrange ¹/₃ of the potatoes in the bottom of a well-oiled, shallow baking dish. Cover with ¹/₃ of the fried onion and ¹/₃ of the sliced tomatoes. Season with salt and pepper to taste, and sprinkle with a little basil and ¹/₃ of the cheese. Repeat the layers until all the ingredients are used up, ending with the cheese. Drizzle with the remaining olive oil. Bake in a preheated 350° F. oven for 30 to 40 minutes or until the top is golden. *Serves 4.*

Burgundy

POTATO SOUFFLÉ
WITH CHEESE
(Soufflé de pommes de terre au fromage)

1 potatoes, peeled and quartered
3 tbsp. hot milk
3 tbsp. light cream
1 tbsp. butter
1/2 cup Gruyère cheese, grated
3 egg, separated
1/4 tsp. freshly grated nutmeg
    salt
    freshly ground black pepper

Bring the potatoes to boil in plenty of lightly salted water. Cook over a moderate heat for 20 minutes or until the potatoes are tender. Force through a sieve or mash with a potato ricer. Add the hot milk, cream, butter, cheese, and egg yolks, and blend well. Season with nutmeg, salt, and pepper to taste. Beat the egg whites stiff and fold into the mixture. Pour into a well-buttered soufflé dish. Bake in a preheated 375° F. oven for 25 to 30 minutes, or until the top is golden and it is nicely puffed. Serve at once. *Serves 4.*

Savoie, Dauphiné

POTATO AND ONION PANCAKES
(Paillassons)

These delicious potato pancakes make a perfect lunch or light supper with a green salad on the side. *Paillasson* literally means "doormat."

1¹/₂	pounds potatoes
1	medium onion
2	eggs
2	tbsp. flour
	salt
	freshly ground black pepper
about ¹/₃	cup olive oil

Peel the potatoes and onion and grate them on a coarse grater into a mixing bowl. Add the eggs and flour and mix well. Season with salt and pepper to taste.

Heat a little of the olive oil in a heavy frying pan. Drop in 3 or 4 heaping tablespoons of the mixture into the frying pan and flatten them with a fork. Cook over a moderate heat until they are golden on both sides. Repeat until the mixture is used. *Serves 3 to 4.*

Bourbonnais, Ninervais

BAKED POTATOES STUFFED WITH EGGS, CREAM, AND CHEESE

(Pommes au calas)

A specialty of the Morvan.

> 4 medium baking potatoes
> 1 tbsp. oil
> 4 tbsp. butter
> 2 egg yolks
> ¼ cup light cream
> 1 cup Gruyère cheese, grated
> pinch of thyme
> salt
> freshly ground black pepper

Scrub the potatoes but do not peel. Pierce each potato in the center with a sharp knife. Brush lightly with oil and bake in a preheated 400° F. oven for 1 to 1¼ hours or until they are soft to the touch. Remove from the oven and cut a lengthwise slit along the top of each potato. Carefully scoop out the pulp without breaking the skins. Place the pulp in a mixing bowl and add the butter, egg yolks, cream, cheese, and thyme. Mix well and season to taste with salt and pepper.

Stuff the potato skins with the mixture. Return to the oven, raise the heat to 425° F., and bake for 15 minutes. Serve hot. *Serves 4.*

Orléannais, Berry

BAKED POTATOES WITH MUSHROOM, CREAM, AND HERBS
(Pommes forestières)

Forestière usually means with mushrooms.

- **4 medium baking potatoes**
- **1 tbsp. oil**
- **1/2 cup light cream**
- **3 tbsp. butter**
- **1 tbsp. fresh parsley, finely chopped**
- **1/4 pound small white mushrooms, thinly sliced**
- **salt**
- **freshly ground black pepper**

Scrub the potatoes but do not peel. Pierce the centers with a sharp knife. Brush lightly with oil and bake in a preheated 400° F. oven for 1 to 1¼ hours or until soft to the touch.

Meanwhile heat the butter in a heavy frying pan and cook the parsley for 1 minute. Add the mushrooms and cook over a moderate heat for 3 minutes or until tender.

Remove the potatoes from the oven and cut a lengthwise slit along the top of each potato. Carefully scoop out the pulp without breaking the skins. Place the pulp in a mixing bowl and add the cream and the mushroom mixture. Mix well, and season to taste with salt and pepper.

Stuff the potato skins with the mixture. Return to the oven, raise the heat to 425° F., and bake for 10 minutes. Serve hot. *Serves 4.*

Rice
(Le riz)

Rice was first brought to Europe by the Moors in the ninth century. However, it was hardly known in France throughout the Middle Ages, although several recipes for rice appeared in Taillevent's *Le Vivandier* (c. 1373), said to be the first French cookbook. By the end of the fifteenth century the cultivation of rice was well established in the Po Valley in neighboring Piedmont, but it did not flourish in France until 1904, when it was finally grown successfully in the Camargue.

The French generally cook rice in two ways: boiled in salted water like pasta and drained well, or prepared as a pilaf. Rice pilaf is more flavorful and very easy to make. First the rice is cooked in butter or oil with an onion, before twice its volume of boiling water is added. Then the rice is simmered in a covered saucepan for 18 to 20 minutes, or until it is tender. The rice should be fluffy and each grain separate. The exact cooking time will depend on the type of rice used. Basmati rice only takes 12 to 15 minutes to cook; long grain brown rice takes about 40 minutes. The pilaf is usually enriched with a little butter at the end of cooking.

All France

R I C E   P I L A F
(Riz pilaf)

The exact amount of liquid will depend on the type of rice used.

1½   **cups long grain rice**
2   **tbsp. olive oil**
1   **small onion, finely chopped**
½   **bay leaf**
3   **cups boiling stock or water**
   salt
   freshly ground black pepper

Place the rice in a sieve and wash well under cold water. Drain well. Beat the olive oil in a heavy-based saucepan and cook the onion over a moderate heat for 5 minutes or until it is translucent. Stir in the rice and the bay leaf and cook for 1 minute, so each grain is coated with oil. Pour in the boiling stock and season with salt and black pepper to taste. Cover, and simmer for 18 to 20 minutes, or until all the liquid is absorbed and the rice is tender but still firm. Remove the bay leaf and serve. *Serves 2 to 4.*

Provence,   Comté   de   Nice

RICE WITH ZUCCHINI
(Riz camarguais aux courgettes)

1½ cups long grain rice
1 pound zucchini
3 tbsp. olive oil
3 cups boiling stock or water
    a grinding of nutmeg
    salt
    freshly ground black pepper
1 tbsp. butter
½ cup freshly grated Parmesan or Gruyère
    cheese

Trim the ends of the zucchini and cut into rounds about ⅛ inch thick. Heat the olive oil in a heavy-based frying pan and sauté the zucchini over moderate heat for 10 minutes or until they start to turn golden, stirring occasionally so they cook evenly. Stir in the rice and cook for 1 minute so each grain is coated with oil. Pour in the boiling stock and season with nutmeg and salt and black pepper to taste. Cover, and simmer for 18 to 20 minutes or until all the liquid is evaporated and the rice is tender but still firm. Stir in the butter and grated cheese and mix lightly. Serve at once. *Serves 4.*

Provence, Comté de Nice

RICE WITH RAISINS, PINE NUTS, AND BLACK OLIVES

(Riz aux raisins et aux pignons)

If you like, freshly grated Parmesan cheese may be served on the side.

¹⁄₄	cup pine nuts
2	tbsp. olive oil
1¹⁄₂	cups long grain rice
4	scallions, thinly sliced
3	cups boiling water
¹⁄₄	cup raisins
¹⁄₄	cup Niçoise or similar black olives, pitted and sliced
	pinch of powdered saffron
	salt
	freshly ground black pepper
2	tbsp. butter

Toast the pinenuts in a heavy frying pan over moderate heat for 5 minutes or until they turn golden. Set aside.

Heat the olive oil in a saucepan and cook the scallions over a moderate heat for 3 minutes. Stir in the rice and cook for 1 minute so each grain is coated with oil. Add the boiling water, raisins, black olives, and saffron, and season to taste with salt and pepper. Cover and simmer for 18 to 20 minutes or until the rice is tender but still firm. Stir in the butter and mix lightly. Serve at once. *Serves 4.*

Provence, Comté de Nice

PROVENÇAL RICE WITH MUSHROOMS
(Riz aux champignons à la Provençale)

In this dish the rice is cooked separately from the vegetables. At the end of cooking the mushrooms and tomatoes are lightly stirred into the rice together with the Gruyère cheese and briefly baked in the oven until the cheese is melted.

4	tbsp. olive oil
1	small onion, finely chopped
1¹/₂	cups long grain rice
3	cups boiling broth or water
	salt
	freshly ground black pepper
2	garlic cloves, finely chopped
3	shallots, finely chopped
2	tbsp. parsley, finely chopped
³/₄	pound small white mushrooms, thinly sliced
	pinch of thyme
4	ripe plum tomatoes, peeled, seeded, and chopped
1	cup Gruyère cheese, grated

Heat 2 tablespoons of olive oil in a saucepan and cook the onion over a moderate heat for 5 minutes or until it is translucent. Stir in the rice and cook for 1 minute so each grain is coated with oil. Pour in the boiling broth and season with salt and black pepper to taste. Cover, and simmer for 18 to 20 minutes or until the rice is tender but still firm.

Meanwhile, heat the remaining olive oil in a frying pan and cook the garlic, shallots, and parsley over moderate heat for 2 minutes. Add the mushrooms and thyme and cook for 5 minutes. Add the tomatoes and cook over fairly high heat for 5 to 7 minutes or until the sauce starts to thicken. Season with salt and pepper to taste. Stir the mushrooms and tomatoes lightly into the rice, together with half of the cheese. Transfer to a well-oiled baking dish and sprinkle over the remaining grated cheese. Bake in a preheated 400° F. oven for 10 minutes or until the rice is heated through and the cheese has melted. *Serves 4.*

Pays   Basque,   Bigorre,   Béarn

R I C E   W I T H   R E D   P E P P E R S ,   B L A C K   O L I V E S ,   A N D   C I L A N T R O
(Rizotto)

If you like, this dish may be served with fresh-ly grated Parmesan cheese on the side.

2	sweet red peppers
2	tbsp. olive oil
2	garlic cloves, finely chopped
1/2	fresh red chili pepper, seeded and finely chopped
1/2	cup fresh cilantro, finely chopped
1	large onion, finely chopped
1 1/2	cups long grain rice
3	ripe plum tomatoes, peeled, seeded, and chopped
1/4	cup black olives, pitted and sliced
3	cups boiling water
1/4	tsp. powdered saffron, dissolved in 1 tablespoon of boiling water
	salt
	freshly ground black pepper
2	tbsp. butter

Remove the fibers and seeds from the sweet peppers and cut into small dice. Heat the olive oil in a saucepan and cook the garlic, chili pepper, and cilantro over a moderate heat for 3 minutes. Add the onion and cook for 5 minutes or until translucent. Stir in the rice and cook for 1 minute, so each grain is coated with oil. Add the tomatoes and black olives and season with salt and pepper to taste. Cook for 1 minute. Pour the boiling water and saffron over the rice. Cover, and simmer for 18 to 20 minutes or until the rice is tender but still firm. Stir in the butter and mix lightly. Serve at once. *Serves 4.*

Burgundy

RICE, TOMATO, AND CHEESE GRATIN

(Rizotto, sauce tomate)

This dish consists of layers of rice pilaf, tomato sauce, and grated Gruyère cheese, topped with breadcrumbs and baked in the oven until the top is golden.

> 1   recipe rice pilaf (see page 232)
> 1   recipe tomato sauce (see page 103)
> 1½ cups Gruyère cheese, grated
> 3   tbsp. whole wheat breadcrumbs
> 2   tbsp. butter

Prepare the rice pilaf as directed on page 232. Spoon ⅓ of the cooked rice onto the bottom of a well-oiled shallow baking dish. Cover with half of the tomato sauce and sprinkle with ⅓ of the grated cheese. Repeat until all the rice, tomato sauce and cheese are used. Sprinkle with breadcrumbs and dot with butter. Bake in a preheated 350° F. oven for 30 minutes or until the top is golden. *Serves 4.*

Pasta
(Les pâtes)

The French have a long tradition of making pasta. Noodles have been made in Alsace since the Middle Ages. Many dishes, especially from Savoie, Provence, and the Comté de Nice, resemble those from across the border in Italy. However, the French have also created many unique dishes such as: *spaghetti au Roquefort* (spaghetti served with a creamy Roquefort cheese sauce), *Macaroni à la cévénole* (macaroni baked with chestnuts, cream, and Gruyère cheese), and *fidés* (a specialty of Savoy made with fresh vermicelli cooked like a risotto). The vermicelli is first fried in butter with onions, then boiling water is added, little by little, until the vermicelli is tender.

TO COOK PASTA
Boil the pasta in plenty of lightly salted boiling water with 1 tablespoon of olive oil; this will prevent the pasta from sticking together. Use 7 pints water to 1 pound pasta. The only way to test if it is ready is to taste it. It should be cooked until it is tender, but still *al dente*, or firm to the bite. Fresh pasta only takes a few minutes to cook, so take care not to overcook it. Drain the pasta in a colander or sieve and serve at once with the sauce of your choice.

Provence, Comté de Nice

EGG NOODLES

(Pâtes aux oeufs)

Egg noodles are widely made in Nice and in the hilly region close to the Italian border. They are usually made with unbleached white or semolina flour, but if you prefer you can use a mixture of whole wheat and unbleached white flour.

> 2 **cups unbleached white or semolina flour**
> 3 **eggs**
> 1 **tsp. water**
> **pinch of salt**

Place the flour in a mound on a large wooden board or table and make a deep well in the center. Work in 1 egg at a time before adding the water and salt. Gradually beat in the flour with a fork, then form into a soft ball. Knead the dough well for 8 to 10 minutes or until it is smooth and elastic. Do not add too much flour or the dough will become hard to roll. If the dough is too dry add another teaspoon or two of water. Wrap the dough in a damp cloth and let it rest for 30 minutes.

Divide the dough into 4. Keep 3 parts of the dough wrapped. With a long rolling pin, roll out one quarter of the dough quickly, making quarter turns to form a circle. Speed is important as the dough will cease to be pliable as it dries out. When the dough is very thin and even, let it dry out for 15 to 20 minutes. This will prevent the dough from sticking when it is rolled up and cut it into noodles of the desired width. Repeat with the remaining portions of the dough, keeping the pieces wrapped until ready to be rolled out.

Provence, Comté de Nice

HERB NOODLES
(Lounjetas d'erbas)

These noodles are made with a mixture of fresh greens and herbs. Choose at least two from the following: Swiss chard, spinach, beet greens, parsley, basil, borage, or chives. Serve them with melted butter and freshly grated Parmesan cheese, or with the sauce of your choice.

Dough: ¼ **pound fresh greens and herbs**
    2 **cups unbleached white or semolina flour**
    2 **eggs**
    1 **tbsp. water**
   ¼ **tsp. salt**

Topping: 4 **tbsp. butter, softened**
    1 **cup freshly grated Parmesan cheese**

Wash the greens and herbs and cook in a covered saucepan for 5 minutes, or until tender. The water clinging to the leaves is sufficient to prevent scorching. Squeeze dry and chop finely. Place the flour in a mound on a wooden board or table and make a deep well in the center. Drop in 1 egg at a time, followed by the greens and herbs, water, and salt. Gradually beat in the flour with a fork, then form into a soft ball. Knead the dough well for 8 to 10 minutes and proceed as for egg noodles on page 239. Roll out the dough very thinly and leave to dry for 15 minutes. Roll up and cut into ¹/₈-inch-wide noodles. Unfold the noodles and spread them out on a large towel or cloth to dry.

Cook the noodles in plenty of lightly salted, boiling water for 3 or 4 minutes, or until they are tender but still firm. Drain and transfer to a heated serving bowl. Dot with butter, toss lightly, and serve with grated cheese on the side. *Serves 4.*

Provence, Comté de Nice

EGG NOODLES WITH BASIL AND GARLIC SAUCE
(Pasta pistou)

Pistou is a garlic and basil sauce—similar to the Italian pesto but without the pine nuts. It is very light and flavorful and is one of my favorite sauces for pasta. Only fresh basil should be used.

Dough:	2	cups flour
	3	eggs
	1	tsp. water
		pinch of salt

Sauce:	2	cups fresh basil
	4	garlic cloves, crushed
	1/4	cup olive oil
		salt
		freshly ground black pepper
	1/2	cup freshly grated Parmesan cheese

Follow the directions for egg pasta on page 239. Roll out the dough very thinly and leave to dry for 15 minutes. Roll up and cut into 1/8-inch-wide noodles. Unfold and spread the noodles out on a large towel or cloth to dry.

To make the sauce, place the basil, garlic, and olive oil in a blender and mix slowly until all the ingredients are chopped. Blend at high speed until the mixture is smooth. Season to taste with salt and black pepper. Meanwhile cook the noodles in plenty of lightly salted, boiling water. Drain and transfer to a heated serving bowl. Pour the basil and garlic sauce over the noodles, toss lightly, and serve at once with grated cheese on the side. *Serves 4.*

Provence, Comté de Nice

EGG NOODLES WITH WALNUT SAUCE
(*Pâtes aux moix*)

Dough:	2	cups flour
	3	eggs
	1	tsp. water
		pinch of salt

Sauce:	¼	cup freshly shelled walnuts
	2	garlic cloves, crushed
		a handful of parsley
	3	tbsp. olive oil
about ¼		cup hot water
		salt
		freshly ground black pepper

Follow the directions for egg noodles on page 239. Roll out the dough very thinly and leave to dry for 15 minutes. Roll up and cut into ⅛-inch-wide noodles. Unfold and spread the noodles out on a large towel or cloth to dry.

Place the walnuts, garlic, parsley, and olive oil in a blender and mix slowly until all the ingredients are chopped. Blend at high speed until the mixture is a smooth paste. Gradually add enough hot water to make a smooth sauce. Season with salt and black pepper to taste.

Meanwhile, cook the noodles in plenty of lightly salted, boiling water. Drain and transfer to a heated serving bowl. Pour over the walnut sauce, toss lightly, and serve at once. If you like, grated cheese may be served on the side. *Serves 4.*

Provence, Comté de Nice

EGG NOODLES WITH PEAS AND CREAM
(Pâtes aux petit pois)

Sometimes Gruyère cheese is used instead of Parmesan cheese.

Dough:
- 2 cups flour
- 3 eggs
- 1 tsp. water
- pinch of salt

Sauce:
- 2 tbsp. olive oil
- 1 medium onion, finely chopped
- 1/2 pound freshly shelled tiny peas
- 1/2 cup heavy cream
- 2 tbsp. butter
- 1 cup freshly grated Parmesan cheese

Follow the directions for egg pasta on page 239. Roll out the dough very thinly and leave to dry for 15 minutes. Roll up and cut into 1/8-inch-wide noodles. Unfold and spread the noodles out on a large towel or cloth to dry.

Meanwhile, prepare the sauce. Heat the olive oil in a heavy saucepan and cook the onion over moderate heat for 5 minutes, or until translucent. Add the peas and 2 tablespoons of water and cook, covered, over a gentle heat for 10 minutes, or until the peas are tender. Add the cream and bring to a boil. Keep hot.

Cook the noodles in plenty of lightly salted boiling water. Drain and transfer to a heated serving bowl. Pour over the sauce, toss lightly, and serve at once with grated cheese on the side. *Serves 4.*

Provence,   Comté   de   Nice

SPAGHETTI WITH ZUCCHINI AND TOMATOES
(Spaghetti aux courgettes)

If fresh plum tomatoes are unavailable, canned plum tomatoes may be used instead.

- 1   **pound zucchini**
- 3   **tbsp. olive oil**
- 2   **shallots, finely chopped**
- 1/2 **pound ripe plum tomatoes, peeled, seeded, and chopped**
-     **salt**
-     **freshly ground black pepper**
- 1   **pound spaghetti**
- 1   **cup freshly grated Parmesan cheese**

Trim the ends of the zucchini and cut into thin rounds. Heat the olive oil in a heavy frying pan and cook the shallots over a moderate heat for 2 minutes. Add the zucchini and cook over fairly high heat until they are golden on both sides. Add the chopped tomatoes and season with salt and black pepper to taste. Cook for 8 to 10 minutes or until the sauce is thickened.

Cook the spaghetti in plenty of lightly salted, boiling water. Drain and transfer to a heated serving bowl. Pour over the zucchini and tomato sauce, toss lightly, and serve at once with grated cheese on the side. *Serves 4.*

Provence, Comté de Nice

SPAGHETTI MENTONNAISE
(Spaghetti Mentonnaise)

A specialty of Menton on the Côte d'Azur.

- 1   red or green sweet pepper
- 3   tbsp. olive oil
- 1   medium onion, finely chopped
- 2   tbsp. fresh basil, chopped
- 1/4   cup dry white wine
- 1   pound ripe plum tomatoes, peeled, seeded, and chopped
      salt
      freshly ground black pepper
- 1/4   cup Niçoise or similar black olives, pitted and sliced
- 1   pound spaghetti
- 1   cup freshly grated Parmesan cheese

Roast the sweet pepper under a hot grill until it is blackened all over. Rinse under cold water and remove the skin. Dice into 1/2-inch squares.

Heat the olive oil in a heavy frying pan and cook the onions and basil over a moderate heat for 3 minutes. Add the sweet pepper and cook for 5 minutes. Add the wine, raise the heat and cook until it is almost evaporated. Add the chopped tomatoes and cook over a fairly high heat for 8 to 10 minutes, or until the sauce starts to thicken. Add the black olives and season with salt and black pepper to taste. Simmer for a few minutes to blend the flavors.

Cook the spaghetti in plenty of lightly salted, boiling water. Drain and transfer to a heated serving bowl. Pour over the sauce, toss lightly, and serve at once with grated cheese on the side. *Serves 4.*

Corsica

CANNELONI
(Canneloni)

Canneloni are large cylinders of pasta that may be made at home or bought commercially. In Corsica they are often stuffed with a mixture of Swiss chard, herbs, and Brocciu cheese—an unsalted fresh cheese made from ewe's milk. Salted dried Brocciu cheese is generally used for grating, but if unavailable Parmesan cheese may be used instead.

Filling:
- 1   pound Swiss chard or spinach
  a handful of parsley, finely chopped
- 1   tbsp. fresh mint, finely chopped
- 1/2   cup dried Brocciu or Parmesan cheese, freshly grated
- 2   eggs
- 1/2   cup Brocciu or Parmesan cheese, freshly grated
- 1/4   tsp. nutmeg, freshly grated
  salt
  freshly ground black pepper

Dough: 2 **cups flour**
3 **eggs**
1 **tsp. water**
pinch of salt

Topping: 2 **cups tomato sauce (see page 103)**
1 **cup dried Brocciu or Parmesan cheese, freshly grated**

Wash the Swiss chard and cook in a covered saucepan over moderate heat for 5 minutes. The water clinging to the leaves is sufficient to prevent scorching. Drain well, squeeze dry, and chop finely.

In a mixing bowl, combine the Swiss chard, parsley, mint, Ricotta cheese, eggs, and $1/4$ cup of grated cheese. Mix well and season with nutmeg, salt, and pepper to taste.

To make the dough, follow the directions for egg noodles on page 239. Roll out the dough very thinly and leave it to dry for 15 minutes. Cut into oblongs 3 inches by 4 inches. Cook in plenty of lightly salted, boiling water. Drain and lay them out on a damp cloth. Spoon a little filling along the edge of each canneloni and roll it up.

Arrange side-by-side on a well-oiled, shallow baking dish. Top with the tomato sauce and sprinkle over the grated cheese. Bake in a preheated 375° F. oven for 15 minutes or until the canneloni are heated through and the cheese is melted. *Serves 6.*

Languedoc, Roussillon

MACARONI BAKED WITH CHESTNUTS, CREAM, AND GRUYÈRE CHEESE
(*Macaroni à la Cévénole*)

A specialty of the Cévennes.

1	pound chestnuts
¹/₂	pound short macaroni
4	tbsp. butter
¹/₂	cup light cream
¹/₄	tsp. nutmeg, freshly grated
	salt
	freshly ground black pepper
³/₄	cup Gruyère cheese, grated

Pierce the chestnuts with a sharp knife and cut a cross on each of the shells. Drop in boiling water and simmer for 10 minutes. Remove a few at a time and peel away the shells and inner skin. It is best to leave the rest in hot water as the skins will harden when cool, and become difficult to peel. Return the peeled chestnuts to the saucepan of boiling water and cook for 15 minutes, or until tender.

Cook the macaroni in plenty of lightly salted, boiling water. Drain and mix with the chestnuts. Place in a well-buttered, shallow baking dish, dot with butter, and pour over the cream. Sprinkle with nutmeg, salt, and pepper to taste. Top with the grated cheese and bake in a preheated 375° F. oven for 15 minutes or until the macaroni is heated through and the cheese is melted. Serve at once. *Serves 4 to 5.*

Dumplings
(Gnocchi)

Various dumplings are made in France, usually with potatoes, semolina or cream-puff pastry. Some are very ancient like the *kaespaetzle* (cheese dumplings) of Alsace. (A similar dish was made in Ancient Rome.) In Savoy potato dumplings, *les rambollets*, are stuffed with prunes or dried figs. In Corsica dumplings are often made with a mixture of Brocciu cheese and spinach.

Cook dumplings, like pasta, in plenty of lightly salted, boiling water. Just before they are cooked they float to the surface where they can be easily removed with a slotted spoon. New, or red-skinned, potatoes are unsuitable for make dumplings.

Dumplings may be served with melted butter and cheese, or the sauce of your choice.

Provence, Comté de Nice

POTATO GNOCCHI
(Gnocchi de trufo)

Potato gnocchi are made with and without eggs. The addition of eggs helps to prevent the gnocchi from falling apart during cooking. However, some cooks claim that gnocchi are lighter if they are simply made with potatoes and flour. The exact amount of flour will depend on the moisture content of the potatoes. Too much flour will make the gnocchi heavy. To test, put one dumpling in boiling water to be sure it holds its shape without falling apart.

2   **pounds Idaho potatoes**
1   **egg yolk**
    salt
    freshly ground black pepper
    about 2 cups flour
4   **tbsp. butter, softened**
1   **cup Parmesan cheese, freshly grated**

Boil the potatoes in lightly salted boiling water for 20 minutes or until they are tender. Drain and remove the skins when they are cool enough to handle. Force through a sieve onto a lightly floured board or work surface. While the potatoes are still warm add the egg yolk, mix thoroughly, and season with salt and black pepper to taste. Work in enough flour to make a soft dough. Roll the dough out into long cylinders about the thickness of your finger, then cut into 1-inch lengths. Press each piece with your index finger against the inside of a fork, forming a crescent shape; this helps the gnocchi to cook properly.

Drop the gnocchi into rapidly boiling, lightly salted water. The gnocchi will float to the surface just before they are cooked. Cook for 1 or 2 more minutes, then remove with a slotted spoon. Transfer to a heated serving bowl, dot with butter, and sprinkle with cheese. Serve at once. *Serves 6.*

Provence,   Comté   de   Nice

Spinach and Potato Dumplings
(Les gnocchi verts)

1¹/₄	**pounds Idaho potatoes**
¹/₂	**pound spinach**
1	**egg yolk**
about ³/₄	**cup flour**
¹/₄	**tsp. nutmeg, freshly grated**
	salt
	freshly ground black pepper
4	**tbsp. butter**
1	**cup Parmesan cheese, freshly grated**

Cook the spinach in a covered saucepan over moderate heat for 5 minutes. The water clinging to leaves is sufficient to prevent scorching. Drain, squeeze dry, and chop finely.

Boil the potatoes in lightly salted water for 20 minutes or until tender. Drain and remove the skins when they are cool enough to handle. Force through a sieve onto a lightly floured board or work surface. While the potatoes are still warm, add the spinach and egg yolk and mix thoroughly. Season with nutmeg, salt, and pepper to taste. Add the flour and blend well to form a soft dough. Roll the dough out into long cylinders about the thickness of your finger and cut into 1-inch lengths. Press each piece with your index finger against the inside of a fork—forming a crescent shape. This helps the gnocchi to cook properly.

Drop the gnocchi into rapidly boiling, lightly salted water. The dumplings will float to the surface just before they are cooked. Cook for 1 or 2 more minutes, then remove with a slotted spoon. Arrange them in a well-oiled, shallow baking dish. Sprinkle with the grated cheese and dot with butter. Bake in a preheated 400° F. oven for 10 to 15 minutes or until the cheese is lightly browned. Serve at once. *Serves 4.*

Corsica

SPINACH AND CHEESE DUMPLINGS
(Storzapreti à la bastiase)

If fresh Brocciu cheese is unavailable, Ricotta cheese may be used instead.

1³/₄ **pounds spinach**
  1 **pound fresh Brocciu or Ricotta cheese**
  1 **egg plus 1 yolk**
¹/₄ **tsp. nutmeg, freshly ground**
     salt
     freshly ground black pepper
     flour for dusting
  2 **cups tomato sauce (see page 103)**
  1 **cup dried Brocciu or Parmesan cheese,**
     freshly grated

Cook the spinach in a covered saucepan over a moderate heat for 5 minutes. The water clinging to the leaves is sufficient to prevent scorching. Drain, squeeze dry, and chop it finely. Place the spinach in a mixing bowl with the fresh Brocciu cheese, egg and egg yolk, nutmeg, and salt and pepper to taste. Mix well. Cover the bowl and refrigerate for 2 hours.

Form the mixture into long sausage shapes about ³/₄ inch in diameter and cut into 1-inch lengths. Dip the gnocchi lightly in flour and drop the dumplings into rapidly boiling, lightly salted water. The dumplings will float to the surface when they are cooked. Remove with a slotted spoon and arrange in the bottom of a well-oiled, shallow baking dish.

Cover with the tomato sauce, and sprinkle over the grated cheese. Bake in a preheated 375° F. oven for 15 minutes or until the cheese is melted. Serve at once. *Serves 4 to 5.*

Alsace, Lorraine

SEMOLINA GNOCCHI
(Gnocchi de semoule)

These little diamond-shaped gnocchi, called *griesschniette* in the Alsatian dialect, are not boiled, but fried in butter—you can use olive oil if you prefer. They are usually served with applesauce and a green salad on the side.

> 4 **cups milk**
> ½ **cup butter**
>   **a grating of nutmeg**
> ½ **tsp. salt**
> 1½ **cups semolina**
> 2 **egg yolks**

Bring the milk to a boil in a heavy saucepan and add half of the butter, the nutmeg, and salt. Very slowly pour in the semolina, stirring constantly to prevent lumps from forming. Cook over a gentle heat until the mixture starts to thicken. Remove from the heat and let cool slightly. Add the egg yolks and blend well.

Spread the mixture out on a baking sheet in a layer about 1-inch thick. Leave to cool. When cold, cut into diamond shapes.

Heat the remaining butter in a large heavy frying pan and fry the gnocchi until they are golden on both sides. Drain on a paper towel and serve hot. *Serves 4 to 6.*

VEGETABLES

LES LÉGUMES

In France vegetables are prepared with much care and attention. They may be served as an accompaniment to the main course, as a course on their own, or as the center of the meal. The French like to eat vegetables very fresh and in season. Vegetables are picked when they are small and full of flavor. *Primeurs*—the first vegetables of spring—are much sought after.

The cooking of vegetables is always imaginative and often surprisingly simple. Vegetables are boiled, steamed, braised, sautéed, puréed, stuffed, stewed, or gratinéed. Great care is taken not to overcook them.

When choosing vegetables look for firmness and a good color. Locally grown vegetables in season always have a finer flavor than those that have been refrigerated and shipped across the world.

Provence, Comté de Nice

ARTICHOKES
BARIGOULE
(Artichauts à la barigoule)

Artichauts à la barigoule is one of Provence's oldest dishes. À la barigoule means "cooked like mushrooms." Originally the artichokes were cooked like mushrooms on a grill over hot coals with a little olive oil, salt, and pepper. Later the artichokes were cooked on top of the stove in an earthenware casserole or tian with chopped onion, garlic, olive oil, salt, and a little water. In recent years a bay leaf, dry white wine, and perhaps a little chopped carrot were added; some recipes include mushrooms. Small violet artichokes are best for this recipe.

12	small violet artichokes
3	garlic cloves, finely chopped
1	medium onion, chopped
4	tbsp. olive oil
1/2	cup dry white wine
1 1/2	cups water
1	bay leaf
2	pinches of thyme
	salt
	freshly ground black pepper

Trim the top 1/2 inch of the artichokes and remove any tough outer leaves. Trim the stems.

Heat the olive oil in a heavy casserole and cook the garlic and onions over a moderate heat for 5 minutes or until the onion is translucent. Pour in the wine and cook over a high heat until it is almost evaporated. Add the water, bay leaf, and thyme, and season with salt and pepper to taste. Bring to a boil, cover, and simmer until the artichokes are tender. The exact cooking time will depend on the size of the artichokes. *Serves 3 to 4.*

Bordeaux, Les Landes

EGGPLANT
BORDEAUX STYLE
(Aubergines à la Bordelaise)

This is a very simple but classic way of serving eggplant. Thick slices of eggplant are sautéed in olive oil until they are golden on both sides, and served garnished with a mixture of sautéed garlic, parsley, and breadcrumbs.

> 2   medium eggplant (about 1 to 1¼ lbs.)
>   salt
>   about ½ cup olive oil
> 3   garlic cloves, crushed
>   a handful of parsley, finely chopped
> 3   tbsp. whole-wheat breadcrumbs
>   freshly ground black pepper

Trim the ends of the eggplants but do not peel. Cut into rounds about ¾-inch thick. Sprinkle with salt and set in a colander for 1 hour to release the bitter juices. Wash off the salt and pat dry with a paper towel.

Heat the olive oil in a frying pan and fry the eggplant slices until they are golden on both sides. Drain on a paper towel. Arrange on a serving dish.

Mix the garlic, parsley, and breadcrumbs together and fry in the same pan for 3 minutes, taking care that the garlic does not burn. Sprinkle over the eggplant slices and serve at once. *Serves 4.*

Provence, Comté de Nice

BOHÉMIENNE
(Bohémienne)

Bohémienne (gypsy style) is a simple eggplant and tomato purée flavored with grated cheese and gratinéed in the oven. It is sometimes called *le gratin estrassaire*. There are several versions of this dish—this one is a specialty of Avignon.

1	pound eggplant
5	tbsp. olive oil
3	garlic cloves, finely chopped
³/₄	pound ripe plum tomatoes, peeled, seeded, and chopped
	salt
	freshly ground black pepper
1	tbsp. flour
3	tbsp. water
¹/₂	cup Parmesan cheese, freshly grated
3	tbsp. whole-wheat breadcrumbs

Peel the eggplant and cut into ¹/₂-inch dice. Heat 3 tablespoons of olive oil in a large frying pan and cook the garlic for 1 minute. Add the tomatoes and eggplant. Cook, covered, over a gentle heat for 30 minutes or until the vegetables are soft, mashing them with a fork as they cook.

Mix the flour with the water, add to the mixture, and simmer for 5 minutes. Stir in the grated cheese. Transfer to a well-oiled, shallow baking dish and sprinkle with breadcrumbs. Drizzle with the remaining olive oil and bake in a preheated 400° F. oven for 15 minutes or until the top is golden. *Serves 4.*

Poitou, Charente

BEETS AND ONIONS
IN VINEGAR SAUCE
(Betteraves à la poitevine)

3 medium beets, baked
2 tbsp. butter
2 medium onions, thinly sliced
1 garlic clove, finely chopped
1 tbsp. flour
1 cup hot water
1 tbsp. wine vinegar
  pinch of cloves
  a grating of nutmeg
  salt
  black pepper, freshly ground

Peel the beets and cut into thin rounds.

Heat the butter in a heavy pan and cook the onions and garlic over moderate heat for 5 minutes or until the onions are translucent. Add the beets and cook over gentle heat for 10 minutes, stirring occasionally until the vegetables are tender. Sprinkle over the flour and cook for 1 minute. Pour in a little of the hot water mixed with the vinegar, stirring constantly, until the sauce starts to thicken. Gradually add more broth until all the broth is incorporated and the sauce is smooth and creamy. Add the cloves and nutmeg, and season to taste with salt and pepper. Simmer for 5 more minutes, and serve hot. *Serves 4.*

Picardy,   Flanders,   Artois

BRUSSELS SPROUTS IN MORNAY SAUCE
(Choux de Bruxelles sauce mornay)

1½   **pounds Brussels sprouts**
2   **tbsp. butter**
2   **cups mornay sauce (see page 100)**
½   **cup Gruyère cheese grated**

Trim the root ends of the Brussels sprouts and remove any yellow-ish leaves. Steam for 8 to 10 minutes or until just tender. Heat the butter in a large frying pan. Add the Brussels sprouts and stir well to coat them evenly in the butter. Cook for 2 or 3 minutes.

Prepare the mornay sauce as directed on page 100. Pour some of the sauce into the bottom of a shallow baking dish. Cover with the Brussels sprouts and pour over the remaining sauce. Sprinkle the grated cheese over the top. Bake in a preheated 400° F. oven for 20 minutes or until the top is golden. *Serves 4 to 6.*

Champagne, Ardennes

RED CABBAGE WITH APPLES, RED WINE, AND JUNIPER BERRIES

(Chou à l'Ardennaise)

Sometimes this dish is made with white cabbage, in which case white wine is used instead of red.

1	small red cabbage
2	tart apples
2	tbsp. butter
2	tsp. juniper berries
1	cup dry red wine (or half wine, half water)
	salt
	freshly ground black pepper
1	tbsp. sugar
2	tsp. wine vinegar

Cut away the hard core and the stem of the red cabbage and shred it finely. Peel, core, and slice the apples.

Heat the butter in a large casserole and add the cabbage, apples, and juniper berries. Pour in the wine, cover, and simmer for 45 to 50 minutes or until the cabbage is tender. Season with salt and pepper to taste. Mix the sugar with the vinegar and add to the cabbage. Simmer for 2 or 3 more minutes. Serve hot. *Serves 4 to 6.*

Bourbonnais, Ninervais, Morvan

VICHY CARROTS
(Carottes à la Vichy)

This is a classic way of preparing carrots in France. Vichy water is generally preferred to tap water as it is said to be good for the liver.

- 1 **pound carrots**
- 2 **tbsp. butter**
- 2 **tsp. sugar**
  about 1 cup water
  salt
  freshly ground black pepper

Scrub the carrots and trim the ends. Cut into rounds about 1/4-inch thick. Place in a saucepan with the butter, sugar, and water. Bring to a boil, cover, and simmer for 20 to 25 minutes, or until the carrots are tender and the liquid is almost evaporated. Season with salt and pepper to taste. Serve hot. *Serves 4.*

Savoie, Dauphiné

CARROTS AND RAISINS
(Carottes aux raisins sec)

1   pound carrots
2   tbsp. butter
2   tsp. flour
1/2   cup hot water
2   tbsp. raisins
    salt
    freshly ground black pepper

Scrub the carrots and trim the ends. Cut into rounds about 1/4-inch thick. Heat the butter in a saucepan and add the carrots. Cover and cook gently for 12 to 15 minutes, or until the carrots are tender and starting to turn golden. Stir in the flour and cook for 1 minute without browning. Add the raisins and the hot water and simmer, stirring constantly, for 5 minutes or until the sauce is thickened and the raisins are tender. *Serves 4.*

Lyonnais

CELERIAC AND POTATO PURÉE
(Purée de céleri ravé)

Potatoes may also be puréed with carro'
beets, or turnips.

> 1 **pound celeriac**
> ¹/₂ **lemon**
> ¹/₂ **pound potatoes**
> ¹/₄ **cup heavy cream or *crème fraîche***
> **(see page 110)**
> 3 **tbsp. butter**
> **salt**
> **freshly ground black pepper**

Peel the celeriac and cut into chunks. Rub all over with lemon juice to prevent discoloring. Peel the potatoes and cut into chunks the same size as the celeriac. Boil the vegetables in lightly salted water for 20 minutes or until tender.

Force through a sieve or mash with a potato ricer and return to the pan. Add the cream and butter and season to taste with salt and pepper. Heat through, stirring constantly. Serve at once. *Serves 4.*

Bourbonnais, Nivernais

CAULIFLOWER WITH SHALLOTS, VINEGAR, AND CREAM

(Choufleur à la Bourbonnaise)

1   small cauliflower
2   tbsp. butter
2   shallots, finely chopped
3   tbsp. wine vinegar
1   cup light cream
     salt
     freshly ground black pepper

Trim the ends of the cauliflower and break into florets. Steam for 7 minutes or until just tender.

Heat the butter in a heavy pan and cook the shallots over a moderate heat for 3 minutes or until they are softened. Add the vinegar and cook until it is reduced by half. Pour in the cream, bring to a boil, and cook until the sauce is slightly thickened. Season to taste with salt and pepper. Transfer the cauliflower to a heated serving bowl and pour over the sauce. Serve at once. *Serves 4 to 6.*

Languedoc,   Roussillon

SAUTÉED
CAULIFLOWER
(Choufleur frit)

This is a very simple but delicious way to prepare cauliflower.

  1 small cauliflower
  3 tbsp. olive oil
    salt
    freshly ground black pepper

Trim the ends of the cauliflower and break into florets. Steam for 5 or 6 minutes or until almost tender. Take care not to overcook it. Heat the olive oil in a heavy frying pan and sauté the cauliflower over a moderate heat until it is nicely browned on both sides. Season with salt and pepper to taste. *Serves 4 to 6.*

Languedoc, Roussillon

FENNEL GRATIN

(Fenouil à la crème)

A specialty of the Comté de Foix.

6   **fennel bulbs**
2   **cups béchamel sauce (see page 99)**
¹/₄ **cup light cream**
1   **cup Gruyère cheese, grated**

Remove the outer stalks and leaves from the fennel bulbs. Trim the bases and cut into wedges. Steam the fennel for 8 to 10 minutes or until just tender.

Prepare the béchamel sauce as directed on page 99, and stir in the cream. Remove from the heat and add half of the Gruyère cheese. Spoon a little of the sauce into the bottom of a shallow baking dish. Arrange the fennel on top in one layer and pour over the remaining sauce. Sprinkle the remaining Gruyère cheese over the top. Bake in a preheated 400° F. oven for 20 minutes or until the top is golden. *Serves 6.*

Provence,   Comté   de   Nice

FENNEL SIMMERED WITH TOMATOES, BLACK OLIVES, AND WHITE WINE

(Fenouil à la Niçoise)

If fresh plum tomatoes are unavailable, canned plum tomatoes may be used instead.

  4   fennel bulbs
  3   tbsp. olive oil
  2   garlic cloves, finely chopped
  3   shallots, finely chopped
  ¼   cup dry white wine
  1   pound ripe plum tomatoes, peeled, seeded, and chopped
  ¼   Niçoise or similar black olives, pitted and sliced
      salt
      freshly ground black pepper

Remove the outer stalks and leaves from the fennel bulbs. Trim the bases and cut into thin wedges.

Heat the olive oil in a large frying pan and cook the garlic and shallots for 2 minutes. Add the fennel and cook for another 2 minutes. Pour in the wine and cook over high heat until it has almost evaporated. Add the tomatoes and black olives and season with salt and pepper to taste. Cover, and simmer for 25 to 30 minutes or until the fennel is tender and the tomato sauce is thickened. Serve hot. *Serves 4.*

Corsica

GREEN BEANS WITH GARLIC AND BASIL
(Haricots verts à l'ail et au basilic)

This dish may also be served at room temperature as an hors-d'oeuvre.

1   **pound green beans**
2   **tbsp. fresh basil, chopped**
3   **garlic cloves, crushed**
3   **tbsp. olive oil**
1   **tbsp. lemon juice**
    salt
    freshly ground black pepper

Top and tail the green beans. Steam for 8 to 10 minutes or until they are tender.

Meanwhile, mix the basil and garlic together in a small bowl. Add the olive oil and lemon juice and mix well. Season with salt and pepper to taste. Place the green beans in a serving dish and pour over the sauce. Toss lightly and serve hot. *Serves 4.*

Corsica

GREEN BEANS SIMMERED WITH LEEKS AND TOMATOES

(Haricots verts et poireaux à la sauce tomate)

1   pound green beans
2   leeks (white part only) thinly sliced
3   tbsp. olive oil
6   ripe plum tomatoes, peeled, seeded, and
    chopped
1   bay leaf
    salt
    freshly ground black pepper

Top and tail the green beans and cut into 2-inch lengths. Trim the root ends of the leeks. Cut in half, lengthwise, and wash away the dirt that collects between the leaves. Slice thinly. Heat the olive oil in a large frying pan and cook the leeks over moderate heat for 3 minutes. Add the green beans, cover, and simmer for 10 minutes, stirring occasionally until tender. Add the green beans, tomatoes, and bay leaf and season with salt and pepper to taste. Cover, and simmer for 30 minutes, or until the vegetables are tender and the sauce is thickened. Serve hot. Serves *4 to 6.*

Bordeaux, Les Landes

HARICOT BEANS SIMMERED WITH SHALLOTS, TOMATOES, AND HERBS

(Haricots blancs à la Bordelaise)

Variations of this dish are also made in Provence and Brittany.

1   cup dried white haricot beans
2   tbsp. butter
2   tbsp. olive oil
4   shallots, finely chopped
3   canned plum tomatoes, forced through a sieve or puréed in a food processor
2   tbsp. fresh parsley, finely chopped
    a few leaves summer savory, chopped
    a pinch of thyme
    a grating of nutmeg
    salt
    freshly ground black pepper

Soak the haricot beans overnight and drain. Place in a saucepan and cover with about 1 inch of water. Bring to a boil, cover, and simmer for 1¹/₂ to 2 hours or until they are tender. Drain, and reserve the cooking liquid.

Heat the butter and olive oil in a saucepan and cook the garlic and shallots over a moderate heat for 3 minutes. Add the puréed tomatoes and herbs and season with nutmeg, salt, and pepper to taste. Add the drained haricot beans and a few tablespoons of the reserved cooking liquid. Simmer, covered, for 10 minutes to blend the flavors. Serve hot. *Serves 4 to 6.*

Provence, Comté de Nice

LEEK AND POTATO STEW

(Le pouare au safran)

Saffron often appears in Provençal cooking—
in sauces, soups, rice, or vegetables stews.

1 **pound leeks**
³/₄ **pound small new potatoes, peeled**
2 **tbsp. olive oil**
2 **garlic cloves, finely chopped**
2 **shallots, finely chopped**
4 **ripe plum tomatoes, peeled, seeded, and
   chopped**
   pinch of powdered saffron
   salt
   freshly ground black pepper

Trim away the root ends of the leeks. Cut in half lengthwise
and carefully wash away any dirt that collects between the leaves.
Cut into 2-inch lengths. Use the whole leek, including the dark
green parts.

Bring the potatoes to a boil in lightly salted water and cook for 20
minutes or until they are tender. Drain and set aside.

Heat the olive oil in a large saucepan and cook the garlic and
shallots for 2 minutes. Add the leeks and cook over a moderate heat
for 5 minutes. Add the tomatoes, and cook, covered, for a further
15 minutes or until the vegetables are tender. Add the potatoes and
saffron and season to taste with salt and pepper. Simmer, uncovered, for 10 minutes to blend the flavors. *Serves 4 to 6.*

Auvergne, Limousin

LENTILS SIMMERED WITH TOMATOES AND RED WINE
(Lentilles à la ponote)

This is an adaptation of a recipe from Le Puy in the Auvergne.

1½ cup Le Puy lentils
4 tbsp. butter
3 shallots, finely chopped
1 medium onion, finely chopped
½ cup dry red wine
1 cup tomato sauce (see page 103)
2 cups vegetable broth or water
1 bay leaf
   salt
   freshly ground black pepper

Soak the lentils for 1 hour and drain. Heat half of the butter in a heavy saucepan and cook the shallots and onion over moderate heat for 5 to 7 minutes or until they start to turn golden. Pour in the wine and cook until it has almost evaporated. Add the lentils, tomato sauce, broth, and bay leaf. Bring to a boil, cover, and simmer for 1 to 1¼ hours or until the lentils are tender. Raise the heat and cook for 10 minutes or until the liquid is almost evaporated, taking care that the lentils do not stick to the bottom of the pan. Just before serving stir in the remaining butter and season to taste with salt and pepper. Serve hot. *Serves 6.*

Franche   Comté

MUSHROOMS
IN CREAM
(Mousserons à la crème)

The *mousseron* is a small creamy colored mushroom with a convex cap. It is found in springtime on the edge of woods and usually grows in a "fairy ring." If unavailable, any other mushroom may be used instead.

> 1   pound mushrooms, sliced
> 2   tbsp. butter
> ¼   cup dry white wine
> ½   cup light cream
>   salt
>   freshly ground black pepper
> 1   tbsp. fresh tarragon

Heat the butter in a heavy frying pan and cook the mushrooms over moderate heat for 5 minutes. Pour in the wine and cook over high heat until it has almost evaporated. Add the cream and cook over gentle heat until it has slightly reduced. Season with salt and pepper to taste. Serve hot sprinkled with tarragon. *Serves 4.*

Poitou, Charente

PEAS SIMMERED WITH SHALLOTS, LETTUCE, AND HERBS

(Petit pois à la vendéen)

In this dish from the Vendée the peas are flavored with a variety of fresh herbs that usually include summer savory, hyssop—called
lisot in the local patois—and parsley. If hyssop
is not available, fresh mint may be used
instead. Tender young peas are best for this
recipe.

2 pounds peas, shelled
1 lettuce heart, shredded
2 shallots, finely chopped
4 tbsp. butter
2 tbsp. fresh herbs, such as parsley, summer
   savory, or fresh mint, finely chopped
½ cup water
   pinch of thyme
   pinch of sugar
   salt
   freshly ground black pepper

Place the peas, lettuce, shallots, half of the butter, herbs, water,
sugar, and seasoning (to taste) in a saucepan. Bring to a boil, cover,
and simmer for 20 to 30 minutes or until the peas are tender, and
most of the liquid is evaporated. Stir in the remaining butter and
correct the seasoning. Serve at once. *Serves 4.*

Champagne, Ardennes

SPLIT PEA AND POTATO PURÉE

(Purée de pois cassés, Sainte–Ménéhould)

Sainte–Ménéhould is a district of the Marne that is well known for its gastronomic specialties.

1   cup split peas
3   medium potatoes, peeled and diced
1   medium onion, chopped
1   garlic clove, crushed
2   tbsp. butter
¼   cup light cream
¼   tsp. freshly grated nutmeg
    salt
    freshly ground black pepper

Soak the peas for 2 hours and drain. Bring to a boil in 2¹/₂ cups of lightly salted water with the potatoes, onion, and garlic. Cover, and simmer for 1¹/₄ to 1¹/₂ hours or until the peas are tender. Drain. and reserve the cooking liquid. Force the vegetables through a sieve or purée in a blender and return to the pan. Dilute with a little of the reserved cooking liquid. Stir in the butter and cream. Season with nutmeg, salt, and pepper to taste and serve. *Serves 6.*

Poitou, Charente

POTATOES SAUTÉED IN WALNUT OIL WITH GARLIC

(Pommes de terre à l'ail)

In the sixteenth century, walnut oil was wide-ly used in cooking. In fact it was so abundant that it even was used to make candles. Later it became rarer and was only used for special occasions.

    2   pounds new potatoes
    5   tbsp. walnut oil
    4   garlic cloves, finely chopped
    3   tbsp. parsley, finely chopped
        salt
        freshly ground black pepper

Peel the potatoes and leave them whole if they are small; otherwise, cut them into lozenge shapes and 1¹/₂-inches long and ³/₄ inch in diameter.

Heat the walnut oil in a heavy frying pan and cook the potatoes, covered, over a gentle heat for 30 to 40 minutes. Shake the pan from time to time so the potatoes cook evenly and are nicely browned all over. When the potatoes are tender, stir in the garlic and parsley and season with salt and pepper to taste. Cook for 3 minutes then serve at once. *Serves 4 to 6.*

Languedoc, Roussillon

POTATOES SIMMERED WITH ONIONS, TOMATOES, AND GREEN OLIVES

(Pommes de terre à la Languedocienne)

2	pounds new potatoes
3	tbsp. olive oil
2	medium onions, thinly sliced
6	ripe plum tomatoes, peeled, seeded, and chopped
¼	cup green olives, pitted and sliced
1½	cups boiling water
	salt
	freshly ground black pepper

Peel the potatoes and slice them thinly.

Heat the olive oil in a heavy saucepan and cook the onions over moderate heat for 5 minutes or until translucent. Add the chopped tomatoes and cook over moderate heat for 5 minutes. Add the potatoes, olives, and boiling water and season with salt and pepper to taste. Simmer covered, for 25 to 30 minutes or until the potatoes are tender and the sauce is thickened. Serve hot. *Serves 4 to 6.*

Provence ,   Comté   de   Nice

R A T A T O U I L L E
(Ratatouïa)

Ratatouille is probably Provence's most famous dish. Recipes vary from region to region. Sometimes the zucchini or sweet peppers are omitted. Some cooks add a pinch of powdered saffron, or serve the dish garnished with black olives. Ratatouille is equally good served hot or cold.

2 small eggplant (about ³/₄ lb.)
3 zucchini
3 sweet peppers
   about ½ cup olive oil
2 medium onions, thinly sliced
3 garlic cloves, finely chopped
1 pound ripe plum tomatoes, peeled, seeded, and chopped
   pinch of powdered saffron
   salt
   freshly ground black pepper

Trim the ends of the eggplant and zucchini and cut them into thin rounds. Sprinkle with salt and set in a colander for 1 hour to release their juices. Wash off the salt and pat dry with a paper towel.

Remove the fibers and seeds from the sweet peppers and cut them into strips. Heat 2 tablespoons of olive oil in a large frying pan and cook the onions over moderate heat for 5 minutes or until soft but not browned. Remove from the pan and set aside. Heat a little more olive oil in the same pan and cook the sweet peppers for 7 or 8 minutes or until tender. Remove from the pan and set aside.

Heat some more olive oil in the same pan and fry the eggplant until golden on both sides. Drain on a paper towel. Repeat with the zucchini. Heat the remaining olive oil in the pan and cook the garlic for 2 minutes. Add the chopped tomatoes and saffron and cook over moderate heat for 8 to 10 minutes or until they start to thicken and make a sauce-like consistency. Arrange all the vegetables in layers over the tomato sauce and stir gently. Season with salt and pepper to taste. Cover, and simmer for 10 minutes. Serve hot or cold. *Serves 4 to 6.*

Provence, Comté de Nice

SPINACH IN CREAM
(Épinards à la crème)

This dish is sometimes served with fried croutons.

- 3 pounds spinach
- 2 garlic cloves, finely chopped
- 2 tbsp. olive oil
- ½ cup heavy cream
- ¼ nutmeg, freshly grated
  salt
  freshly ground black pepper

Wash the spinach and cook in a covered saucepan over moderate heat for 5 minutes. The water clinging to the leaves is sufficient to prevent scorching. Drain and chop finely.

Heat the olive oil in a heavy saucepan and cook the garlic for 1 minute. Do not let it brown. Add the chopped spinach and simmer for 2 or 3 minutes. Stir in the cream and season with nutmeg, salt, and pepper to taste. Heat thoroughly and serve at once. *Serves 4.*

Provence, Comté de Nice

SPINACH WITH PINE NUTS AND ORANGE FLOWER WATER

(Espinousos a l'aiga-passera e ai pignoun)

> 2 pounds spinach
> 2 tbsp. butter
> 2 tbsp. olive oil
> 1/4 cup pine nuts
> 1 or 2 tbsp. orange flower water
>   a grating of nutmeg
>   salt
>   freshly ground black pepper

Wash the spinach carefully and cook in a covered saucepan over moderate heat for 5 minutes. The water clinging to the leaves is sufficient to prevent scorching. Drain well.

Heat the butter and olive oil in a large frying pan and cook the pine nuts over moderate heat until they start to turn golden. Add the spinach and orange flower water and season with nutmeg, salt, and pepper to taste. Stir well. Simmer for 2 or 3 minutes to blend the flavors and serve at once. *Serves 4.*

Provence, Comté de Nice

ZUCCHINI WITH TOMATOES AND BASIL
(Courgettes aux tomates et au basilic)

Use the smallest zucchini you can find as they have the finest flavor.

1½ **pounds zucchini**
4   **tbsp. olive oil**
2   **garlic cloves, finely chopped**
1   **medium onion, chopped**
1   **pound ripe plum tomatoes, peeled, seeded, and chopped**
10 **basil leaves, chopped**
    salt
    freshly ground black pepper

Trim the ends of the zucchini and cut into rounds ⅛-inch thick. Heat the olive oil in a large frying pan and cook the garlic and onion over moderate heat for 7 minutes or until the onion is starting to turn golden. Add the zucchini, cover, and cook gently for 30 minutes, stirring occasionally until tender. Add the tomatoes and season with salt and pepper to taste. Cook, uncovered, over moderate heat for 10 minutes. Add the basil and simmer for 5 more minutes. Serve hot. *Serves 6.*

Languedoc,   Roussillon

ZUCCHINI   GRATIN

(Carbassous à la crème)

In the Languedoc "baby" zucchini are called *carbassous.*

> 2   pounds "baby" zucchini
> 2   cups béchamel sauce (see page 99)
> 3   tbsp. whole-wheat breadcrumbs
> 2   tbsp. olive oil

Steam the zucchini for 7 or 8 minutes or until they are tender. Cut into fairly thick rounds and arrange them in the bottom of a well-oiled shallow baking dish.

Prepare the béchamel sauce as directed on page 99, and pour over the zucchini. Sprinkle with breadcrumbs and drizzle with the olive oil. Bake in a preheated 400° F. oven for 15 to 20 minutes or until the top is golden. *Serves 4 to 6.*

DESSERTS

LES DESSERTS

The French usually end their meals with cheese followed by fresh fruit. Sometimes a fresh or dried fruit compote is served, or a baked custard, mousse, or ice cream. Yogurt or a fresh cheese such as *petit suisse* is often served sprinkled with sugar and topped with fresh fruit.

For a dinner party or special occasion a sweet soufflé, a fruit-filled crêpe or a light pudding might be served. Cakes and pastries are generally served at teatime. They are seldom made at home, but are usually bought at the local *patisserie*, where the quality is always very good. However, I have included in this chapter a few simple cakes and tarts that can easily be made at home.

Normandy

APPLE SPONGE CAKE
(Beurré Normande)

- ¼ cup raisins
- 2 tbsp. Calvados or brandy
- 3 apples
- 2 tbsp. butter
- 4 eggs, separated
- ½ cup sugar
- 1 cup whole wheat pastry flour
  grated rind of 1 lemon
- 2 tbsp. hot water

Butter a 9-inch springform pan and dust with flour.

Soak the raisins in Calvados and let stand for 30 minutes.

Peel, core, and slice the apples fairly thickly. Heat the butter in a large frying pan and sauté the apples over a moderate heat for 5 minutes or until they start to turn golden, but still hold their shape.

Beat the egg yolks with the sugar until light and fluffy. Stir in the flour, raisins, Calvados, lemon rind, and hot water, and blend well. Pour into the prepared pan and bake in a preheated 350° F. oven for 30 to 35 minutes or until a knife comes out clean from the center of the cake. *Serves 6.*

Alsace, Lorraine

CHOCOLATE
ALMOND CAKE
(Gâteau chocolat de Nancy)

A specialty of Nancy. This delicious light chocolate cake is perfect for a special occasion.

    4   ounces semi-sweet chocolate
    4   tbsp. butter
    ½   cup sugar
    4   eggs, separated
    1   tbsp. flour
    ¾   cup almonds, finely ground in a blender
        pinch of salt

Butter a 9-inch springform pan and dust it with flour.

Melt the chocolate in a bowl over hot, not boiling, water then set aside to cool.

Cream the butter and sugar together until light and fluffy. Add the chocolate and blend well. Add the egg yolks, one at a time, blending well after each addition. Stir in the flour and ground almonds. The mixture will be firm. Beat the egg whites stiff with a pinch of salt and fold into the chocolate mixture. Pour into the prepared pan and bake in a preheated 325° F. oven for 45 minutes or until a knife comes out clean from the center of the cake. Let cool for 5 minutes in the pan, then invert onto a cake rack to cool completely. *Serves 6.*

Lyonnais

HAZELNUT CAKE
(Gâteau aux noisettes)

This cake is equally good made with almonds or walnuts.

        6   eggs, separated
        1   cup sugar
        1   cup hazelnuts, finely ground in a blender
             grated rind of 1 lemon
 1 or 2   tbsp. rum
       ³/₄   cup whole-wheat pastry flour

Butter a 9-inch springform pan and dust it with flour.

Beat the egg yolks and sugar until light. Stir in the ground hazelnuts, lemon rind and rum and blend well. Beat the egg whites stiff and fold one quarter of them into the hazelnut mixture. Fold in the flour, then fold in the remaining egg whites. Pour into the prepared pan and bake in a preheated 325° F. oven for 40 to 50 minutes or until a knife comes out clean from the center of the cake. *Serves 8.*

Burgundy

SPICE BREAD
(Pain d'épice)

Several towns in France are famous for their spice bread, especially Rheims and Dijon. In the past the people of Rheims were so fond of spice bread that they were nicknamed *mangeurs de pain d'épice* (spice-bread eaters).

Pain d'épice is traditionally made with honey, flour, and spices. It is usually made with rye flour in Rheims and a mixture of rye and wheat flour in Dijon. Sometimes a little molasses or candied orange rind is added to enhance the flavor.

  1 **cup whole wheat pastry flour**
3/4 **cup rye flour (not rye meal)**
  1 **tsp. cinnamon**
1/2 **tsp. ginger**
1/4 **tsp. nutmeg, freshly grated**
    pinch of cloves
    pinch of salt
    pinch of black pepper
2/3 **cup clear honey**
  2 **tbsp. sugar**
  1 **egg yolk**
  1 **tbsp. orange flower water**
    grated rind of 1 orange
  2 **tsp. baking soda**
1/2 **cup hot water**

Butter an 8-by-4^1/$_2$-by-3-inch loaf pan and line it with wax paper. Combine the whole wheat and rye flour, spices, salt, and pepper in a bowl and set aside.

Mix the honey, sugar, egg yolk, orange flower water, and grated orange rind in a large bowl. Dissolve the soda in the hot water and add to the honey mixture. Stir in the dry ingredients and blend well. Turn into the prepared pan and bake in a preheated 325° F. oven for 45 to 50 minutes or until a knife comes out clean from the center of the loaf. Let cool and serve sliced with butter. *Serves 6 to 8.*

Savoie, Dauphiné

COFFEE WALNUT CAKE
(*Gâteau Grenoblois*)

There are many versions of this delicious coffee walnut cake from Grenoble. Some cooks use crushed *biscottes* instead of the flour, others fill the cake with a rum-flavored *crème patissière*. I prefer to serve the cake plain, or simply topped with a dollop of whipped cream, flavored with rum.

- 1/2 cup whole wheat pastry or unbleached plain white flour
- 1/2 cup walnuts, finely ground in a blender
- 1/4 tsp. baking powder
- 1/2 cup sugar
- 4 tbsp. butter, melted
- 2 eggs, separated
- 2 tbsp. rum
- 1 tsp. instant coffee, dissolved in 2 tbsp. of hot water

Butter an 8-inch springform pan and dust it with flour.

Combine the flour, ground walnuts, and baking powder in a bowl and set aside.

Beat the sugar and melted butter until light and fluffy. Add the egg yolks one at a time, blending well after each addition. Stir in the rum. Fold in the dry ingredients alternately with the coffee. Beat the egg whites stiff and fold into the mixture. Pour into the prepared pan. Bake in a preheated 325° F. oven for 45 minutes or until a knife comes out clean from the center of the cake. *Serves 6 to 8.*

A l s a c e ,   L o r r a i n e

APPLE TART
(Chaudée)

Apricots, cherries, greengage and mirabelle plums, peaches, and pears may be prepared the same way.

Sweet shortcrust pastry:
- 1¹/₂ **cups whole wheat pastry or unbleached white flour**
- 2 **tbsp. sugar**
  pinch of salt
  pinch of cinnamon
- 2 **egg yolks**
- 6 **tbsp. butter, slightly softened**

Filling: 2 **pounds tart apples**
- ¹/₄ **cup sugar**
- 2 **egg yolks**
- ¹/₂ **cup heavy cream**
- ¹/₄ **tsp. vanilla extract**

Place the flour on a work surface and make a well in the center. Drop in the sugar, salt, cinnamon, egg yolks, and butter cut into small cubes. With your fingertips work in the flour and enough iced water to make a smooth ball. Wrap in foil and refrigerate for 45 minutes before rolling out.

Place the dough on a lightly floured work surface and knead briefly. Roll out into a circle about 12 inches in diameter and ¹/₈-inch thick. Carefully roll the dough around the rolling pin and unroll it on to a well-buttered 9- to 10-inch pie plate. Trim away any excess dough and flute the edges with a fork. Prick the bottom in a few places. Cover the dough with a sheet of foil and fill it with dried beans; this prevents the pie shell from puffing up while baking.

Bake in a preheated 400° F. oven for 8 to 10 minutes. The pastry should have shrunk away slightly from the sides of the pie plate. Remove from the oven and carefully remove the foil and dried beans.

Peel, core, and slice the apples fairly thickly. Arrange the slices in overlapping circles over the partially baked pie shell. Sprinkle with half of the sugar. Bake in a preheated 375° F. oven for 20 minutes. Remove from the oven.

Beat the egg yolks and the remaining sugar in a bowl until light. Stir in the cream and vanilla extract. Pour the mixture over the apples and return to the oven. Bake for a further 20 minutes or until the custard is set. Serve hot or cold. *Serves 6 to 8.*

Alsace, Lorraine

MIRABELLE PLUM TART

(Tarte aux mirabelles)

Lorraine is famous for its fine fruit, especially
the delectable, amber-colored mirabelle plum,
which is also used to make plum brandy.

Sweet shortcrust pastry with almonds:

1¼	cups whole wheat pastry or unbleached white flour
2	tbsp. ground almonds
	pinch of salt
2	tbsp. sugar
6	tbsp. butter, slightly softened
1	egg, beaten

Filling: 1½ pounds mirabelle or any other, preferably golden, plums

¼ cup sugar

For the glaze: 3 tbsp. apricot jam

3 tbsp. plum brandy, *eau-de-vie* or kirsch

2 tbsp. ground almonds

Place the flour on a work surface and make a well in the center.
Drop in the ground almonds, salt, sugar, and butter cut into small
cubes, and the beaten egg. With your fingertips work in the flour to
make a smooth ball. Wrap in foil and refrigerate for 45 minutes
before rolling out.

Place the dough on a lightly floured work surface and knead it
briefly. Roll out into a circle about 12 inches in diameter and ⅛-inch

thick. Carefully roll the dough around the rolling pin and unroll it on to a well-buttered 9- to 10-inch pie plate. Trim away any excess dough and flute the edges with a fork. Price the bottom in a few places. Cover the dough with a sheet of foil and fill it with dried beans; this prevents the pie shell from puffing up while baking.

Bake in a preheated 400° F. oven for 8 to 10 minutes. The pastry should have shrunk away slightly from the sides of the pie plate. Remove from the oven and carefully remove the foil and dried beans.

To prepare the filling, cut the plums in half and remove the stones. Arrange in the partially baked pastry shell and sprinkle with sugar. Return to the oven, reduce the heat to 375° F. and bake for 30 minutes. Remove from the oven.

Heat the apricot jam with the plum brandy over a moderate heat for a few minutes until it has dissolved. Remove from the heat and stir in the ground almonds. Spoon over the plums and bake at the same temperature for 15 more minutes or until the top is golden. *Serves 6 to 8.*

Berry, Orléanais

PEAR AND CREAM PIE
(Le poirat)

This simple country pie is filled with pears and cream. A similar pie called *piquenchagne* is made in Bourbonnais.

Shortcrust pastry:
- 2¼ cups whole wheat pastry or unbleached white flour
- pinch of salt
- 10 tbsp. butter (5 oz.)
- about 6 tbsp. iced water

Filling:
- 1½ pounds pears
- ¼ cup sugar
- freshly ground black pepper
- ½ cup heavy cream

Prepare the shortcrust pastry as directed on pages 160–161. Remove the dough from the refrigerator and place on a lightly floured work surface. Divide the dough into two balls, one slightly larger than the other. Roll out the larger ball into a circle about 12 inches in diameter and ⅛-inch thick. Carefully roll the dough around the rolling pin and unroll it on to a well-buttered 9-inch pie plate. Trim away any excess dough.

Peel, core, and slice the pears and arrange in concentric circles in the pie shell. Sprinkle the sugar and a grinding of black pepper. (This is said to improve the flavor of the pears.)

Roll out the second ball of dough into a circle about 10 inches in diameter and ⅛-inch thick. Place over the pie and flute the edges with a fork. Make a hole about 1 inch in diameter in the center of the pie to allow any steam to escape. Bake in a preheated 375° F. oven for 35 to 40 minutes or until the pears are tender and the pastry is golden. Remove from the oven and pour in the cream through the hole in the center of the pie. Return to the oven and bake for a further 5 minutes. Serve hot. *Serves 8.*

Burgundy

PUMPKIN PIE
(Tarte au potiron)

This delicious pumpkin pie is flavored with vanilla and grated lemon rind.

Shortcrust pastry:

1¹/₂	cups whole wheat pastry or unbleached white flour
	pinch of salt
6	tbsp. butter
2 or 3	tbsp. iced water

Filling:	1	cup cooked pumpkin purée
	1	cup whipping cream
	2	eggs
	¹/₂	tsp. vanilla extract
		grated rind of 1 lemon

Prepare an 8-inch partially baked pie shell as directed on pages 160–161.

Place the pumpkin purée, whipping cream, eggs, sugar, vanilla extract, and lemon rind in a bowl and mix well. Pour into the partially baked pie shell and bake in a preheated 375° F. oven for 35 to 40 minutes or until the tart is lightly browned and a knife comes out clean from the center of the pie. *Serves 4.*

Auvergne, Limousin

CHERRY CLAFOUTIS
(Clafoutis Limousin)

In Limousin *clafoutis* is made with a variety of small black cherry with a tiny pit called *la franche noir*. The pits are never removed as it is said that if the skin of the cherry is broken the flavor would be lost.

1   **cup milk**
1¹/₂ **pounds small black cherries**
1   **cup whole wheat pastry or unbleached white flour**
1   **cup sugar**
     pinch of salt
4   **eggs**
3   **tbsp. butter, melted**
2   **tbsp. kirsch or brandy**

Scald the milk and leave to cool. Wash the cherries, remove the stems and arrange in the bottom of a well-buttered, shallow baking dish.

Combine the flour, sugar, and salt in a large bowl and make a well in the center. Drop in the eggs, melted butter, warm milk, and kirsch and blend well. The mixture should have the consistency of a pancake batter. Pour over the cherries and bake in a preheated 350° F. oven for 40 to 50 minutes or until a knife comes out clean from the center of the pudding. *Serves 6.*

Lyonnais

PEAR CLAFOUTIS
(Clafoutis aux poires)

Clafoutis is made in many regions of France from Périgord to Lyonnais. Not only cherries are used, but also prunes, plums, apricots, pears, strawberries, and blackberries. In this recipe from Lyonnais the batter is richer and more like a cake.

1	pound firm, slightly underripe pears
2	eggs
1/3	cup sugar
1¼	cup whole wheat pastry or unbleached white flour
1	tsp. baking powder
2	tbsp. brandy
2/3	cup light cream

Peel and core the pears and cut into slices. Combine the flour and baking powder in a bowl and set aside.

Beat the eggs and sugar together until light. Add the flour mixture alternately with the cream and blend well. Stir in the pears and the brandy. Pour into a well-buttered, 8-inch pie dish and bake in a preheated 350° F. oven for 35 to 40 minutes. *Serves 4.*

Alsace, Lorraine

BEGGARMAN
(Le bettelmann)

Le bettelmann is a kind of bread pudding or cake that may be served hot or cold. It may be made with apples or cherries.

1 **pound tart apples**
 juice of ½ lemon
8 **slices of bread (about 8 oz.)**
1 **cup milk, scalded**
4 **eggs, separated**
1 **cup sugar**
2 **tbsp. Calvados or kirsch**
1 **tsp. vanilla extract**
½ **cup raisins**
2 **tbsp. butter**

Butter a 9-inch-by-3-inch-round cake pan and dust it with flour.

Peel, core, and slice the apples and sprinkle them with lemon juice. Set aside.

Place the bread in a large bowl and pour over the hot milk. Let it soak in, then mash well with a fork. Add the egg yolks, sugar, Calvados, and vanilla and blend well. Beat the egg whites stiff and fold into the mixture. Pour into the prepared pan and dot with butter. Bake in a preheated 375° F. oven for 1 hour or until a knife comes out clean from the center of the pudding. Serve hot or cold. *Serves 6 to 8.*

Alsace, Lorraine

APPLES LORRAINE
(Apples Lorraine)

This simple pudding consists of layers of
sliced apple, sugar, raisins, and breadcrumbs.
It is said to be of Jewish origin.

2	pounds apples
½	cup sugar
¼	cup raisins
1	cup whole wheat breadcrumbs
4	tbsp. butter
	grated rind of 1 lemon
½	cup hot water

Peel, core, and slice the apples thinly. Arrange a layer of apples in
the bottom of a well-buttered baking dish. Sprinkle with a little
sugar, raisins, breadcrumbs, and grated lemon rind. Dot with butter.

Repeat until all the ingredients are used. Pour in the hot water and
bake in a preheated 350° F. oven for 40 to 50 minutes or until the
apples are tender and the top is golden. *Serves 4 to 6.*

Pays Basque, Béarn, Bigorre

FRENCH TOAST
WITH RUM
(Pain perdu au rhum)

Pain perdu (literally, "lost bread") is made all over France. Sometimes it is flavored with orange flower water or vanilla. In Lorraine it is often served topped with mirabelle plums.

1 **cup milk**
3 **tbsp. rum**
6 **slices whole wheat bread**
2 **eggs, beaten**
about ¼ **cup olive oil (for frying)**
sugar for dusting

Mix the milk and rum together in a bowl. Soak the bread slices in the milk mixture for a few minutes. Dip each slice in beaten egg and fry in hot olive oil until golden on both sides. Serve at once sprinkled with sugar. *Serves 6.*

Normandy

APPLE PANCAKES
WITH CALVADOS

(Crêpes aux pommes)

Apple pancakes make a delicious breakfast or dessert. Serve them with a squeeze of lemon juice and sprinkle with sugar.

> ³/₄ **cup whole wheat pastry or unbleached white flour**
> 1 **tbsp. sugar**
> **pinch of salt**
> **pinch of cinnamon**
> 2 **eggs**
> 1 **tbsp. Calvados or brandy**
> **about 1 cup milk**
> 2 **apples**
> 1 or 2 **tbsp. peanut or olive oil**
> **sugar for dusting**

Combine the flour, sugar, salt, and cinnamon in a bowl. Make a well in the center and drop in the eggs and Calvados. Mix well with a wooden spoon. Gradually add the milk, beating constantly, to form a smooth batter the consistency of thin cream. Let stand for 2 hours before using.

Peel, core and slice the apples thinly, and add to the batter. Heat a little oil in a heavy 8-inch frying pan and pour in 3 tablespoons of batter including some of the apple slices. Quickly tilt the pan in all directions so the batter evenly coats the pan. Cook for 1 or 2 minutes on each side. Slide on to a warm plate and sprinkle with sugar. Serve at once. Lightly oil the pan again and repeat until all the batter and apples are used. *Serves 2 to 4.*

Anjou, Touraine

OMELETTE SOUFFLÉ
WITH COINTREAU
(Omelette soufflé au Cointreau)

Cointreau is an orange-flavored liqueur that was created in Angers in 1849 by Eduard–Jean and Adolphe Cointreau.

3   egg yolks
4   egg whites
1/3 cup sugar
2   tbsp. Cointreau
    grated rind of 1 orange

Butter a shallow baking dish and dust it with sugar. Beat the egg yolks and sugar together until very light. Add the Cointreau and grated orange rind and mix thoroughly. Beat the egg whites until stiff and fold into the egg yolk mixture. Turn into the prepared baking dish and bake in a preheated 400° F. oven for 15 to 20 minutes or until the center is set. *Serves 3 to 4.*

Brittany

STRAWBERRY SOUFFLÉ
(Soufflé Plougastel)

Although it is called a soufflé, this dish is more like an omelette soufflé. Plougastel is famous for its wild strawberries.

> sugar for dusting
> 4   ounces (¹/₄ pint) strawberries
> 6   eggs, separated
> 4   tbsp. sugar
>   a few drops of vanilla extract
> 4   tsp. flour

Butter a shallow baking dish and dust it with sugar.

Wash and hull the strawberries and mash them well with a fork. Beat the egg yolks with the sugar and vanilla extract until light. Add the mashed strawberries and flour and mix thoroughly. Beat the egg whites stiff and fold into the strawberry mixture. Pour into the prepared baking dish and bake in a preheated 375° F. oven for 15 to 20 minutes or until the center is set. *Serves 4.*

Languedoc, Roussillon

PEACH FRITTERS
(Beignets aux pêches)

A specialty of the Comté de Foix.

 4 ripe peaches
 2 tbsp. sugar
 1/4 tsp. cinnamon
 3 tbsp. rum
 1 1/4 cups whole wheat pastry or unbleached
   white flour
   pinch of salt
 1 tbsp. olive oil
   about 1 cup water
 1 egg white
   oil for deep frying
   sugar for dusting

Peel the peaches, cut in half, and remove the pits. Place in a bowl and sprinkle with sugar and cinnamon. Pour over the rum. Cover, and marinate for 1 hour.

Meanwhile, prepare the batter. Combine the flour and salt in a bowl and make a well in the center. Pour in the olive oil and water and mix well to form a smooth batter, the consistency of thin cream. Let stand for 1 hour. Just before using, beat the egg white stiff and fold into the batter. Dip the peach halves into the batter and fry in hot oil until golden on both sides. Drain on a paper towel, dust with sugar, and serve at once. *Serves 4.*

Lyonnais

APPLES FLAMBÉED WITH RUM
(Pommes mariadel)

This is very quick and easy to prepare.

 2   pounds tart apples
 ¼   cup sugar
     grated rind of 1 lemon
 2   tbsp. butter
 ¼   cup rum

Peel, core, and slice the apples. Arrange in layers in a baking dish. Sprinkle each layer with sugar and grated lemon rind. Dot with butter and bake in a preheated 350° F. oven for 25 to 30 minutes or until the apples are tender, and any liquid from the apples has evaporated. Warm the rum gently in a small saucepan. Pour over the apples and set alight. Serve at once. *Serves 4.*

Alsace, Lorraine

BAKED APRICOTS WITH KIRSCH
(Abricots à l'alsacienne)

If you like, this dish may also be served cold.

 1   pound ripe apricots
 ⅓   cup sugar
 ¼   cup hot water
 2   tbsp. kirsch

Cut the apricots in half and remove the pits. Arrange cut side down in a shallow baking dish. Sprinkle with half the sugar and pour in the hot water. Bake in a preheated 200° F. oven for 25 to 30 minutes or until the apricots are tender. Remove from the oven. Pour in the kirsch and sprinkle over the remaining sugar. Place under a hot grill for a few minutes to lightly caramelize the sugar. Serve at once. *Serves 4.*

S a v o i e ,   D a u p h i n é

S A V O Y   B A K E D
P E A R S
(Poires cuites à la Savoyarde)

This is a very simple but delicious way of preparing slightly unripe pears.

> 2 **pounds slightly unripe pears**
> ¹/₄ **cup sugar**
>   **a pinch of cinnamon**
> 2 **tbsp. hot water**
> ¹/₄ **cup heavy cream**

Peel and core pears and cut them into 8 equal-sized wedges. Arrange in one layer in a shallow baking dish. Sprinkle with sugar and a good pinch of cinnamon. Dot with butter. Bake in a preheated 375° F. oven for 40 minutes or until the pears are tender and the juice is syrupy. Remove from the oven and spoon over the cream. Bake for 2 or 3 more minutes or until the cream is heated through. Serve at once. *Serves 4.*

Burgundy

PEACH AND BLACK-CURRANT COMPOTE

(Cômpote de pêches au cassis)

6   peaches
¹/₄   cup black currants
¹/₄   cup sugar
1¹/₂   cups water
2   tbsp. cassis liqueur

Peel the peaches, cut in half, and remove the pits. Bring the black currants, sugar, and water to a boil in an enamel saucepan. Add the peach halves and cook gently until tender. Transfer the peaches with a slotted spoon to a glass serving bowl. Boil the cooking liquid and black currants down to a syrupy consistency and pour over the peaches. Let cool to room temperature. Stir in the cassis and chill thoroughly before serving. *Serves 6.*

Anjou, Touraine

PEARS SIMMERED IN RED WINE WITH CINNAMON

(Poires belle Angevine)

This dessert is named after a variety of pear that grows in Anjou called *belle Angevine*.

4 firm, slightly unripe pears
1 cup good quality red wine
$^1/_4$ cup sugar
$^1/_2$ cinnamon stick

Peel the pears, cut in half lengthwise and remove the cores. Place in a heavy saucepan with the wine, sugar, and cinnamon stick. Bring to a boil, cover, and simmer for 45 to 50 minutes. Slow simmering removes any bitterness from the wine. Remove the pears with a slotted spoon and place them in a glass serving bowl. Boil the cooking liquid down to a syrupy consistency. Remove the cinnamon stick and pour the syrup over the pears. Chill thoroughly before serving. *Serves 4.*

Burgundy

MELON WITH RASPBERRIES AND CASSIS
(Melon au cassis)

2 small ripe melons, such as canteloupe
1 cup raspberries (8 oz.)
4 tbsp. sugar
4 tbsp. cassis liqueur

Cut the melons in half and remove the seeds. Scoop out the flesh, taking care not to damage the shells. Cut into small dice. Add the raspberries and sprinkle with sugar. Pour over the cassis and toss lightly. Fill the melon halves with the mixture and refrigerate for at least 1 hour before serving. *Serves 4.*

Alsace, Lorraine

WILD
STRAWBERRIES
WITH KIRSCH AND
CREAM

(Fraises des bois, Lorraine)

This is one of the most delicious ways of serving strawberries.

> 1   pint strawberries
> 4   tbsp. sugar
> 4   tbsp. kirsch
> 1   cup whipping cream

Wash and hull the strawberries and place them in a glass serving bowl.

Dissolve 3 tablespoons of sugar in the kirsch and pour over the strawberries. Toss lightly. Refrigerate for 1 to 2 hours. Just before serving whip the cream with the remaining sugar until stiff, and spoon over the strawberries. *Serves 3 to 4.*

Paris, Ile-de-France

CHOCOLATE MOUSSE

(Mousse au chocolat)

This is a very light and creamy chocolate mousse.

4 ounces semi-sweet chocolate
1 cup whipping cream
1 tbsp. Grand Marnier or brandy
2 tbsp. sugar
2 egg whites

Melt the chocolate with 2 tablespoons of the cream in a bowl over hot, not boiling, water. Remove from the heat and stir in the Grand Marnier. Whip the remaining cream with the sugar until stiff and fold into the chocolate mixture. Beat the egg whites until stiff and fold into the mixture. Spoon into individual glass dishes and refrigerate for at least 4 hours before serving. *Serves 4.*

Pays   Basque,   Béarn,   Bigorre

ORANGE FLAN
(Flan à l'orange)

A "flan" can mean several things in France, from a savory custard tart to a thick custard. This flan from the Pays Basque is a simple crème caramel flavored with orange flower water and orange liqueur.

For the caramel:	¹/₄	**cup sugar**
	2	**tbsp. water**

For the flan:	2¹/₄	**cups milk**
	¹/₄	**cups sugar**
	3	**eggs plus 2 yolks**
	2	**tsp. orange flower water**
	2	**tbsp. orange liqueur, such as Curaçao or Cointreau**

Place ¹/₄ cup of sugar and the water in a small, heavy saucepan and cook over moderate heat for 4 to 5 minutes or until the sugar darkens and starts to caramelize. Pour into a 1-quart mold or soufflé dish, tilting the dish in all directions until the caramel evenly lines the bottom and a little way up the sides of the mold. Set aside.

Scald the milk. Do not let it boil or the custard will curdle. Remove from the heat and set aside. Beat the eggs and egg yolks with the remaining sugar until light. Gradually add the hot milk, orange flower water, and orange liqueur. Pour through a fine sieve into the prepared mold.

Set the mold in a pan of hot water and place in the lower third of a preheated 325° F. oven and bake for 40 to 45 minutes or until a knife comes out clean from the center. Let cool at room temperature, then chill for several hours before unmolding. *Serves 4 to 6.*

L y o n n a i s

PEACH ICE CREAM

(Glace aux pêches)

This ice cream is equally good made with bananas or strawberries.

¹/₂	**pound ripe peaches**
¹/₄	**cup sugar**
1 or 2	**tbsp. peach brandy or kirsch**
1¹/₄	**cups whipping cream**

Peel the peaches, cut in half, and remove the pits. Force through a nylon sieve or purée in a food processor. Add the sugar and peach brandy. Whip the cream until stiff and fold into the peach purée. Pour into a mold and freeze for 2 or 3 hours or until firm. *Serves 4.*

Poitou, Charente

BRANDY PARFAIT
(Parfait au cognac)

A parfait is a kind of frozen mousse or cream. Originally it was made with coffee, but today it may be made with nuts, chocolate, fruit, or liqueur—like the following recipe from Charente.

    1   egg yolk
    ¼   cup sugar
    3   tbsp. cognac or brandy
    1   cup whipping cream

Whisk the egg yolk, sugar, and cognac in a bowl over hot, not boiling, water until the mixture starts to thicken. Remove from the heat.

Whip the cream lightly and fold into the egg yolk mixture. Pour into a mold and freeze for 2 or 3 hours until firm. *Serves 2 to 4.*

INDEX